Case Studies in

Strategic Management

Pearson Casebook Series

Case Studies in Strategic Management
A Practical Approach

Sanjay Mohapatra

Professor

Xavier Institute of Management

Bhubaneshwar, Odissa

Pearson

Assistant Editor—Acquisitions: Anant Kapoor
Editor—Production: Jennifer Sargunar

ISBN 978-81-317-5984-4

First Impression

Published by Dorling Kindersley (India) Pvt. Ltd, licensees of Pearson Education in South Asia.

Head Office: 7th Floor, Knowledge Boulevard, A-8(A), Sector 62, Noida 201 309, UP, India.
Registered Office: 11 Community Centre, Panchsheel Park, New Delhi 110 017, India.

Compositor: Diacritech
Printed in India at Repro India Limited

CONTENTS

FOREWORD

Balanced scorecard (BSC) is an effective tool for making accurate and fast decisions. A disciplined and scientific approach to strategic management is crucial to higher profitability and business transformations. It is difficult to imagine strategic advantage and operational efficiency in the knowledge economy without the use of BSC. In its role as a strategic tool, BSC integrates corporate objectives into decision-making processes. There are several books that portray the importance of BSC, its strategic alignment with corporate objectives and its usage of technology to enable business to achieve higher productivity and to reduce the cost of operations. However, to the best of my knowledge, no other book has provided a better framework for designing BSC that aligns management information system (MIS) with strategic corporate objectives.

With increased competitions, complexities of business operations, decision-making processes and the underlying technologies have increased manifold. As business spreads to remote areas across geographical boundaries, executives are often not clear about the decisions that need to be made. Such confusion arises from the inability to monitor, manage and analyse vast range of processes and the transaction data generated from these processes. This book attempts to provide a framework for simplifying the data collection processes and designing an effective MIS so that adequate information is available for making appropriate decisions. The book also includes a slide deck that can be used by the instructors for class preparation.

With his extensive background in implementing information systems in a many leading corporations in India and abroad, Sanjay has provided many relevant cases that can be adopted for implementation. I am confident that this book will be an extremely useful resource to practitioners, NGOs and organizations that are involved in MIS development.

Sambit Samal
Senior Product Manager, SQL Server, Microsoft
Redmond, WA, USA
MBA, University of North Carolina, Chapel Hill
B.Tech., Institute of Technology, Banaras Hindu University

PREFACE

According to Johnson *et al.* (1999), strategic management is the management of the direction and scope of an organization over the long term, which is advantageous to the organization as it facilitates the optimal utilization of resources within a dynamic market environment to meet the needs of all its stakeholders including customers, the environment, investors, employees and regulatory authorities. This is a change from the traditional thought process, which emphasizes that organizations need to work towards the fulfilment of investors' goals alone, that is, making profits. Based on this backdrop, it can be argued that there are three broad steps in strategic management: analysis of the present situation, designing a strategy based on available choices and implementation of that strategy. Analysis of the present situation implies understanding the strategic position of the organization with respect to its environment, available resources, culture, mission and business goals. Designing a strategy based on available choices implies the formulation of a strategy from a decision tree where the best possible option is selected based on the medium- and long-term returns expected from investment. These returns can be linked to financial returns known as returns on investment (ROIs). Finally, any strategic decision can be successful only if its implementation is carried out effectively. For implementation to be effective, we need to monitor the progress of implementation using a management information system (MIS). Through the MIS, progress of each performance metric can be tracked against each goal.

For designing the MIS, once corporate objectives are derived, metrics are defined for all the functions/departments that will be integrated with the vision, mission and corporate objectives of the organization. The metrics thus defined indicates the variables for which data need to be collected. The data need to be collected at periodic intervals using organization-wide tools. This will bring in consistency and integrity in data collection. The responsibility of data collection will be defined, and the role so defined will be indicated clearly in the MIS. Thus, all the MISs designed in this book consist of metrics (derived from corporate objectives), data to be collected, roles that will publish the data and frequencies at which these data must be collected. For each case study, a sample MIS report has been illustrated to make the idea clear to the students. The approach is feasible and can be used by students as well as practitioners.

In the knowledge economy era, where resources are limited, the use of strategic management to optimally utilize resources is a necessity. In this book, it has been demonstrated how strategy can be developed using scientifically sound psychology theory and the consideration of all stakeholder objectives. Through different perspectives, as indicated in a balanced scorecard, strategy is designed and it will result in interventions that would ensure the growth and prosperity of the concerned organization. This will improve strategic competence and also increase market capitalization. This competency translates into the ability of the executives in the organization to acquire, store, recall, interpret and act upon relevant information so that both short-term and long-term goals are achieved. This will ensure that the organization tides over short-term problems and achieves its long-term vision. The chapters of this book demonstrate that strategic management is primarily cognitive in nature and can be used in vastly different areas with consistent success. The perspectives described here have been drawn from multiple levels of management processes, which have been developed from different domains.

The rapidly changing and evolving market conditions in the knowledge economy put tremendous pressure on key individuals and groups as they seek to fulfil long-term business goals by skilfully steering their organizations amid the volatility in the market. This book is based on previous research, work experience in different domains for over two decades and organizational psychology. The book identifies a number of ways in which business challenges can be met in different industries. Thus, the book can be seen as providing enough overview of the process and procedure of scientific and systematic strategic management and providing execution techniques (through MIS) that increase the deployability of the strategies discussed.

Whereas considerable research has gone into developing strategic models and theories, legitimizing the psychology of strategy management processes and mapping the organization boundary conditions, there is still a gap between the application of theory and the theory itself, more so in the developmental sectors. There is a considerable time gap before which the research in strategic management will have noticeable application in developmental sector that too in a developing country like India. The maturity and knowledge, which is available in corporate sectors is lacking in developmental sectors and theory applied in better established areas of corporate sectors, have so far not been applied in social sector. In particular, there are many non-trivial methodological hurdles that have not yet been confronted, and many of the frameworks, tools and techniques discussed in this book are yet to be adequately scrutinized through empirical research. Many of the procedures currently in use for mapping strategic knowledge are yet to be screened in terms of their effectiveness in developmental sector. That is why this book has been provided with illustrated procedures that elicit conceptual knowledge being mapped to different organizations.

Although these forms of conceptual, non-conscious knowledge are yet to be tested in the field, they have been tested in classroom environments and have also been presented to industry experts. As a result, the case studies and practice depicted in different chapters have been verbally accepted by industry experts, and they will be deployed in their respective organizations. Although no written communication is available to this effect, it gives immense satisfaction to the author that these have been found suitable and that organizations are willing to accept the same. A cursory glance at the voluminous material in this book (15 case studies in the developmental sector, which have applied balanced scorecard techniques and used MIS to monitor the progress of critical success factors), which has been based on experimental psychology and the wider field of management sciences, reveals that we can delineate many forms of knowledge and apply them with satisfying results. It is clear that although the results of applications of these concepts are yet to be reported, the concepts are getting their due notice. Although this could be the starting point for the organizations covered in different chapters of this book, it is required for them to investigate further and study the results of the implementations in the years to come.

The book presents a wide range of case studies from different sectors, such as fertilizers, insurance, developmental activities, microfinance, nongovernmental organizations (NGOs) and bank operations. Each chapter describes the industry overview, how to arrive at the corporate strategy using the balanced scorecard technique, metrics to be measured so as to track the progress of a set of corporate objectives, definitions of variables for measuring these metrics, and a sample MIS report.

This book, unlike other books on strategic management, is much shorter in length, concise in its writing and to the point when describing the applications of balanced scorecard. It also describes the steps to be adopted for strategic management in the same way as a faculty would describe them the classroom. In other words, students can not only easily understand the discussed approaches but also apply them in other case studies. Practitioners also can benefit from this book and can emulate the approaches in their own organizations. For this book, the guiding principle is different. The principle is to question oneself whether a concept can help students in analyzing the case studies and business situations.

The book is also based on two decades of corporate experience, which was gained by the author while working as a consultant for different clients. The author has primarily been a consultant helping organizations to define their strategies, aligning them with business goals and then ensuring that they are being implemented effectively to reap the benefits of business alignment. In the process, proper monitoring mechanisms were developed in all these organizations, which helped them to track the values of different metrics with respect to their defined business goals. This principle has been applied in all the case studies mentioned in this book and, hence, in each case study the strategies are aligned with business goals and then an effective MIS is designed to monitor the progress of alignment. Each chapter also discusses ROI, which makes the analysis a cross-functional integrated analysis.

Each chapter has discussion questions that can be used by the instructor as discussion topics for participants. At the end of the chapter, references for further reading are also provided.

The real-life examples covered in this book are from India, but the concepts can be used in any organization. These case studies can be used by practitioners as examples for designing MISs in their own organizations. These case studies can be taught in strategic management courses, MIS courses, insurance certification programs, postgraduate diploma courses, executive MBA programmes, Bachelor of Engineering (BE; IT specialization) courses, the Master of Computer Applications course and the Master of Science (computer science) course. The case studies can also be taught in financial management courses as well as in Management Development Programmes (MDPs, where senior executives from developmental sectors are the target audience), workshops held for executives in NGOs and training sessions for capacity building in developmental areas.

The case studies can be used to illustrate the following themes:

- Developing a strategy that would help in aligning corporate goals with operational strategy in the case of mergers and acquisitions.
- To understand how the balanced scorecard can be a strategic tool in helping insurance companies to increase their reach to the financially backward segment of the population and at the same time be able to control and monitor premium payments.
- To understand how an effective strategy can arrive at metrics that can help in the effective monitoring of loan repayment in the agricultural sector.
- To understand how the proposed balanced scorecard can help in quantifying research projects in a research organization like RMRB.
- To understand how to describe information flow at different levels and use the same for designing strategy in the mutual fund sector.
- To understand how strategic focus can help to provide value for money to the customers of Pantaloons.
- To understand how Tata Chemicals Limited can use the balanced scorecard to identify areas of improvement and thus make decisions to reduce its cost of operations.
- To understand how a strategy based on different perspectives can meet all the objectives of stakeholders in RPG.

For practitioners, using the case studies described in this book a framework for designing strategy can be developed. Depending on the industry and the organization, the framework can have the following sections: introduction to the industry, where the organization stands in the industry, its vision, its mission, the use of the balanced scorecard technique to derive corporate objectives and corporate objectives derived from the organization's mission. Then define metrics that would measure the progress of these objectives, define roles that would collect data as well as define the periodicity of publishing these data and provide a sample MIS report to give the students a feel of MIS reports.

ONLINE WEB RESOURCES

Online Web resources for instructors are available in the book's Companion Web site www.pearsoned.co.in/sanjaymohapatra. They include PowerPoint slides and Case Teaching Notes that aid instructors in teaching.

PowerPoint Slides: Each chapter has a PowerPoint slide highlighting the key concepts discussed in that chapter.

Case Teaching Notes: Each Case Teaching Note comprises Case Overview, Target Audience, Sources of Data, Learning Objectives and Lead Questions.

Sanjay Mohapatra

ACKNOWLEDGEMENTS

This book was made possible by the support and encouragement of my well-wishers, students and family members. It is not possible to name each and every one here, but I would like to thank many of them who remain at the top of my mind. I start by acknowledging the contributions made by my colleagues Soumya Mahapatra, Sushila Nayak and Alok Pani. All of them have helped me in different ways for the timely completion of this book. I also thank the IGI Global publishing house for their detailed review and excellent comments that challenged me to better my performance.

This book is a collection of cases which have been tested in my class. These cases have been discussed and presented in the class during the course. I am proud that I got the opportunity to teach such a brilliant batch of students who made teaching a memorable and pleasant experience. Although it would make this section lengthy, I would like to name each and every student of my class for the part played by them in publishing this book.

I thank the following students: Abhishek Bhati, Ajoy Deb, Amit Gupta, Amrit Singha, Ankur Sharma, Anshuman Niranjan Nayak, Anuj Jindal, Anup Kumar Singh, Anupam Satpathy, Aparajita Mahendra, Bipin Bachkhati, Chitra Nayak, Deotima Goswami, Dipti Ranjan Mohanty, Garima Jain, Jagnyabalkya Mahapatra, Jay Shankar Prasad, Ketaki Kishor Narkar, Kiranjyoti Mahasuar, Komal Agarwal, Kumar Anubhav

M. Udai Krishna Rao, Jagdale Yogesh Hanmant, Monalisha Mahapatra, Mukti Narayan Rai, Neha Srivastava, Nitish Kumar, Nivedita Sowle, Alok Gupta, Param Brahma Mohapatra, Parul Agarwal, Pavithra C., Pawan Kumar Yadav, Prabodha Kumar Biswal, Premjit Singh Laikhuram, Prerna Ruchi, Pritika Ojha, Priyanka Kothari, Puspak Sengupta, Rakesh Kumar, Ramani Ranjan Padhi, Rathod Puspendra Sinh, Ritesh Pandey, Sainath Suni, Saphallya Misra, Sasmita Patnaik, Saumya Ranjan Swain, Saurabh Singh, Sherel Jeevan Joseph Mendonsa, Shitanshu Shekhar, Anshuman, Shubhankar Das, Sk. Mosharaf Hossain, Soumya Kanta Dwibedy, Arvindra Kumar Singh, Surabhi S. Shahi, Swarup Ranjan Nayak, Sweta Kumari, Tarakarama Rao Raghupati, Vijay Rangarajan, Vivek Kumar, Gayatri Patnaik, Sanjeev Gonsalves S. J. and Sudeep Vaidya.

Last but not the least, I thank Sambit Samal of Microsoft, United States, for his support and for agreeing to write the foreword of this book.

Sanjay Mohapatra

INTRODUCTION

BSC PERSPECTIVES

In the current fast-moving knowledge economy, there is cut-throat competition. Organizations are competing with each other at the strategy, tactical and operational levels to outperform each other. At the strategy level, organizations need to look at all the possible directions so that they leave no stone unturned. The traditional focus in strategy management was on forming strategy on financial parameters only; in modern times, this is insufficient for an organization to progress towards achieving its vision. Apart from financial parameters, the organization also needs to monitor its operational efficiencies and long-term drivers of success.

There are many techniques available for scientific and systematic strategic management. Kaplan and Norton (1996) propose the balanced scorecard (BSC) approach for strategy design, which covers all angles of strategic management. BSC is a conceptual framework for translating an organization's strategic objectives into action through a set of performance indicators, targets and initiatives, which are distributed among four perspectives: financial, customer, internal business processes, and learning and growth. For the implementation of scorecard to be successful, it is essential that all departments and individuals in turn develop their own scorecards, such that everyone works towards a common set of objectives.

In most organizations, functional departments are not aligned with business needs and there is a significant gap between the business's expectation of value and its perception of value delivered. This is primarily because the measures and performance indicators in these functions are not derived from business goals. As a result, strategies formed for department heads and executives there under fail to see the bigger picture and these individuals work in silos. In addition, in a knowledge economy the role of technology is important as investments in information technology are seen today as imperative and strategic to the future of all organizations. Given the rise in investments and the consequent prominence of the IT function, it has become necessary to create a new role called Chief Information Officer (CIO) who would be able to justify the investments made and the value delivered. Arriving at measurable indicators of value delivery is central to the success of this implementation.

Whereas the measurement of progress on operational and customer orientation perspectives is relatively easy, the delivery on corporate contribution (financial) and future orientation (learning and growth) perspectives throws up certain challenges. Further complication also arises from the rapid changes occurring in the availability of technologies, resulting in possible risks on account of uncertainties. The theory of 'new information economics' with certain structured framework provides mechanisms to effectively overcome these challenges.

Designing a strategy alone is not enough; the execution and monitoring of progress of key performance indicators with respect to business goals is important as well. In addition to the scorecard that would show the progress made on initiatives, the CIO needs to put in place a management information system (MIS) to capture the value delivered by the initiatives on all the four perspectives. The MIS will collect data and track the progress based on these data for all stakeholders in the organization.

This ensures that the organization captures and communicates the total value delivered rather than the value captured on the primary perspective only.

Using this approach in strategic management, the organization is now in a position to effectively monitor the progress it is making towards achieving its strategic objectives. However, in order for the organization to be able to succeed in the identified initiatives, it is essential that the groups as well as all the stakeholders involved in the implementation process share the same vision and objectives of the organization. In this, technology can play a big role in the current knowledge economy. This would need the use of tools that would help in understanding business models, the underlying processes and organizational dynamics to be able to ensure business value delivery. Thus the implementation of a BSC approach supported by techniques of value measurement and appropriate processes of solution delivery would be central to the business value delivery to customers.

BSC APPROACH TO BUSINESS VALUE DELIVERY

As mentioned in the preceding section, the traditional focus on financial parameters is currently insufficient to power organizations to a path of sustainable and predictable growth. It is essential that businesses measure performance through financial as well as certain non-financial indicators that are critical to the survival of the business.

BSC is a conceptual framework for translating an organization's strategic objectives into action through a set of performance indicators, targets and initiatives, which are distributed among four perspectives: financial, customer, internal business processes, and learning and growth.

- Customer perspective: How do customers see an organization?
- Process perspective: What must the organization excel in?
- Organization perspective: Can the organization continue to improve and create value?

BSC provides a comprehensive view of the business to its management using the critical measures identified by the management. A well-made scorecard will have a unity of purpose that ensures the measures are directed towards achieving a unified strategy. In order to evolve an effective scorecard, the following points need to be kept in mind: Strategy needs to be based on a clear set of cause-and-effect relationships and the drivers that create a desired outcome. It also helps to ensure that strategy balances out the contradictory forces (for example, long-term profitability versus short-term gains); strategy needs to create a differentiated value proposition and the planned initiatives need to provide an adequate infrastructure and processes to enable the delivery of strategy. The measures identified need to provide an effective monitoring mechanism for the assumptions underlying the strategy and the successful implementation of the same.

Please see Table 1 for the different perspectives in a BSC. BSC provides a comprehensive view of the business to the management using the critical measures identified by the management. A well-made scorecard will have a unity of purpose that ensures the measures are directed towards achieving a unified strategy. In order to evolve an integrated and effective scorecard, the following salient points need to be kept in mind:

- Corporate strategy needs to be based on a clear set of goals and objectives, which have been aligned with the organization's vision.
- During strategy formulation, all the contradictory forces (for example, long-term profitability versus short-term gains) should be considered and balanced out to provide a focused direction for the stakeholders in the organization.

- In addition, corporate strategy needs to create a differentiated value proposition to the customers.
- The management should provide adequate infrastructure investment and support for defining processes to enable the delivery of strategy.
- Last but not the least, an effective MIS should be defined so that the measures identified can provide an effective monitoring mechanism for the assumptions underlying the strategy and the successful implementation of the same.

Table 1 *BSC perspectives*

	Strategic Themes	Strategic Objectives	Strategic Measures	Initiatives
Financial	Financially strong	F1 Return on capital employed F2 Existing asset utilization F3 Profitability F4 Industry cost leader F5 Profitable growth	ROCE Cash flow Net margin rank (versus competition) Full cost per gallon delivered (versus competition) Volume growth rate versus industry Other business revenue and margin	Diversity into new business B2B implementation to derive supply chain Efficiencies Penetrate new markets
Customer	Delight the customer Win-win dealer relationships	C1 Continually delight the targeted consumer C2 Build win-win relations with dealers	Share of segment in selected key markets Mystery shopper rating Dealer gross Profit growth Dealer survey	Web-based services for better customer services Dealer Connectivity Dealer Conference and relationship building
Internal	Build the franchise Increase customer value	I1 Innovative products and services I2 Best-in-class franchise teams	New product return on investment (ROI) New product acceptance rate Dealer quality score	Build the franchise Monthly monitoring system
	Operational excellence	I3 Factory performance I4 Inventory management I5 Industry cost leader I6 On spec—on time	Yield gap Order fulfilment Inventory levels Run-out rate Activity cost versus competition Perfect orders	Benchmark Factory systems Implement the SCM Planning solution Complete vendor integration
	Good Neighbour	I7 Improve Education Health Alliance (EHA)	Number of environmental incidents Days away from work rate	Organization-wide safety and quality drive Actively participate in an international forum of EUropean Society (EUS)

(Continued)

Table 1 (*Continued*)

	Strategic Themes	Strategic Objectives	Strategic Measures	Initiatives
Learning and growth	Motivated and prepared workforce	L1 Climate for action L2 Core competencies and skills L3 Access to strategic information	Employee survey Strategic competency availability Strategic information availability	Personal BSC (%) Implementation of a performance development program Organization-wide intranet

FRAMEWORK FOR DESIGNING MIS

The case studies developed in this book follows a framework. The framework is derived as follows: From vision and mission, corporate strategies are derived. Corporate objectives can be derived using (1) SWOT (strengths, weaknesses, opportunities, threats) analysis, (2) benchmarking exercise, (3) brainstorming exercise, (4) BSC technique, (5) scenario analysis or any other technique. In this book, all the case studies use BSC techniques as these are very systematic and scientific techniques and as they cover all the functional areas. The following paragraph describes in detail the BSC technique:

Once the corporate objectives are derived, metrics are defined for all the functions/departments, which are integrated with the vision, mission and corporate objectives of an organization. The metrics thus defined indicate the variables for which data need to be collected. Data need to be collected at periodic intervals using organization-wide available tools. This brings in consistency and integrity in data collection. The responsibility for data collection is defined and the role so defined is indicated clearly in the MIS. Thus, the MISs designed in this book consist of metrics (derived from corporate objectives), data to be collected, role that will publish the data and the frequency at which these data will be collected. For each case study, a sample MIS report has been illustrated to make the study clear to the students. The approach is feasible and can be used by students as well as practitioners.

CONCLUSION

In order for an organization to effectively achieve its objectives, it is essential that the objectives of every business unit, team and individual of the enterprise are linked with organizational objectives. Hence, it would be useful for each level of the organization to have a scorecard of its own.

Hence, each functional head would also need to have his or her own BSC. Table 2 shows the BSC for an IT manager. The stronger the link between the BSC of the IT head and that of the organization, the higher the prominence of the function. The IT head would hence have to align his or her scorecard to the corporate scorecard to ensure the delivery of organizational objectives.

Most organizations have a significant gap between actual value delivered and the business's expectations of value delivered. To overcome this, value management techniques must be used to optimize IT investments, facilitating business efforts to create, measure and manage value.

Table 2 *Functional BSC (IT head's scorecard)*

	Strategic Themes	Strategic Objectives	Strategic Measures	Initiatives
Financial	Business contribution	F1 Control of IT expense F2 Business value of new IT projects F3 Business value of the IT function	Percentage of projects within budgets IT budget percentage turnover IT overheads Financial evaluation based on net present value/ROI, etc. Business evaluation based on information economics Involvement in strategic projects	Ensure IT infrastructure for foray into new markets Monthly value monitor for all the key projects
Customer	Delight the internal customer Delight the external customers	C1 Continually delight the targeted consumer C2 Build win-win in relations with dealers	Share of segment in selected key markets Mystery shopper rating Dealer gross profit growthDealer survey	Web-based services for better customer services Dealer connectivity Dealer conference and relationship building
Internal	Operational excellence	I1 Efficient software management (internal and third party) I2 Effective issue resolution I3 Factory performance I4 Inventory management I5 Industry cost leader I6 On spec–on time	Delivery of projects within budget, on time and within spec Component reuse achieved Percentage downtime of hardware Response times per category of users Average time between system failure and lead time for service Percentage users trained Reduction in overhead expenses	Help desk establishment for resolution on all development projects Activity value Analysis study to identify areas for cost reduction
Learning and growth	Motivated and prepared workforce to answer future challenges	L1 Continuous training program L2 Hone core competencies and required skills L3 Access to strategic information	Employee survey Strategic competency availability Strategic information availability Asset value	Personal BSC (percentage) Implementation of a performance development program Organization-wide intranet

FURTHER READINGS

1. Performance-Based Management, Eight Steps to Develop and Use IT Performance Measures Effectively, 1996, http//www.itpolicy.gsa.gov/mkm/pathways/pathways.htm, 2008
2. Measuring and Improving Corporate Information Technology through the Balanced Scorecard, October 2000, http://is.twi.tudelft.nl/ejise/vol1/issue1/paper3/paper.html, 2008
3. META Group Research, Increasing IT Value through Effective Portfolio Management, IT Performance Engineering & Measurement Strategies, 2000, http://www.metagroup.com, 2008
4. Dave Pollard and Ron Buckle, Ernst & Young Canada, Multi Level Balanced Scorecards: Aligning Performance Measurement for Individuals, Teams Business Units and Whole Organizations, *Perform Magazine*, 13 October 2000, http://www.pbviews.com/magazine/articles/pollard.html, 2008
5. L. Lapide, What About Measuring Supply Chain Performance? *AMR Research*, October 2000, http://lapide.ASCET.com, 2008
6. Procurement Executives' Association, *Guide to a Balanced Scorecard Performance Management Methodology*, Procurement Executives' Association, October 2000.
7. R. S. Kaplan and D. P. Norton, *The Balanced Scorecard: Translating Strategy into Action*, New York: Harvard Business Press, 1996.

1

CASE STUDY ON RMRB INTERNATIONAL: STRATEGIC DIRECTION FOR A RESEARCH ORGANIZATION

INTRODUCTION

Established in 1971, RMRB International is a pioneer in market research in India. It is a member of the Kantar Group, WPP's information, insight and consulting division. RMRB's footprint extends across 11 countries—India, Pakistan, Bangladesh, Sri Lanka, Dubai, Saudi Arabia, Egypt, Singapore, Malaysia, Korea and England.

With over 1,200 full-time staff, RMRB provides high-quality conceptualization, strategic thinking, execution and interpretation skills. RMRB International is the only research company in India that offers such a wide range of research-based services to its clients. RMRB International's areas of specialization include consumer market research (both quantitative and qualitative), industrial market research, business-to-business (B2B) market research, social and rural market research, media research, retail research on consumer panels.

RMRB INTERNATIONAL'S DIVISIONS

RMRB International has been offering for over 35 years both general as well as specialist research services to clients in India and overseas.

RMRB International operates from its five full-service offices in Mumbai, Delhi, Kolkata, Chennai, and Bengaluru, and it is supported by 15 other regional centres in the collection of survey information.

RMRB International has eight specialist units:

- Probe Qualitative Research (PQR)
- Media and Panel Group

- Customer Satisfaction Management and Measurement (CSMM): Partners in managing stakeholder relationships
- BIRD: Research-based consultancy for B2B and technology markets (*http://www.rmrbint.com/divisions/index.html - 3#3*)
- eTechnology Group at RMRB
- Social and Rural Research Institute (SRRI)
- RMRB MindTech Systems: Software development house
- Abacus Market Analytics: Data Processing House (*http://www.rmrbint.com/divisions/index.html - 4#4*)

PQR

RMRB has a division named Probe Qualitative Research, which is one of India's leading qualitative research groups. The division has expertise in qualitative research and draws its strength from highly trained and skilled executives. Over the years, based on its experience, PQR has innovated tools that help its customers in product innovation, communication and brand development.

Media and Panel Group

The Media and Panel Group of RMRB International is a pioneer in the field of media research in India. The Group also runs one of the world's largest household panels with over 70,000 households in urban and rural India, chronicling changing consumption habits across the country.

CSMM: Partners in Managing Stakeholder Relationship

The CSMM is an independent, specialist unit of RMRB International and the exclusive member of the Walker Global Network (WGN) for the Indian subcontinent. As a specialist unit of RMRB International, CSMM provides the widest field coverage with five full-service offices and 15 field offices in Delhi, Kolkata, Mumbai, Chennai, Bengaluru, Hyderabad, Kochi, Pune, Patna, Ahmedabad, Guwahati, Bhubaneswar, Lucknow, Indore and Ludhiana. CSMM services clients from India and neighbouring countries. In addition, through its associate AMRB, a company with headquarters in Dubai and operating throughout the Middle East and North Africa, CSMM provides Walker proprietary tools throughout the region.

BIRD: Research-based Consultancy for B2B and Technology Markets

BIRD is a research-based consultancy arm for B2B and technology markets. Operating from four locations in India, viz, Mumbai, New Delhi, Bengaluru and Chennai, BIRD has been advising clients from India and across the globe since the last 35 years.

eTechnology Group at RMRB

As technology evolves and creates new opportunities, barriers to progress arise. Some problems are technical, economic or policy-related, whereas the hardest problems combine all three aspects in any country. By maintaining a continuous link with industry and constantly monitoring markets, we can understand the trend of technology markets. The eTechnology Group at RMRB constantly monitors technology trends in information technology (IT), Internet, telecom and convergence space, helping Indian and international companies alike. It also has a partnership with the Yankee Group, United States, to represent the Indian market internationally.

SRRI

SRRI specializes in social research and in conducting research on emerging rural markets. It has staff with special expertise in conducting knowledge, attitudes and practice (KAP) studies on health and sanitation, water, environment and other fields, in India as well as internationally.

RMRB MindTech Systems—Software Development House

MindTech Systems is a client-servicing-oriented specialized software unit of Media & Panel, Mumbai, facilitating solutions to critical business questions. MindTech Systems has been providing business solutions since 2000 and has thus acquired an extensive expertise in market research applications. Having based themselves on the features demanded by a large number of companies, we have created innovative, user-friendly applications. Our solutions help clients to convert market research knowledge to actions.

Abacus Market Analytics: Data Processing House

Using standard state-of-the-art analytics, graphics, statistical software and tested work quality processes, Abacus delivers exceptional quality working to stringent deadlines at highly competitive prices.

SECTORS RESEARCHED BY RMRB

RMRB International has been a pioneer in conducting market research exercises for several sectors. Today, there is hardly any sector that RMRB International has not researched. From potato wafers to personal computers (PCs), cigarettes to cellular phones, alcohol to air conditioners and bubble gums to building materials, just name it and we have researched it:

1. Agriculture and agricultural products
2. Alcohol
3. Automotive sector
4. Building and construction
5. Consumer durables
6. Household care
7. IT, telecom, and the Internet
8. Industry and business
9. Media and entertainment
10. Social and rural sectors
11. Tobacco
12. Engineering sector
13. Education sector
14. Processed food
15. Sports goods and accessories
16. Healthcare
17. Finance, banking and insurance
18. Energy and environment
19. Telecom

SERVICES OFFERED BY RMRB

The depth and breadth of services that we provide is extensive, and they include research and advisory services in the following areas:

1. Advertising, promotion and media research
2. B2B and industrial research
3. Corporate and employee research
4. Channel and retail research
5. Product and packaging research
6. Pricing research
7. Strategic market research

SYNDICATED OFFERS

TGI INDIA—Single-Source Marketing, Communication and Planning Tool

RMRB International has launched Target Group Index (TGI) in India, an international product from Kantar Media Research (KMR); KMR is WPP's specialist global research agency offering media research services. KMR offers TGI in 36 countries, and TGI is widely used by advertising agencies, media owners and advertisers round the world.

TGI will be the largest single-source database offered in India till date, combining products, brands, media, demographics and lifestyles. TGI INDIA covers more than

- 200 categories
- 3,000 brands
- 15 radio stations
- 125 television channels
- 250 press titles
- 100 lifestyle statements

Truly, TGI's analysis possibilities are limitless!

ITOPS

ITOPS covers news related to PCs and software markets in India. This is a half-yearly report that provides details on all hardware related to PC such as local area networks (LANs), printers, uninterruptible power supply (UPS), networking products and operating systems. The report also provides details on market penetration, total number used, market potential, etc., of these products. Based on survey, the report specifies the most popular brands in PCs and IT products in Indian market. The data are collected from 8,000 business establishments and more than 6,000 end users from about sixteen cities in the country. The report was first published in 1997, and it has become popular among its readers. In April 2009, the report was in its ninth round. The report is sponsored by the Manufacturer's Association of Information Technology (MAIT).

Syndicated Series in Internet Usage in India

Syndicated series report discusses the Internet usage in different sectors in India. It was started in 1998 and covers issues related to the Internet market, viz, International Organization for Standards (ISOs), content providers, portals, venture capitalists and investors. The series publishes reports about issues and challenges with respect to all stakeholders concerned, viz, Internet service providers (ISPs); content providers; marketing organizations trying to use Internet as a vehicle for reaching out to buyers, web portals, investors, venture capitalists, Internet kiosks, etc. The report gives detailed information about Internet usage by households and businesses along with the broadband usage status of Indian markets, consumers' content preferences, cross-media consumption, etc. The report is prepared by surveying 16,000 households, 30 cities, 65,000 individuals and 10,000 business houses. As a result of such a detailed coverage, this report has become a bestseller and has already sold 250 volumes since its inception.

Telecom Report

One more report that the firm publishes is on telecommunication. This report gives a detailed analysis of present and future telecom market in India. The report discusses present penetration levels of cellular, landline and wireless local loop (WLL) services. The report gives detailed usage information for local and STD calls made from all different modes of telephony. Since this report uses data from more than 16 cities and covers both households and business houses, it is quite popular and is used for preparing telecom marketing strategy by many firms.

National Food Survey (NFS)

The NFS is a comprehensive study on food habits and consumption across urban India. Over the past two decades, NFS has completed four rounds with the last one, NFS4: The Convenience Foods Handbook Study, conducted in September 2007. NFS is one of the most comprehensive studies in terms of categories and information coverage, providing marketers with baseline information on food purchase behaviour.

Patient Pulse

Patient Pulse is a unique two-in-one product from RMRB International specially designed to provide you the advantages of syndicated research and exclusively customized research.

Patient Pulse has 12-city four-zone coverage. It includes exhaustive information on common ailments, treatment methods, key influencers with respect to treatment methods and consumers' attitudes towards treatment methods, as well as awareness of brands, their stocking levels and more.

Further, Patient Pulse is designed to help you satisfy your exclusive information needs by allowing you to ask the patients three questions of your choice. The answers to these questions will be confidential and shared only with you. Hence, this is very helpful if you want to gauge the pulse of a patient.

VISION

The vision of RMRB is to consistently exceed client expectations through high-quality work, integrity, innovativeness and the building of a culture that promotes professional and personal growth opportunities.

MISSION

The two missions of RMRB is to study social issues with commitment, expertise, objectivity and an orientation towards actionability; and to set up databases and develop research expertise for marketing in rural India, about which hitherto there has been a paucity of data.

PARENT COMPANY

WPP is one of the world's largest communication services groups. It is made up of leading companies in the following areas: advertising; media investment management; information, insight and consultancy; public relations and public affairs; branding and identity; healthcare communications; direct promotion and relationship marketing; and specialist communications.

WPP has 253 companies working under it. The few important companies under WPP are

- 10AM Communications (advertising)
- Addison Corporate Marketing (branding and identity)
- AGB Nielsen Media Research (consultancy)
- Kantar Group (market research)

RMRB International is a daughter company of the Kantar Group.

KANTAR GROUP

Kantar group consists of following ventures

1. Added value group
2. AMRB
3. BMRB
4. BPRI
5. Cannondell Associates
6. Centre partners
7. Everystone
8. Focalyst
9. FUSION 5
10. GLENDINNING
11. Henley Centre HeadlightVision
12. RMRB
13. Kantar operatives
14. KMR Group
15. Lightspeed Research
16. Management ventures
17. Mattson Jack Group
18. Millward Brown
19. Research International

20. RMS
21. TGI
22. Ziment Group

Stakeholders and Their Objectives

Clients—to get quality research that is close to ground situation, in order to get value for money

Kantar group—to be the apex global player in market research and provide clients with the most satisfactory solution

Public at large—quality research that can help markets to provide the public the maximum satisfaction at the most effective price

Financial institutions—proper utilization of their funds

Clients include the following:

1. *Bilateral/United Nations agencies/banks*: CARE Ford Foundation, Micronutrient Initiative, SIDA, UNICEF, USAID, WHO, World Bank
2. *Advocacy/consultancy*: BASICS, Pathfinders International, Population Council, the Futures Group, the Policy Project
3. *Central and state governments in India*: Andhra Pradesh Forest Department, Department of Adult Education, Department of Women and Child Development, Ministry of Rural Development, Ministry of Health and Family Welfare, Ministry of Forests and Environment
4. *Social marketers*: Commercial Market Strategies, Population Services International (PSI), Program for Appropriate Technology in Health (PATH)
5. *Development/relief non-governmental organizations (NGOs) in India*: International Federation of Red Cross, Rajiv Gandhi Foundation, SIFPSA, World Vision
6. *Private companies*: DuPont, Hindustan Latex, Hindustan Lever, ITC, Reckitt Benckiser, Tata Chemicals, Thompson Social, Wipro
7. *Some agri clients of RMRB International*: Monsanto, ProAgro India Ltd., Syngenta, Rallis India Ltd.

The process for research has been depicted in Figure 1.1. Define the problem, decision alternatives and research objectives. Clarity on the following points helps to define the problem appropriately:

1. What is to be researched (the content, the scope)?
2. Why is it to be researched (decisions that must be made)?

Research plan development: The next step in carrying out marketing research involves taking decisions for developing a plan for efficiently gathering the required information. The manager (marketing manager) should know the total cost involved for carrying out the research. This will help managers in approving the total cost against the approved budget. The research plan, which can be prepared, will consist of information on different factors such as *data sources, research approaches, research instruments, sampling plan and contact methods*.

Data Sources

For any research, either primary or secondary data sources or a combination of both are required. *Secondary data* are data that were collected for a prior purpose and already exist somewhere. *Primary data* are data gathered for a specific purpose or for a specific research project. Researchers usually start

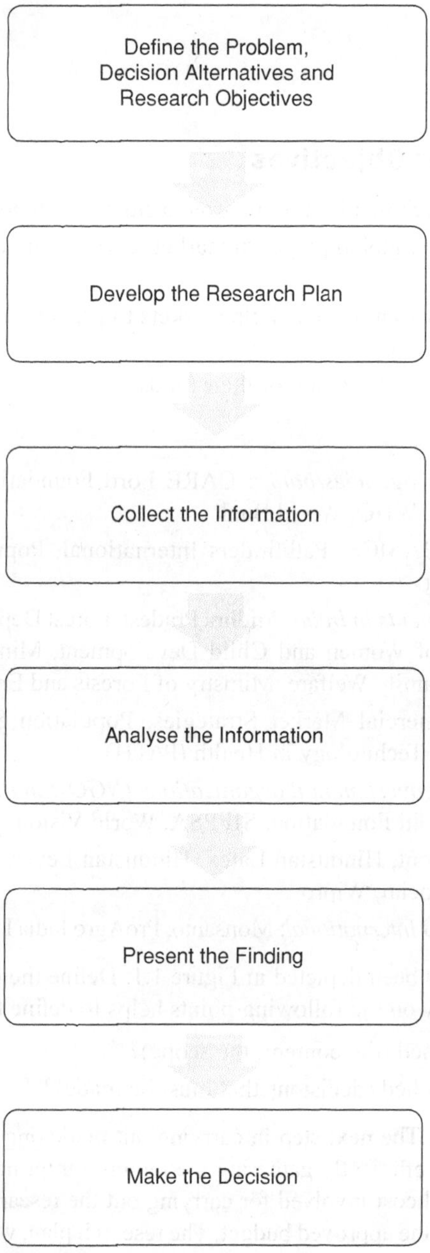

Figure 1.1 *Process Flow for Research*

data collection by collecting secondary data and then progressing to primary survey, if required. In this way, the cost of data collection can be reduced.

A *customer* or *prospect database* is an organized collection of comprehensive data about individual customers, prospects or suspects that are current, accessible and actionable for marketing purposes such as lead development.

Research Approaches

Usually primary data are collected in several ways such as observation, focus group research, conducting surveys, behavioural data collection and experiments.

- *Observational research*: Fresh data can be gathered by observing the relevant actors and settings.
- *Focus group research*: A *focus group* is a gathering of 6–10 people who are invited to spend a few hours with a skilled moderator to discuss a product, service, organization or some other marketing entity.
- *Ethnographic research*: This is a particular observational research approach that uses concepts and tools from anthropology and other social science disciplines to provide an in-depth understanding of how people live and work.
- *Survey research*: Surveys are best suited for descriptive research. Companies undertake surveys to learn about people's knowledge, beliefs, preferences and satisfaction, and to measure these magnitudes in the general population.
- *Behavioural data*: *These data are usually captured by* noticing and recording the purchase behaviour of customers in a store. These data can also be recorded from different recorded sources such as catalogue purchase records and customer databases. By analysing these data first-hand information can be prepared on consumer behavioural pattern, which can increase accuracy in decision making for marketing managers. When customers visit different places for purchasing goods, they exhibit preferences for different brands and buy products based on perceived value for money. For customers, value for money is determined by brand equity, price tag, sales promotions, etc. These data are captured to aid in making future policy decisions.
- *Experimental research*: This method is used to do research in a controlled environment. The results are also statistically and scientifically valid. In this approach the assumption is that each pattern of purchase behaviour has a cause, and experimental research records the cause and effect relationships. Usually, based on past literature and data, hypotheses are developed and these hypotheses are tested when conducting controlled experimental research. The key to success in this experiment is selecting samples that represent the actual target population, simulating the correct purchase environment, identifying and controlling different parameters that affect purchase behaviour and checking if the final results exhibit statistical significance.

Research Instruments

There are three main research instruments:

1. Questionnaires
2. Qualitative measures
3. Technological measures

Sampling Plan

The sampling plan consists of the following:

1. Sampling unit: Who should we survey?
2. Sample size: How many people should we survey?
3. Sampling procedure: How should we choose the respondents?

Contact Methods

The major contact methods are as follows:

1. Mail questionnaire
2. Telephone interview
3. Personal interview
4. Online interview

Collect the Information

The data collection phase of marketing research is generally the most expensive and the most prone to error. In the case of surveys, four major problems arise:

1. Some respondents will not be at home and must be recontacted or replaced.
2. Other respondents will refuse to cooperate.
3. Still others will give biased or dishonest answers.
4. Some interviewers will be biased or dishonest.

Analyse the Information

Researchers now compute averages and measures of dispersion for major variables and apply some advanced statistical techniques and decision models in the hope of discovering additional findings.

Present the Findings

Researchers present findings that are relevant to the management for making major marketing decisions. They also consider ways to present the research findings in as understandable and compelling a fashion as possible.

Make the Decision

Research findings provide only additional information and insight to managers. Depending on their confidence in the findings, managers decide to use them, discard them or decide to carry out more research.

RMRB INTERNATIONAL'S DIVISION: SRRI

The SRRI was set up in 1990 with the objective of establishing a specialist unit to give focus and identity to two aspects of research that RMRB International had, in fact, been actively involved in for several years, namely, social research and research of and for rural markets.

SRRI uses a combination of desk research, qualitative research techniques such as focus group discussions and participatory research, as well as quantitative research techniques. In addition, SRRI approaches each research subject with an open mind and adapts market research techniques to suit the special requirements of illiteracy, poor articulation, language and dialects of subjects.

SRRI has two distinct missions that guide its operations: to study social issues with commitment, expertise, objectivity and an orientation towards actionability; and to set up databases and develop research expertise for marketing in rural India, about which hitherto there has been a paucity of data.

SRRI is guided by its mission specialists in conducting social research and rural research. Social research deals with research on causes and issues that can contribute to actions that bring about social change. Rural research pertains to research in, of and for rural areas, both for resolving social issues as well as for rural marketing.

Coverage

SRRI takes pride in having the resources to conduct data collection in almost any part of the country. It can undertake several nationwide surveys almost simultaneously and at a much faster rate than other similar institutions. In the last three years, we have undertaken four nationwide surveys and our presence is felt in almost all parts of India.

In the flowchart shown in Figure 1.2, we can see how RMRB takes a project and provides the final result to a client. First, a client sends a request to RMRB. If the request is feasible then it is send to the research wing to prepare questions and target samples. Otherwise, the request is send back to the client. If the client is satisfied with the questionnaire, then it is send to the field officer to carry out the interview. But, if the client is not satisfied with the questionnaire, then it is send back to the research wing for modification or change. If the field officer is able to conduct the interview properly, then the collected information is send to the analysis department. If the field officer fails to conduct the interview properly, then questionnaire is send back to the research wing. From the analysis department, information is send to research wing for interpretation using various tools, and then the final output is given to the client.

The following section gives a sample questionnaire prepared by RMRB on global warming.

Sample Questionnaire

This questionnaire is solely for academic purposes. We are conducting a survey to reveal the understanding of people from different age groups, backgrounds and cultures on global warming. Please feel free to express yourself. Honestly, it will take just 2 minutes of your precious time!

Name ________________________________

Age ________________________________

State ________________________________

Religion ________________________________

Highest educational qualification ________________

Gender ________________________________

Occupation ________________________________

Designation ________________________________

Question 1. Do you feel that some kind of change has been happening in our environment in the last five years?

a. Yes

b. No

c. Did not notice

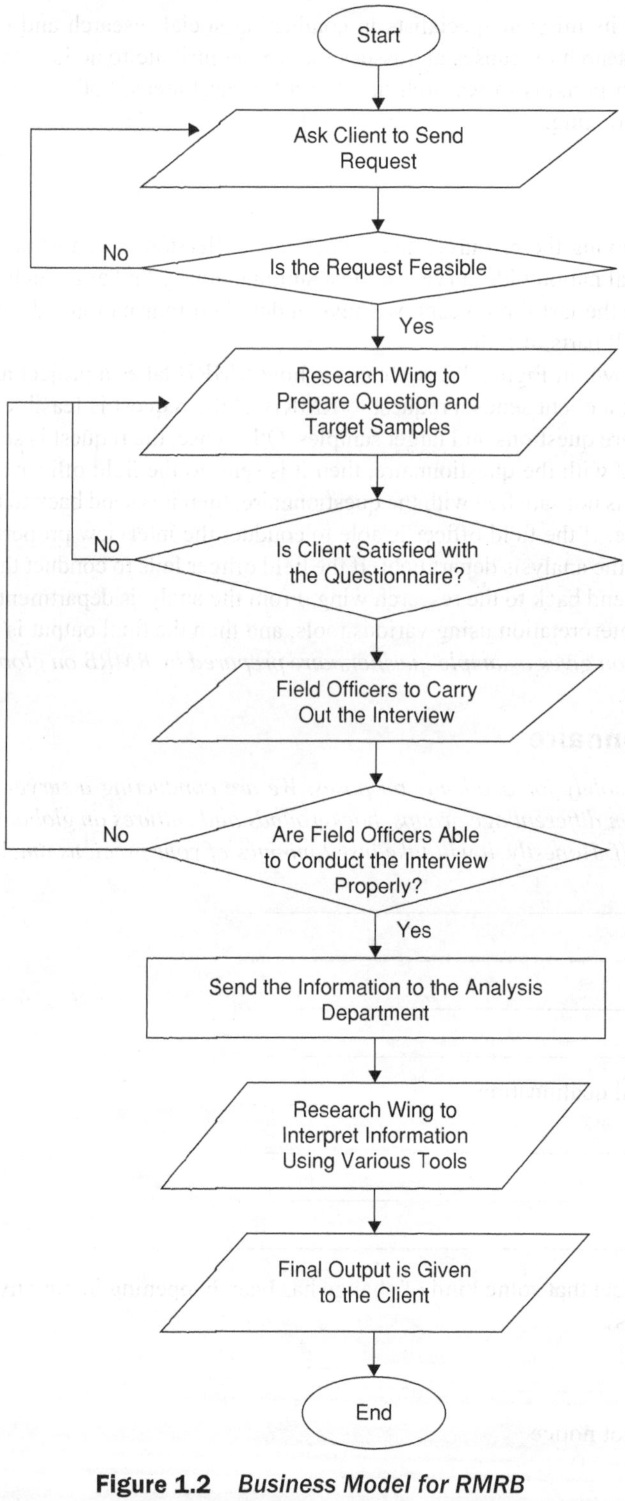

Figure 1.2 *Business Model for RMRB*

Question 2. Have you heard about global warming/climate change?

a. Yes
b. No
c. Did not notice

Question 3. Do you think that you can individually combat the issue of carbon emissions?

a. Yes
b. No
c. No idea

Question 4. Do you reuse waste paper?

a. Yes
b. No
c. No idea

Question 5. Do you think that by adjusting air conditioners to moderate temperatures we can reduce carbon emissions?

a. Yes
b. No
c. No idea

Question 6. Do you think that brand campaigning by various organizations, such as Honda, to reduce carbon emissions has helped in making people aware about the issue?

a. Yes
b. No
c. No idea

Question 7. What do you understand by the term 'carbon footprint'?

a. No idea
b. Carbon produced by each individual because of personal activities
c. Attempts by organizations or the government to reduce carbon emissions

Question 8. According to you, which of the following is the best way to reduce carbon emissions?

a. Plant more and more tress
b. Travel by public transport
c. Reduce per capita electricity consumption by encouraging the utilization of renewable sources of energy such as wind, solar and bio oil
d. All the above

Question 9. Do you think that it will have an impact if the government is strict about reducing carbon emissions?

a. Yes
b. No
c. No idea

Question 10. If you are paid for planting trees, which in turn curbs carbon emissions, will you be motivated to do so?

a. Yes

b. No

c. No idea

Question 11. Was Dr. R. K. Pachauri's winning of the Nobel prize helpful in generating awareness about global warming?

a. Yes

b. No

c. No idea

Question 12. Do you feel that an individual's energy needs have an effect on carbon emissions?

a. Yes

b. No

c. No idea

Question 13. Have you heard of 'Kyoto Protocol'?

a. Yes

b. No

c. No idea

Question 14. Do you feel bothered about various talks, discussions, etc., about climate change?

a. Yes

b. No

c. No idea

Question 15. Do you feel that renewable sources of energy will be of great help to combat global warming?

a. Yes

b. No

c. No idea

THANK YOU!

INFORMATION SECURITY

To make sure that sensitive information is accessible only by authenticated personnel, various arrangements are made. These arrangements are discussed in detail in the following sections.

Firewalls

Firewalls are hardware devices or software programs or combinations of both located at the network gateway, which control traffic of the data entering a network or a system, thus protecting the private network based on set guidelines and rules.

Cryptography

Cryptography refers to the practice and study of hiding information. This means even if somebody is able to access the secure information, he or she will not be able to use it as it is hidden. The following terms are important in cryptography:

Until modern times, cryptography referred almost exclusively to *encryption*, the process of converting ordinary information (plain text) to unintelligible gibberish (that is, *cipher text*). Decryption is the reverse process, converting unintelligible cipher text to plain text. A cipher (or *cypher*) is a pair of algorithms that creates the encryption and the decryption. The detailed operation of a cipher is controlled both by the algorithm and, in each instance, by a *key*. A key is a secret parameter (known only to the communicants ideally) for a specific message exchange context. Keys are important, as ciphers without variable keys are trivially breakable and therefore less than useful for most purposes. Historically, ciphers were often used directly for encryption or decryption, without additional procedures such as authentication or integrity checks.

In colloquial use, the term 'code' is often used to mean any method of encryption or any concealment of meaning. However, in cryptography *code* has a more specific meaning; it means the replacement of a unit of plain text (that is, a meaningful word or phrase) with a code word (for example, 'apple pie' replaces 'attack at dawn'). Codes are no longer used in serious cryptography, except incidentally for such things as unit designation, since properly chosen ciphers are both more practical and more secure than even the best codes and better adapted to use in computers as well.

Security Keys

A message encrypted with a recipient's public key cannot be decrypted by anyone except the recipient who possesses the corresponding private key. This is used to ensure confidentiality.

In public key cryptography, there are two keys that are used to access a system. These two keys are usually alphanumeric numbers that are mathematically related to each other. Whereas one key encrypts the access, the second key decrypts it. A person trying to access a system in an unauthorized manner must know both the keys for accessing the system. There are private and public keys, and usually the owner of the system uses one of the keys to decrypt while the other key is used to encrypt the system.

DERIVATION OF OPERATIONAL STRATEGY

Please refer to Annexure for balanced scorecard details.

The corporate objectives are as follows:

1. To provide quality research
2. To offer the most competitive market price
3. To bring new clients to the fold

The business strategy includes the following:

1. Comparative advantage
2. Cost advantage
3. Market dominance

The operational strategy is as follows:

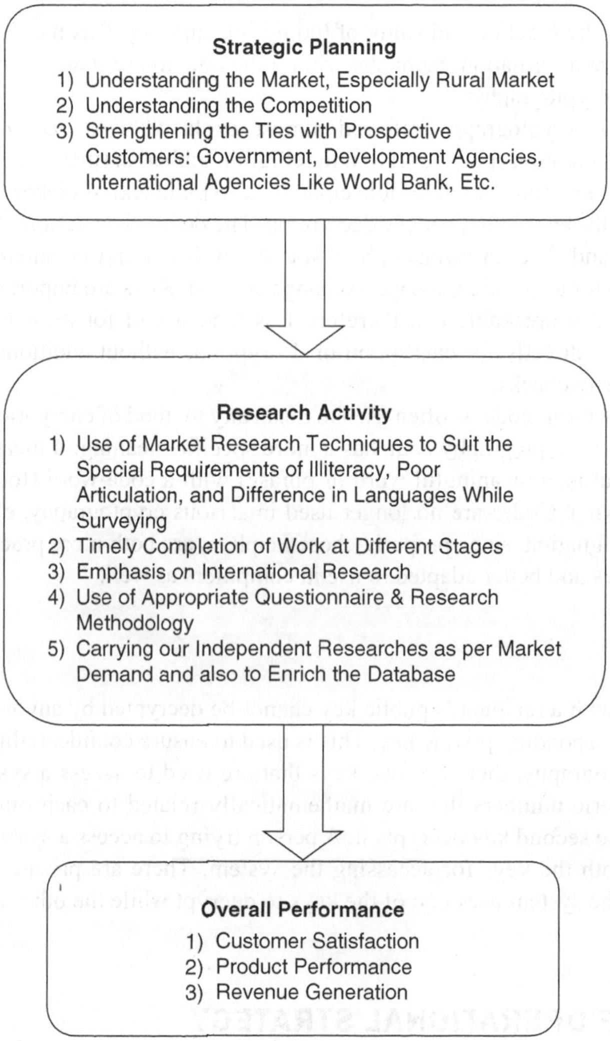

Figure 1.3 *Process of Aligning Operational Strategy to Corporate Objectives*

Operational strategy needs to be aligned with business goals. This will result in achieving business results as desired by the organization. Figure 1.3 shows the alignment.

METRICS

1. *On time reporting factor*: This metric is useful for determining the timeliness of report update by field offices to the head office. Twice a week the field offices have to update the head office about the progress made in various projects, that is, on Mondays and Thursdays. Its time period can be quarterly, half yearly or yearly.

$$\text{OTR} = \frac{\text{Number of times report was received on time}}{\text{Total number of weeks}}$$

2. *Time efficiency factor*: This metric depicts how time efficient an organization is in carrying out the projects of its clients. It shows the capacity of the organization to meet project deadlines.

$$T = \frac{\text{Number of projects completed on time}}{\text{Total number of projects received (during a period)}}$$

3. *Overall client loyality*: Creating, maintaining and enhancing customer relationships is essential to sustain business success. Overall customer loyalty goes beyond customer satisfaction and quality management, and focuses on customer commitment and loyalty to the organization. It is calculated as follows:

$$\text{OCL} = W_1 \times C_1 + W_2 \times C_2 + K + W_n \times C_n$$

$$W = \frac{\text{Weightage of projects by the client}}{\text{Total number of projects of RMRB}}$$

$$C = \frac{\text{Number of projects offered to RMRB}}{\text{Total number of potential projects for RMRB of the client}}$$

4. *Employee Attrition Rate (EAR)*: The EAR is a tool that provides a fast, affordable way to measure the level of employee commitment and identify factors affecting employee commitment. EAR is not just an 'employee satisfaction' survey; it provides you with information on how to increase turnover and implement programs that have the greatest impact on employee commitment and satisfaction. It provides benchmarks for measuring ongoing improvement efforts and activities.

$$E = \frac{\text{Number of employees who left the company during a given period}}{\text{(Employee strength at the beginning of the period + Employee strength at the end of the period)/2}}$$

5. *Cost-effectiveness factor*: Cost effectiveness is a factor that shows how effective an organization has been in completing a given project within its allocated budget.

$$\text{CE} = \frac{\text{Total cost incurred during a project (AC)}}{\text{Total budget allocated to this project (EC)}}$$

6. *Periodicity*: The time allocated to data collection, analysis and report preparation depends upon
   i. Nature of the project
   ii. Project duration

   Report updating is done by field offices to the research department every Monday and Thursday for continuous evaluation in order to update the client on a regular basis.

DESIGN OF MANAGEMENT INFORMATION SYSTEM (MIS)

As RMRB is a market research organization, the design of MIS is such that it caters to the needs of not only the organization per se but also the clients, partners and other stakeholders simultaneously.

In India, RMRB has four branch offices, each located at different cities in the eastern, western, northern and southern parts of the country. The branch offices further have control over the regional field offices. These field offices are 15 in number, and each field office comes under the purview of its respective branch office.

To enable information sharing among all the field offices and to connect them to all the branch offices, a central server is located at one of the branch offices. All field offices coming under the purview of one branch office are connected to that branch office through extranet connectivity. The extranet is used for security purposes. As we know, market research data collected at various times are crucial and even a slight lapse in security can result in huge monetary loss as well as loss of reputation for the organization. Thus, in order to ensure optimum security and safety of the system, the branch office is connected to field offices using extranet connectivity.

Further, all the branch offices are connected to the central server, which as mentioned already is located at one of the branch offices. The server keeps a record of all information that is required in the organization. The RMRB server is a computer dedicated to providing one or more services over a computer network, typically through a request–response routine. These services are furnished by specialized server applications, which are computer programs designed to handle multiple concurrent requests. By driving down infrastructure costs, improving time to market and shifting user resources towards the development of new applications and services, RMRB server helps to accelerate the cost-effective deployment of converged services.

As RMRB is a market research organization, the output of research is given to the clients in the form of presentations or as information stored in compact discs or digital versatile discs (DVDs). Thus, usually connectivity is required with the clients just to send and receive emails and timelines and to share information. These clients are connected to the RMRB server through the Internet, as the information required to be shared is not very sensitive. And it is through other secure means that the final output of research is delivered to them.

However, depending upon the demand of clients and the kind of research done, it becomes essential at times to share important information with clients on a real-time basis using IT. As the information that needs to be shared is important and sensitive, such clients are given extranet connectivity to ensure security. An extranet is a private network that uses Internet protocols, network connectivity and possibly the public telecommunication system to securely share part of an organization's information or operations with suppliers, vendors, partners, customers or other businesses. An extranet can be viewed as the part of a company's intranet that is extended to users outside the company (for example, normally over the Internet). It has also been described as a 'state of mind' in which the Internet is perceived as a way to do business with a preapproved set of other companies B2B, in isolation from all other Internet users.

MIS FOR THE RESEARCH DEPARTMENT

As RMRB is basically a research-oriented organization, we will concentrate more on the MIS that cater exclusively to the needs of the company's research department. There are four departments in any branch office of RMRB; they are

- Research department
- Field department

- Commerce department
- Analytics department

The four departments in a branch office are connected to each other through the company intranet. As an intranet is a private computer network that uses Internet protocols and network connectivity to securely share any part of an organization's information or operational systems with its employees, it best suits the security need of various departments. As an intranet is built from the same concepts and technologies as those used for the Internet, such as client and server systems running on the Internet protocol suite (TCP/IP), the flow of information is lucid, fast and secure.

The most important issue that is associated with the research department of RMRB is security. At times, research content is so sensitive that the need of the client is that the content should not be accessible even to the other departments and offices of the company except the one that is actually conducting the research on the subject. A situation like this creates a challenge for the MIS in that the four departments have to share the same intranet but only limited information from the research department should be accessible to the rest of the departments. Thus, it becomes crucial for the organization to take care of security issues. So the MIS design should be such that only the part of information that is to be shared should flow through the network; the rest should be inaccessible to the other departments sharing the same intranet system.

DISCUSSION QUESTIONS

1. How are business processes different in a market research organization than those in a marketing services organization?
2. How do you measure the success of research projects?
3. How are corporate objectives set for research activities?
4. How does MIS help in measuring the success of research activities?

ANNEXURE

Perspective	Performance
Financial perspective	
Research performance perspective	
Operational perspective	
Learning and growth perspective	
Total performance	

(*Continued...*)

Strategy Tree and Scorecard Details:

Perspective	**Goal**	**Weight (× 10)**	**Description**	**Performance (%)**	**Measure Unit**	**Target Values**
Financial Perspective		3				
	Percentage of research quantum received from the government	4		Funding received from the government to support research activities.	%	40%
	Proportion of income from research	2.5	It means the percentage to total income associated to research income.	%	100%	
	Research income per academic staff	3.5	Research income divided by number of academic staff.		Rs (in thousands)	100
Total Performance in Group			**Financial Perspective**			
Research Performance Perspective		3				
	Number of international research publications	It refers to the number of international research publications in a year.		#	50	
	Number of research grants sanctioned	2	It means the number of research grants sanctioned in a year (on a scale of 1 to 10).		Score	10
	Number of national research publications	4	It refers to the number of national research publications in a year.		#	200

Total Performance in Group			**Research Performance Perspective**		
Operational Perspective		2			
	Research output of research assessment exercise (RAE)	3	It refers to research output of RAE.	%	100%
	Number of higher degree by research completions per 10 research staff	3	It means the number of higher degree by research completions per 10 research staff.	#	25
	Number of external contracts for research facilities	3		Score	10
Total Performance in Group			**Operational Perspective**		
Learning and Growth Perspective		2			
	Percentage increase in student involvement	3	It means percentage increase in student involvement in the research activities undertaken.	%	100%
	Number of feedbacks	2	Number of feedbacks received from students regarding the research initiatives comprised of suggestions (on a scale of 1 to 10).	Score	10

(*Continued...*)

Strategy Tree and Scorecard Details: (...*Continued*)

Perspective	Goal	Weight (× 10)	Description	Performance (%)	Measure Unit	Target Values
	Number of research initiatives undertaken	3	Independent research studies undertaken.		Score	10
	Proportion of research active staff	2	Number of researchers divided by the total number of staff.		%	40%
Total Performance in Group			**Learning and Growth Perspective**			

2

Case Study on Merger and Acquisition: Coromandel Fertilisers Limited

Integrating Business Entities in a Merger and Acquisition Successfully through Strategic Information System

VISION

The vision of Coromondel Fertilisers Ltd. (CFL) is to be the leader in the phosphatic fertilizer industry, producing high-quality fertilizers at a low cost and satisfying all stake holders.

MISSION

The mission of CFL is to enhance the prosperity of farmers by supplying quality farm inputs and related services to ensure value for money.

COMPANY PROFILE

CFL was established in 1961 with a licence approval from the Government of India. Under this licence, IMC, Chevron Chemical Company and E.I.D. Parry (India) Ltd. were entered into a partnership. To enhance the visibility of CFL among farmers, in 1970, the brand 'Gromor' was introduced as the marketing symbol. Over the years, CFL evolved, and during the period 1995–99, E.I.D. Parry (India) Ltd. bought the stakes of the other two partners.

CFL chose the inorganic growth route for its growth, and it acquired Ficom Organics Ltd. (Ficom) and Godavari Fertilisers and Chemicals Ltd. (GFCL). Then, CFL followed the route by merging Ficom and its wholly owned subsidiary Rasilah Investments Ltd. in April 2006 and GFCL in April 2007. By these acquisitions, CFL has maintained its position as the second-largest phosphatic fertilizer producer in India.

HOLDING STRUCTURE

Figure 2.1 is the holding structure of the parent group.

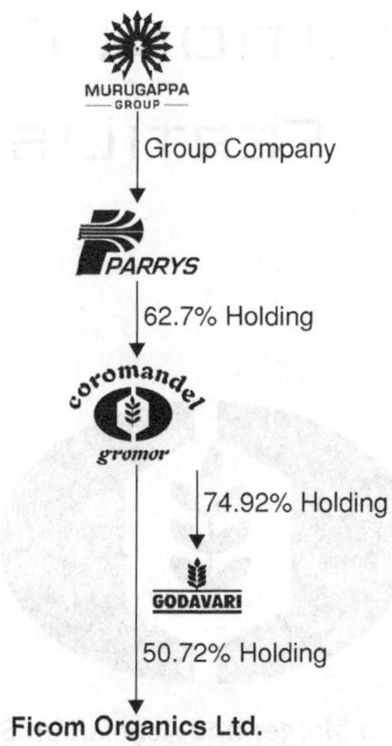

Figure 2.1 *The Holding Structure of the Parent Group*

BUSINESS DIVISIONS

Phosphatic Fertilizers

The major produce of CFL is phosphatic fertilizers in India. CFL has a combined production capacity of 23.10 lakh tonnes of complex fertilizers, 8.15 lakh tonnes of diammonium phosphate and 1.32 lakh tonnes of single super phosphate (SSP). It produces phosphatic fertilizers of various grades, complex fertilizers and SSP and also manufactures potash, another key plant nutrient, which are sold under the well-established brand names 'Gromor', 'Godavari', 'Paramfos', 'ParryGold' and 'Parry Super'. CFL has dealer networks in Andhra Pradesh, Karnataka, Tamil Nadu, Maharashtra, Orissa, Chhattisgarh, parts of Uttar Pradesh, Madhya Pradesh and West Bengal.

Pesticides (Plant Protection)

The pesticides division is a growing business, and in the last financial year, it registered a turnover growth of 26% over the previous year. Of these, endosulfan and malathion continue to be the major contributors to the turnover. Co-marketing tie-ups with leading MNCs help the company in accessing speciality chemicals and strengthening its portfolio in new crop segments such as wheat.

Speciality Nutrients

Speciality nutrients including 'bentonite sulphur' (Gromor Sulphur), water-soluble fertilizers and other micronutrients are getting a major thrust from CFL, enabling the company to provide a wide range of farm inputs and services to the farming community through a balanced fertilization.

Plant Locations

Figure 2.2 shows locations of CFL plants throughout the country.

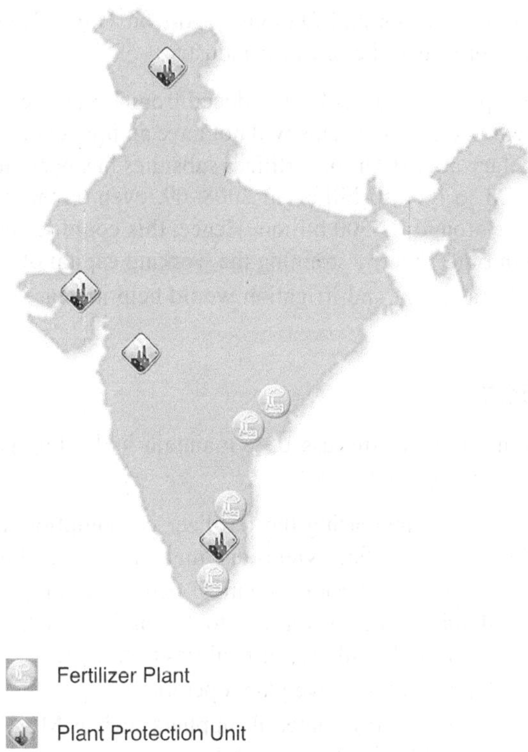

Figure 2.2 *Plant Locations of CFL*

INDUSTRY OVERVIEW

Agriculture is the predominant occupation of about 65% of the Indian population. While it grew at 2.6% in 2007–08, the desired growth was 4%. Agriculture always draws greater attention from the government, yet a lot needs to be done. One of the prime factors which will foster growth in this sector is the fertilizer consumption. Over the past seven years, the overall fertilizer consumption increased by 26%, but still there is an enormous scope for further increase.

In recent years, international prices of food, fuel and edible oils have increased, thereby underlining the importance of stability in domestic price and growth in agricultural sector in ensuring food security to a large human population. This also stresses the role of government subsidies in making agriculture a viable occupation.

In the case of fertilizer sector, demand outstrips supply, because there is not enough production to meet the demand. The major factor contributing to low production is non-availability of raw materials such as sulphur, rock phosphate, phosphoric acid, sulphuric acid and potash.

The Indian pesticides industry is dominated by multinationals. The industry took a hit as Bt cotton adoption reached a new high with 65% of the total acreage of land cultivated in India used for genetically modified varieties. The bane of the pesticides industry became the boon for the fertilizer industry because genetically modified varieties require fertilizers extensively.

The latest CRISIL Research Analysis and Outlook report on Union Budget 2008–09 makes the following observations with reference to the fertilizer industry:

- The customs duty on phosphoric acid has been reduced from 7.5 per cent to 5.0 per cent, whereas on sulphur from 5 per cent to 2 per cent. This will not have an impact on margins as product prices are regulated. The budgetary allocation for fertilizer subsidies has been increased marginally from Rs 305 billion in 2007–08 to Rs 310 billion in 2008–09, even as the estimated subsidy bill for 2008–09 is expected to be around Rs 500 billion. Hence, this could result in arrears if the balance subsidy is not provided in time, thereby straining the working capital of fertilizer companies.
- Greater thrust on agricultural credit and irrigation would help increase the fertilizer consumption in the long run.

BUSINESS STRATEGY

Operating in an industry environment as discussed, to maintain its leading position in the phosphatic fertilizers, CFL adopted the following strategies:[3]

- Educate farmers on the need for increasing the fertilizer consumption and providing a balanced nutrition to crops in order to improve farm yields and maintain soil health.
- Set up rural retail centres called 'Mana Gromor Centres' selling the company's fertilizers, pesticides and speciality nutrients with other products directly to the rural population. These centres will also impart technical training and provide soil testing facilities to farmers.
- Initiate brand-building activities and improve plant operations.
- Long-term tie-ups with international raw material suppliers such as M/s Foskor (South Africa) and M/s Groupe Chimique Tunisien (Tunisia) to enable the company to maximize the production.
- Improve infrastructure and supply chain to reduce costs.
- Increase revenue and profitability from non-subsidy-related activities.

Apart from aforementioned strategies, CFL took inorganic growth route by acquiring and controlling stakes in Ficom in 2006 and GFCL in 2007.

Ficom is a technical-grade pesticides manufacturing company. It is one of the world's three manufacturers of technical-grade malathion, an agrochemical, and is an export-oriented company. With its acquisition, CFL has got an opportunity to expand its own export market.

GFCL was a leading phosphatic fertilizer manufacturing company with its plant located at Kakinada, Andhra Pradesh. According to CFL Chairman and Vice-chairman and Director (strategic) of Murugappa group, A. Vellayan, 'Both the companies have a lot of synergies. The combined entity would become the second largest manufacturer of phosphatic fertilizers in India after IFFCO and would have a combined turnover of more than Rs 4,000 crore' (Director's Annual Report, 2007–08). The areas of synergies include raw material processes, geographical presence, combined marketing strength, a wide range of products, including high-end and low-end phosphatic products and sulphur, and easy penetration in deep pockets of Andhra Pradesh, Tamil Nadu, Karnataka, Maharashtra and Orissa.

UNDERSTANDING THE TERM MERGER AND ACQUISITION (M&A)

An acquisition, or a takeover, is the purchase of one company, referred to as the 'target', by another company. Acquisition may be either friendly or hostile. In order to acquire the target company, the buyer company buys a majority of the shares or the assets of the target company, thereby taking control over the target company.

Acquisition indicates the management control of a buyer company over its target company. Merger, on the other hand, is the consolidation of two companies into one company. Either the target company loses its identity or the combination of both the companies gives place to a new identity for the consolidated one. Mergers are, generally, voluntary and involve stock swaps. The shareholders of the existing companies are compensated by swapping their shareholding with equal-value shares of the new entity.[10] As is clear from this discussion, merger results in a new company and a new branding.

M&As: A BUSINESS STRATEGY

Globalization has changed the way business is conducted today. Companies do not operate in isolation. Domestic and global economic environment play a crucial role in day-to-day business decisions that executives make. 'Competition' and 'staying ahead' are the two objectives on which managers focus always. To grow the business, building new production capacities will be the obvious choice. But, actually, it is not so. The change that companies have to implement these days is so rapid that green-field projects are the last thing on a management's agenda. A company having a pile of cash reserves or facing a tough competition in the marketplace would prefer to acquire another company for some of the following business concerns:

- *Eliminate competition*: The easiest thing a company can do to eliminate a competitor is to make the competitor its own part by acquiring the competitor.
- *Increase market share*: Increasing the customer base is a challenge, and by acquiring another firm which operates in the same line of its business, a company can add a whole new group of customers to its base overnight.
- *Cost efficiency*: Managing costs is a Herculean task, but by combining two companies, a big pool of resources, such as suppliers, warehouses, production plants, distributors and retailers, is generated, which can significantly help in bringing cost efficiency by removing the common resources.
- *Improve product lines*: With the consolidation of businesses, the management gains the ability to remove brands which are getting duplicated post-merger.

- *Acquire the needed resources*: Setting up a new supply chain from scratch may be troublesome for the management, whereas a company can simply acquire its suppliers or distribution channels to align them for its own business objectives.
- *Achieve wider market penetration*: It may take years for a company to enter a market and create a good recognition for its products and services. Consolidation with another company allows a company to enter into such markets.
- *Cross-selling*: One may observe that some companies buy other companies which are not operating, in the real sense of the words, in the same line of business. Yet, this makes a lot of sense for the company because it can then offer its own products to the customers of its target company.
- *Obtaining proprietary rights to products or services*: Companies that create a niche market for their products and services are quite often the acquisition targets of rival firms that wish to dominate by having all the major brands or products under their blanket.
- *Business synergies*: Companies which are futuristic in nature look for strategic buyouts which can bring significant business synergies in almost all the functional areas, so as to launch into another growth trajectory by building a sound base in the present.
- *Avoid being a takeover target*: It is a classic case of a fish that fearing itself to be eaten up by another one attacks back and eats the assumed threat. Companies are no different from this fear, and to manage this fear, they increase their business size by acquiring other companies similar to the line of their business.

SOME ISSUES IN M&As

M&As are fraught with risks which are not quite visible as managements rush to make them happen. With the realization over time that so many of the mergers have failed, companies pay attention to the following issues while the mergers are underway:

Cultural Integration

Culture consists of long-standing, largely implicit shared values, beliefs and assumptions that influence behaviour and attitudes in a company (or a society). Culture influences the behaviour of people and people's interpretation of their own actions. For a successful cultural integration, organizations should consider the following aspects:

- Culture should be considered a major component of all the change-management initiatives.
- Owners of both companies need to be involved in the integration process to represent their views.
- Cultural integration should be measured by tying it to tangible business results.
- If cultures are different, it should be assessed whether the elements can be integrated. If integration is problematic, separate core competencies of each company should be retained.
- A decision-making process that has not been hampered by cultural differences should be implemented, and this can be achieved by identifying decision makers for each area of the integration.
- If retaining the employees is a goal of integration, then an effort must be made to secure their loyalty, just as customer loyalty must be reinforced. Emphasis should be on making the acquiring company's brand attractive, in terms of the career opportunities, rewards and the sense of identity that it offers to the 'acquired' employees. Thus, employee loyalty must be secured through building a common employee brand.
- Interfaces for critical business integration points that help create business value should be designed or improved.

Talent Assessment

With the new entity replacing the older ones, there is a need to re-look at the competencies that are required at various functional levels. Talent in both the integrating entities should be assessed for job fits.

Speed of Integration

There are certain business benefits which accrue only if the integration is achieved in a time frame. If this time limit is breached, the various stakeholders pose questions to the management regarding the logic behind going ahead for the merger.

Strategy Integration

Pre-merger, companies devise their own strategies to work in a business environment. These strategies may fall in-line or out of line with each other. Once the firms are combined, it is quintessential that all the functions should 'row in the same direction'. This calls for an integration of the business strategies at all levels.

Customer Service and Systems Integration

All organizations run their own systems aimed at achieving organizational objectives. At the front end, customer service is of prime importance. Post-merger, the consolidated entity should continue to deliver the same levels of customer service to maintain customer loyalty and good image. All these can be achieved through a proper integration of systems.

Supply Chain Synergy

Integration creates a pool of resources in each segment of a supply chain. To make the integration effective, supply chain synergies have to be achieved to make the integration profitable and leaner.

MANAGING THE CHANGE DURING INTEGRATION

Integration is essential for the success of any merger, and it has various dimensions such as cultural integration, systems integration and process integration. It is frequently observed that integration is preceded by chaos, as no one knows what to do. The organization has grown overnight: there are new employees to take care of, new supplier and vendor relations to be managed and a plethora of processes to be streamlined. In such a scenario, managing the change during integration assumes utmost importance.

As organizations come together to function as a single entity, the change-management teams must develop a systematic plan for helping individuals and teams to transition to their new roles, or new place in the complete organization structure. The same applies to managing the change in systems and processes.

Change management involves processes and tools for assisting this transition. On its process side, it is critical to building awareness of the need for a change. Educating and training the staff is helpful in making them aware of the happenings in their organization and managing their anxieties. Managers and supervisors can also act as coaches for effectively bringing this transformation. On the tools side, the organization can use measurement systems for assessing the change and its impact on various aspects of the organization. Through skill development and rewards programme, organizations can make employees an important stakeholder in the success of the organizational integration.

Kurt Lewin proposed a model, known as Unfreeze-Change-Refreeze, for change management. In this three-stage model, the first stage is 'Unfreeze', which calls for dismantling the existing mindset about the change itself. The second stage, 'Change', involves the actual change. This is a period of confusion and transition. The old ways of doing things do not hold good, and one does not know which new ways will replace the older ones. The third stage, 'Freeze', leads to crystallization of a new mind-set, a new view of the organization. A similar approach to change was proposed by Hughes, who made reference to 'Exit' (departing from an existing state), 'Transit' (crossing unknown territory) and 'Entry' (attaining a new equilibrium).

Whatever be the approach, the objective of the change-management process for integration during a merger is to bring order to the chaos among the individuals and stability in processes.

STAGES IN M&A INTEGRATION

Metrus Group has defined four stages in M&As that can make or hinder the outcome of the integration process:[5]

Pre-planning: At the very onset, a buyer company should effectively identify the target M&A candidates that will fit on multiple important dimensions of success, not only on the financial ones.

Due diligence: During due diligence, onus should be on gathering information on culture, leadership, organizational capabilities and customers. There typically exists a plethora of information about the human capital, hidden cultural black holes, management talent, leadership strength and philosophy, customer focus, and values that go well beyond the financial and market data that are being analyzed.

The after-close evaluation and integration planning: After the closure of a deal, new information keeps getting discovered, and conflict over assumptions, resources, style and roles is frequent. At this stage, development of an integration strategy should begin followed by development of an integration scorecard that measures all the important elements that must be tackled during this period, with clear success targets, accountabilities and monitoring.

Integration implementation: Clear strategic metrics, such as customer loyalty, employee commitment and core process cycle times, are critical to ensure that the limited resources of the organization are focusing on the really important activities—activities that produce value in the new context. Ongoing monitoring of these metrics and integration tracking are essential to efficiently and effectively complete the integration with the expected value.

BUSINESS PROCESS

The business process in a manufacturing setup is shown in Figure 2.3.

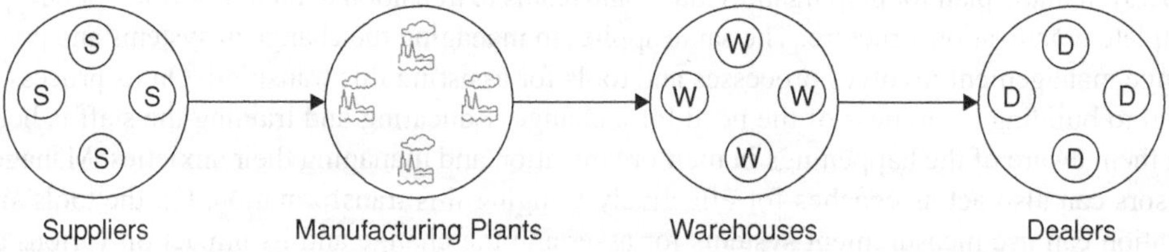

Figure 2.3 ***High-level Business Flow***

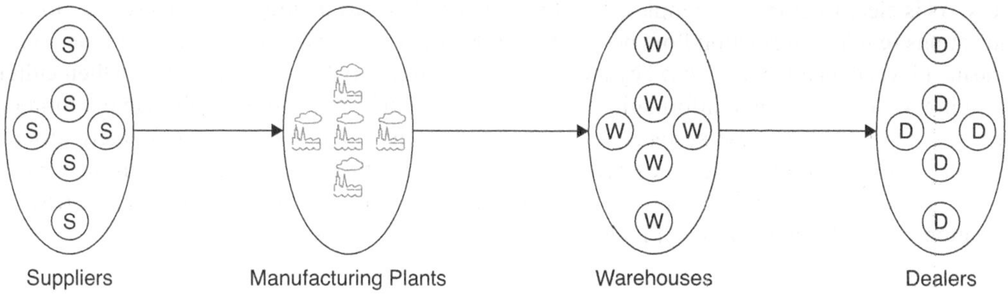

Figure 2.4 *Alignment after M&A*

Once the merger is complete, an organization is faced with a scenario in which two or more similar processes exist. The goal of an integration plan is to bring all the suppliers together. Same treatment has to be done for production facilities, warehouses and front-end dealers. Of course, at each stage of this process, there is a dire need to trim resources to achieve operational efficiencies. Consequently, the organization sets on a quest for finding out the partners who will stay with it in the future, and rest of the partners would cease to be part of the process. Next challenge would be to stabilize the process as new entrants will have to adjust to the process. This would require a great deal of synergies in the IT systems and operations. Once the dust settles down, the stabilized business process will flow exactly like the previous one, except that there would be a new set of partners at each stage, reflecting a mix of new and old partners (Figure 2.4).

MAJOR STAKEHOLDERS

In any M&A activity, all the major stakeholders should be identified because the integration will be successful in real terms only if the activity can provide realizable gains to all the stakeholders. In the case of CFL, the following stakeholders have been identified:

- Employees of CFL
- Farmers
- Shareholders
- Government
- Dealers
- Suppliers

MANAGEMENT INFORMATION SYSTEM (MIS) FOR INTEGRATION

A MIS consists of a network of all communication facilities used within an organization for collecting, storing, manipulating and disseminating data or information. These systems provide the management with status reports and enable objective decision making.

An organization is an amalgamation of various business functions, and these functions have to work together to achieve organizational goals. These functions are tied together by the need of information about each other. For example, the finance department requires information about the purchase orders that the inventory department places with a vendor, or the human resource department requires information from the production department regarding the vacancies so that they can plan their recruitment process. As is clear from these examples, an information system has to integrate all these functions. All organizations require information flow between their departments to run their day-to-day functions.

The next level of challenge is posed by mergers of two companies that differ not only in their cultures but also in their objectives and information systems. Even if both companies use the same information system software, the way these systems collect and deliver information may be completely different. Thus, there arises the need to align the organizations by aligning their information systems and training the combined workforce on these new systems, wherever needed. In sample MIS report sections, the information system for integrating CFL and its acquisitions will be discussed.

OBJECTIVES OF A MIS

- *To streamline the information flow between the merged entities*: Information flow is the basic ability of a MIS, but in an M&A scenario, it assumes a greater role in order to achieve cost efficiencies.
- *To help the company to manage relationships with all the existing and newly added stakeholders*: With addition of new stakeholders at each level of the supply chain to the existing ones, for an organization, it is crucial to manage the relationship with all the partners and enable them to fulfil their own organizational goals.
- *To assist the management in deciding which all suppliers it need, which are the strategic warehouse locations and which all dealers it should be related to post-merger*: As the number of partners at each stage increases, an organization should decide the partners with whom the business will be continued. The MIS will assist the management in identifying partners from whom sourcing will happen.
- *To cut down operational costs of the combined entities*: Separate companies have their own costs, but as a consolidated entity, some duplicate costs occur. MIS will help reduce operational costs by identifying wastage and common costs.

PRE-INTEGRATION STRATEGIC INFORMATION SYSTEM

With reference to the business process, the whole supply chain at CFL is depicted in Figure 2.5.

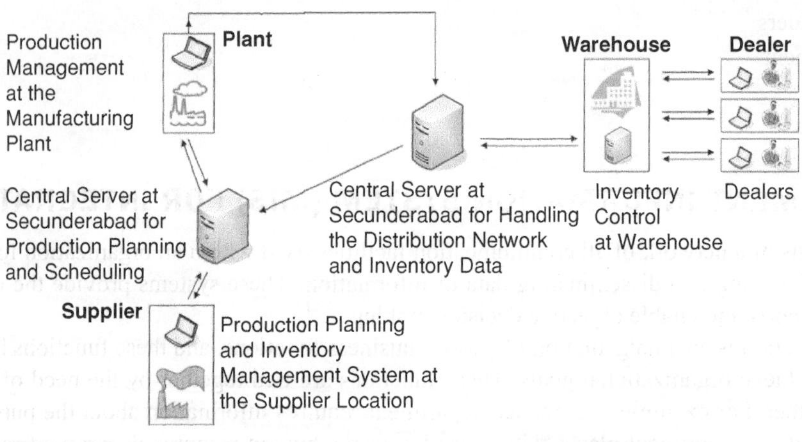

Figure 2.5 *Information System—Pre-merger*

The information system consists of two central servers at Secunderabad, the headquarters of CFL; one server functions as the production planning and scheduling server, whereas the other one functions as the distribution network and the inventory data server at the plants and the warehouses.

The production planning and scheduling server gets a regular update from the inventory management server about the inventory levels. Based on the estimation of the market demand and existing inventory levels at the plants and the warehouses, the server plans the production schedule and allocates targets to the various plants. On the sourcing part, it places the purchase order to the suppliers according to their supplying capacities and quotations. Once the fertilizers or pesticides are produced at the plants, the information is updated on the inventory management server. This server maintains the records of the stock levels at warehouses and gets regular updates from them. As per the demand, the products are moved to various warehouses, and the same gets updated in the system. The warehouses keep a record of the stock levels of their dealers and the dealers place their orders with the warehouses as per their stock needs, and the same is updated in the inventory control system at the warehouses. The inventory records at the warehouses may be manually or electronically kept, depending on the infrastructure availability.

STRATEGIC INFORMATION SYSTEM FOR PROCESS INTEGRATION

Once the merger is complete, the new partners need to be integrated with the existing information system in order to keep the business process stable while adding new entities to the information system. This will entail re-coding of the existing software or tools being used by various entities and even phasing out the existing IT infrastructure and bringing in the systems which have versions similar to the existing IT infrastructure.

The integration process will necessarily include some key decision points, which are shown by numbers in Figure 2.6, which will be coded as business logic in the information systems:

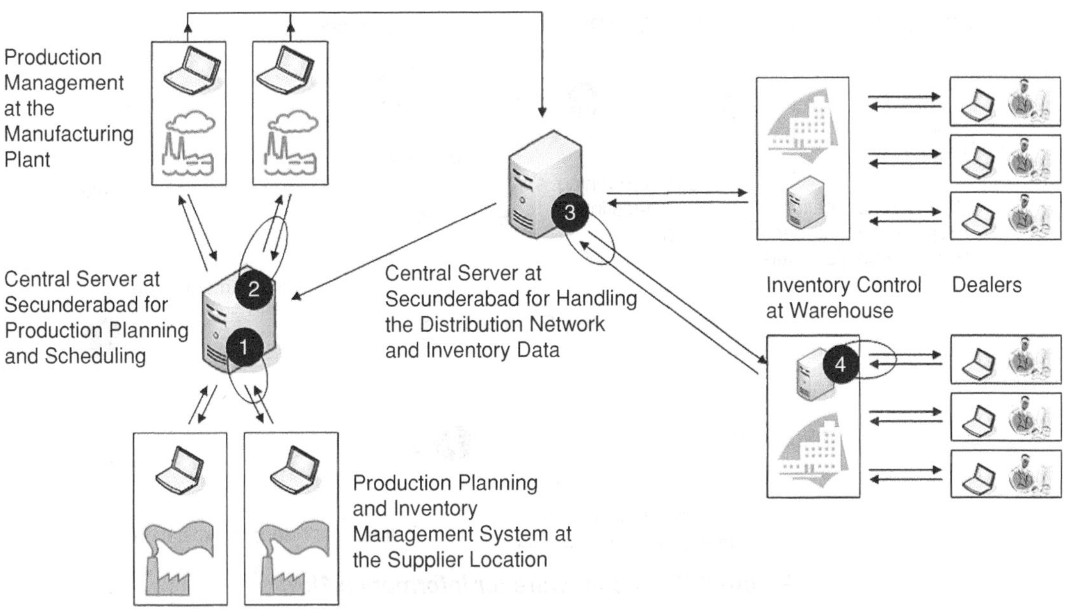

Figure 2.6 *Strategic Information System for Process Integration*

Decision point 1: It is to be decided which supplier to place the order with.
Decision point 2: It is to be decided which plant has to produce what and in what amount.
Decision point 3: It is to be decided which warehouse has to be supplied what amount.
Decision point 4: It is to be decided which dealer will be getting the orders serviced.

ARCHITECTURE FOR STRATEGIC INFORMATION FLOW

CFL has implemented SAP R/3 enterprise-wide; therefore, its suppliers connect to its systems through an EDI interface. This communication happens over an extranet. All the production plants of the company are connected through an intranet. This infrastructure also includes the production planning and scheduling server and the distribution network and inventory data handling server. The plants communicate data to the server through Business Application Programming Interfaces (BAPIs) or Remote Function Calls (RFCs). These are the functions in SAP ABAP programming language used for communicating data remotely. The architecture is depicted in Figure 2.7.

All the communication discussed till this point is electronically transmitted. The dealers use telecommunication to exchange information with the warehouses. The warehouse managers communicate information to the headquarters through telecommunication or emails over the Internet. The data, thus, received is manually entered in the server managing the distribution network and the inventory data. Through RFCs, this data is updated on the production planning server.

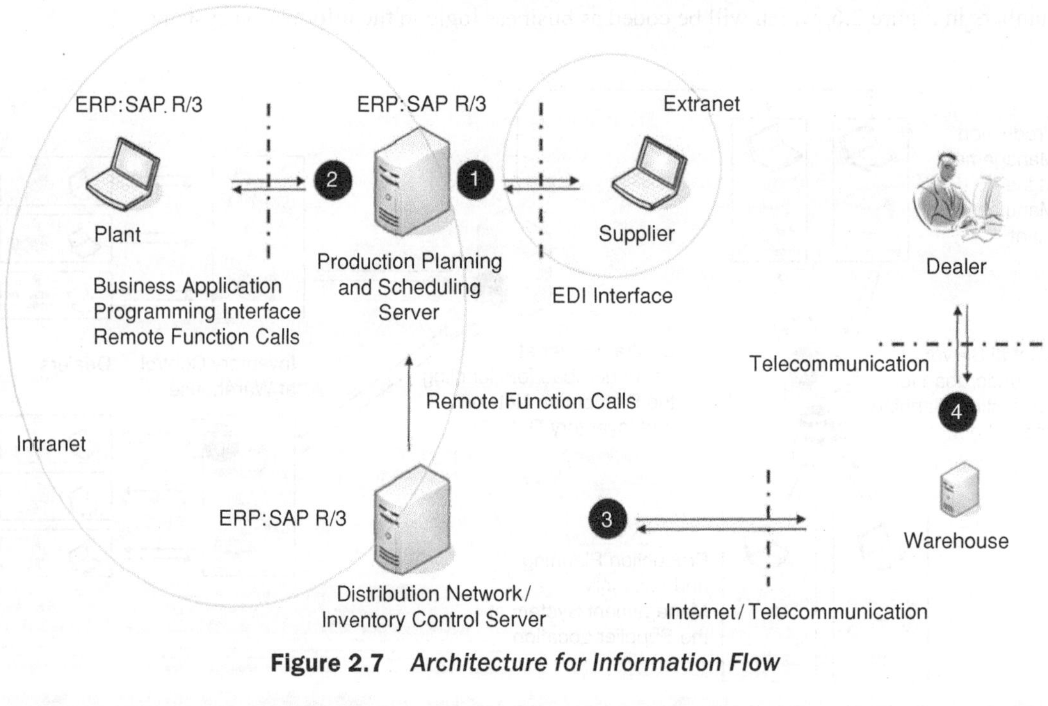

Figure 2.7 *Architecture for Information Flow*

BALANCED SCORECARD FOR M&A

We cannot improve what we cannot measure. Keeping this in mind, CFL has developed a balanced scorecard to measure the performance of the M&As. The balanced scorecard is provided in Table A1.

Since the business process here is slightly different in the fact that it measures factors for the success of integration, some perspectives have been modified to reflect the business processes for which the scorecard has been designed. In an M&A case, the scorecard measures the performance based on four perspectives. These perspectives and related goals are listed in Table 2.1.

Table 2.1 *The balanced scorecard for M&As*

Perspectives	Goals
Financial perspectives	Number of independent sources of funds
	Per cent of shares exchanged
	Operational savings
	Tax considerations
Human resources issues	Cross-cultural training
	Clearly defined roles
	Operational and technical training sessions
	Per cent of job losses
Operations perspectives	Product continuation
	Product restructuring
	Per cent increase in market shares
	Integrated activities
Partner compatibility	Goal compatibility
	Proposed time duration for mergers or acquisitions
	Number of compliances required
	Pay-back period

Financial perspective deals with the financing part of the M&A process and the proposed savings that CFL would make. Human resources issues are measured through initiatives taken by the company for building a common culture and also through any job losses that may take place or attrition.

Through the operations perspective, post-merger, an attempt is made to capture product-related performance issues and the market size the company operates in. Another important perspective regarding M&As is the partner compatibility. The very logic of the M&A is measured through the progress made on the non-financial reasons for the M&A.

BUSINESS LOGIC

This section discusses the decision points mentioned in the section 'Strategic Information System for Process Integration'. Each decision point is having a business logic for management decision making aided by quantifiable metrics to support decision making. These are listed below.

Supplier Identification Metrics

- Quality
- Production capacity
- Pricing
- Proximity to production plants
- Lead time
- Logistics
- Scale-up capability
- Business relations

Production Plant Identification Metrics

- Product
- Production capacity
- Technology
- Lead time
- Logistics
- Cost of operations
- Scale-up capability
- Employee relations

Warehouse Identification Metrics

- Proximity to dealers
- Storage capacity
- Inventory turnover
- Number of dealers associated
- Cost of operations
- Scale-up capability
- Logistics
- Proximity to production plants
- Lead time

Dealer Identification Metrics

- Sales volumes
- Storage capacity
- Proximity to warehouses
- Time to service
- Business relations

MEASUREMENT OF KEY PARAMETERS

This section discusses key parameters which are measured to support the decision making through the information system. The users of these metrics have been listed alongside. The periodicity of use of these metrics has also been listed. The decision points implemented for suppliers and dealers are provided in Tables 2.2 and 2.3, respectively.

Table 2.2 *Measurements for suppliers*

S. No.	Metrics	Formula	Role	Periodicity
1	Quality	$\frac{\text{Material composition}}{\text{Specified composition}}$	Quality manager	Sampling on arrival
2	Production capacity	$\frac{\text{Material supply capacity}}{\text{Demanded quantity of the material}}$	Plant manager	Half-yearly review
3	Pricing	$\frac{\text{Quoted price by a supplier}}{\text{Lowest quote by a competitor}}$	Finance manager	Tender issue
4	Proximity to production plants	$\frac{\text{Distance to travel for supplier}}{\text{Distance to travel for competitor}}$	Material handling manager	Tender issue
5	Lead time	$\frac{\text{Time to deliver for a supplier}}{\text{Time to deliver for a competitor}}$	Production manager	Tender issue

Table 2.3 *Measurements for dealers*

S. No.	Metrics	Formula	Role	Periodicity
1	Sales volume	$\frac{\text{Sales by a dealer}}{\text{Sales by a competitor}}$	Marketing manager	Daily (in season) Weekly (in off season)
2	Storage capacity	$\frac{\text{Storage capacity of a dealer}}{\text{Storage capacity of a competitor}}$	Warehouse manager	Quarterly
3	Proximity to warehouses	$\frac{\text{Distance to deliver for a dealer}}{\text{Distance to deliver for a competitor}}$	Material handling manager	Half yearly
4	Time to service	$\frac{\text{Total time to supply goods}}{\text{Total no. of customers}}$	Warehouse manager	Monthly

A SAMPLE MIS REPORT

A sample MIS report is provided in Tables A2 and A3.

For suppliers, the report has the following fields:

- Supplier Name
- Supplier Code

- Material Composition
- Supply Capacity
- Quoted Price
- Distance from the Production Plants
- Delivery Time

For dealers, the report has the following fields:

- Dealer Name
- Dealer Code
- Sales (April)
- Sales (May)
- Sales (June)
- Storage Capacity
- Distance from Warehouses
- Service Time

BUSINESS BENEFITS OF MIS

Leaner supply chain of the consolidated company: By streamlining the supply chain and manufacturing operations and proper resource utilization, the supply chain has become leaner.

Effective control of operational costs: The integrated information system provides opportunities for controlling operational costs at each stage of the business process.

Better distribution network: With the identification of relevant warehouses and dealers and also proper distribution of products, the MIS has improved the performance of the distribution network.

Efficient utilization of plant capacities: As the number of plants being handled by the system increased along with the product portfolio, it has given an additional strength in terms of decision-making power for deciding production schedules for various plants based on demand and cost efficiencies.

Improvement in quality of raw materials from suppliers and CFL's products: The MIS assesses the quality of raw materials from suppliers, thus identifying the best sourcing point. Improvement in quality of raw materials is translated into better product quality in CFL.

Ability to scale up production operations: As and when required, the production can be scaled up using the integrated information system through an assessment of the capacity of the plants.

Better logistics: The information system provides the ability—in terms of what to deliver, when to deliver, and how to deliver—to streamline logistics for the merged entities.

Inventory control: Inventory control through the information system helps manage the complete set of inventory of the consolidated company.

ECONOMIC BENEFIT PROJECTION

The primary objective of any M&A is to achieve certain financial gains. These gains can be viewed on the balance sheet of the company.

The assumption underlying a merger is that a consolidated company can achieve more economic value than separate entities. This can be verified by using previous years' profit after tax (PAT) for separate companies and forecasted PAT for a future period. The sum of these separate forecasted PATs can be compared to that of the combined entity for the same period.

CFL merged Ficom with itself in 2006 and GFCL in 2007. To verify the economic gains, the PAT of the consolidated CFL in 2007–08 can be compared with the sum of the individual forecasted PATs of Ficom, GFCL and CFL. Two years prior to merger, Ficom was making losses which were increasing over the years. So, it is assumed that either Ficom made losses in 2007–08 or CFL was helping turning around the company. For the purpose of simple linear regression analysis, the year 2002–03 is given the serial number 1, and the following years are in series. The result of the study is provided in Table 2.4.

Table 2.4 *Financial results after M&A*

Financial Year	S. No.	Ficom PAT (rupees in lakh)	GFCL PAT (rupees in lakh)	CFL PAT (rupees in lakh)
2002-03 (actual)	1		-1,362	2,703
2003-04 (actual)	2		715	4,311
2004-05 (actual)	3	-110.58	1,709	6,919
2005-06 (actual)	4	-1,496.50	2,610	8,355
2006-07 (actual)	5		4,929	10,074
2007-08 (forecasted)	6		**6,063.3 (A)**	**12,108.2 (B)**
Total forecast				**18,171.5 (A + B)**
Actual PAT in 2007-08				**20,976**
Net difference between the actual and forecasted PAT				**2,804.5**

The forecasted PAT for GFCL and CFL in 2007–08 is Rs 6,063.3 lakh and Rs 12,108.2, respectively, and their sum is Rs 18,171.5 lakh. The actual PAT, which is available in the balance sheet of CFL, is Rs 20,976 lakh. The actual PAT is Rs 2804.5 lakh more than the forecasted PAT.

Accuracy of the Forecast

The R^2 value is a measure of the accuracy of regression analysis. The closer it is to 1, the more accurate is the forecast. For GFCL, the R^2 value is 0.9704. The analysis is shown in Figure 2.8. For CFL, the R^2 value is 0.9915, and the analysis is shown in Figure 2.9. It can be inferred that the forecasted PATs are accurate to a large extent. Thus, the calculated increase in PAT post-merger is also accurate to this extent.

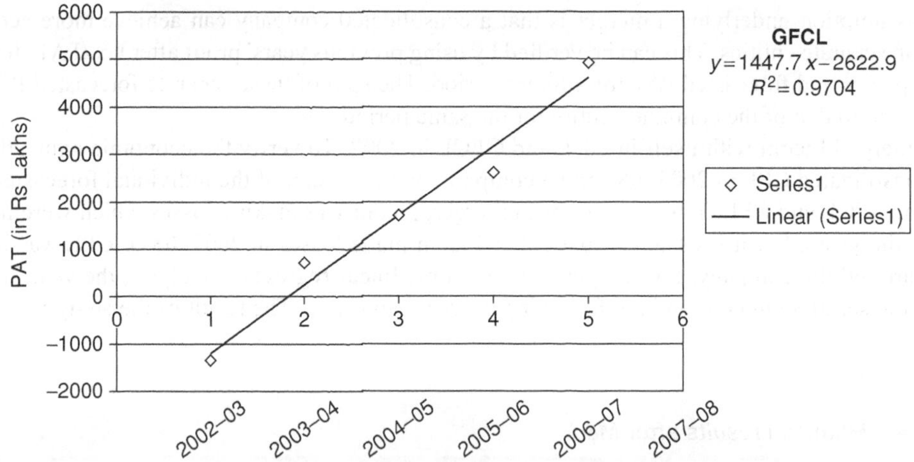

Figure 2.8 *Regression Analysis for GFCL*

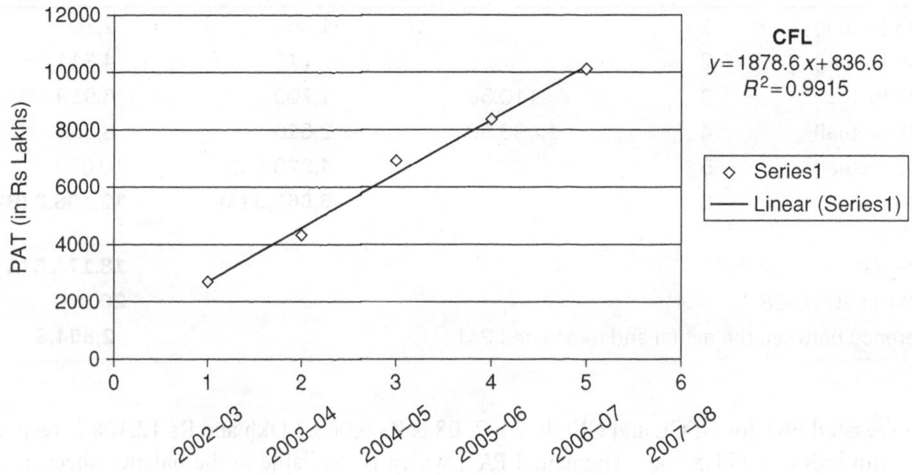

Figure 2.9 *Regression Analysis for CFL*

SUMMARY

- *Given the business environment, the management of CFL ensured the vision and mission of the organization is achieved in letter and spirit.*
- *CFL maintains its dominant position in the fertilizer and related inputs business through the acquisition and merger of Ficom and GFCL with itself.*
- *Our projections indicate that the information system designed to achieve the process integration helped CFL to increase its consolidated PAT by Rs 2804.5 lakh in the financial year 2007–08.*
- *The MIS is futuristic in functionality; CFL will continue to use the system for its acquisition-led inorganic growth.*

DISCUSSION QUESTIONS

1. What are the factors need to be considered for any M&A situation?
2. What are the factors that decide success or failure of a merger?
3. How does MIS help to track the success or the failure of an M&A?
4. What are the benefits of MIS in M&A situations?

BIBLIOGRAPHY

1. *www.cflindia.com*
2. *www.gfcl.co.in*
3. *CFL Annual Report 2007–08.* www.cflindia.com/ar032008.pdf.
4. *GFCL Annual Report 2006–07.* http://gfcl.co.in/GFCLAR_0607.pdf.
5. *Metrus Group, Mergers, Acquisitions, Joint Ventures, and Internal Integrations.* www.metrus.com/issues/mergers.html.
6. *Deloitte Consulting, Cultural Issues in Mergers and Acquisitions*, 2008, www.deloitte.com/dtt/article/0,1002,sid=26551&cid=187847,00.html.
7. *Wikipedia.org, Change Management.* http://en.wikipedia.org/wiki/Change_management_(people).
8. *Balanced Scorecard for M&A*, 2006, www.strategy2act.com/solutions/mergers_and_acquisitions_excel.htm.
9. *Balanced Scorecard Basics*, 2007, www.balancedscorecard.org.
10. *Mergers and Acquisitions: Boon or Bane?* 2008, http://www.uwsp.edu/BUSINESS/CWERB/2ndQtr01/SpecialReportQtr2_01.htm.
11. *CRISIL Research Analysis and Outlook Report on Union Budget 2008–09*, 2008, http://im.sify.com/sifycmsimg/mar2008/Finance/14613337_CRISIL-Research-Union-Budget-2008-09.pdf.
12. *The Financial Express article on CFL, GFCL merger,* 2008, http://www.financialexpress.com/news/Murugappa-to-merge-CFL-GFCL-for-better-synergy/206228/.

ANNEXURE

Table A1 *Balanced scorecard for measuring the performance of M&As*

Key Performance Indicators (KPIs) are the quantitative measures of expressing the parameters used to evaluate and manage the crisis that can emerge in the process of M&As. These can be formed in various dimensions.
Perspectives:
Financial perspective
Human resources issues
Operations perspective
Partner compatibility

(Continued...)

Table A1 (*...Continued*)

Scorecard includes four categories, 16 indicators					
Strategy tree and scorecard details:					
Perspective	**Goal**	**Weight (× of 10)**	**Description**	**Performance (%)**	**Target Values**
Financial perspective	Number of independent sources of funds		Various independent sources from which the funding of M&As can be done to avoid over-reliance on the single source		
	Per cent of shares exchanged		Per cent of shares given in exchange to the merging company according to their value		
	Operational savings		Total savings in operational costs due to merging the operations		
	Tax considerations		Total savings in taxes due to merging the companies		
Total performance in group			**Financial perspective**	**A**	
Human resources issues	Cross-cultural training		Number of training sessions provided to employees to make them easily understand the different organization cultures		
	Clearly defined roles		Per cent of employees who are clearly illustrated about the goals they are going to perform in the organization		
	Operational and technical training sessions		Number of training sessions provided to employees to bring them to same level on operational and technical issues		
	Per cent of job losses		Per cent of employees who had to lose their jobs due to the merger		
Total performance in group			**Human resources issues**	**B**	

Operations perspective	Product continuation	Per cent of existing products to be continued by the organization after the M&A	
	Product restructuring	Per cent of products restructured by the organization for effectively meeting the customers' needs and organizational goals	
	Per cent increase in market shares	Per cent of market size for the products before and after the merger	
	Integrated activities	Number of operations which have been integrated among the merging companies	
Total performance in group		**Operations perspective**	**C**
Partner compatibility	Goals compatibility	Number of goals that are compatible with the other partner	
	Proposed time duration for merger or acquisition	The proposed time duration for comfortably merging the business functions	
	Number of compliances required	Number of legal compliances required for the merger to complete	
	Pay-back period	The time required for the combined entity to deliver the business benefits envisaged in the pre-integration planning	
Total performance in group		**Partner compatibility**	**D**
	Total performance in group	Balanced scorecard for measuring the performance of M&As	A + B + C + D

Source: www.strategy2act.com.

Table A2 *Sample MIS report for suppliers*

S. No.	Name of the Suppliers	Supplier Code	Material Composition	Supply Capacity	Quoted Price (Rs)	Distance from the Production Plant	Delivery Time
1	ABC Ltd.	S563	Chemical: 97% Moisture: 3%	0.6 MT	2,400	406	16
2	LMN Ltd.	S874	Chemical: 97.4% Moisture: 2.6%	0.3 MT	2,412	268	10
3	XYZ Ltd.	S472	Chemical: 97.2% Moisture: 2.8%	0.67 MT	2,300	374	14

Table A3 *Sample MIS report for dealers*

S. No.	Name of the Dealers	Dealer Code	Sales (April)	Sales (May)	Sales (June)	Storage Capacity (Metric Tons)	Distance from Warehouses (km)	Service Time (hr)
1	ABC Sons	D76309	324	573	533	60	38	2
2	LMN Pvt. Ltd	D19835	275	401	293	26	42	2.5
3	XYZ Fertilizers	D83700	466	768	703	110	87	2

3

Case Study on Tata Chemicals Limited: Growth with Responsibility

INTRODUCTION TO TATA CHEMICALS

Tata Chemicals Limited (TCL) is India's leading manufacturer of inorganic chemicals. It also manufactures fertilizers and food additives. Incorporated in 1939, the company has an annual turnover of more than Rs 3,000 crore and is part of the Rs 65,000-crore ($14.25 billion) Tata group, India's foremost business conglomerate.

In the six decade since its inception, TCL has been setting benchmarks for its competencies in technology capabilities, thus, being recognized as a leader in the industry. True to its leadership style, it recognizes its social commitment as part of its sustainable business development strategy. It engages its resources in meeting needs of society at large through ethical means to achieve high standards of business performance.

TCL has an integrated unit at Mithapur in Gujarat, India (this state is situated in the western part of the country). One of the outputs of the integrated chemical complex is iodized salt with a purity of 99.8 per cent, which is the highest level of purity in India as of now. The company also produces synthetic soda ash and has a leading market share in the country. It also has a fertilizer unit in Babrala in Uttar Pradesh (a state in the northern part of India), where the state-of-the-art technology is used to manufacture urea. Through energy-efficient technology, the plant reduces production cost and pollution, for which TCL has won several awards in environmental conservations as well as in safety domains. TCL also has a fertilizer complex at Haldia, West Bengal, India (in the eastern part of the country) where it manufactures DAP/NPK-based fertilizers. The fertilizers are sold with the brand name 'Tata Paras' and have captive markets in West Bengal, Jharkhand, Bihar and Orissa. The Haldia plant has production capacity of more than 1.2 million tonnes per annum and currently, it is the only manufacturing unit for DAP/NPK. Please refer Figure 3.1.

VISION

The vision of TCL is to provide a better and enriched quality of life through products and services that are essential to society at large.

MISSION

To achieve our vision, we will strive to be the most trusted and respected organization by all stakeholders. We will prosper by:

- Improving value for money to our customers
- Having a competitive edge at global level and being a leader in all geographical area
- Meeting objectives of all stakeholders
- Conducting business for the society
- Constantly innovating to maintain the competitive edge

VALUES

- Excellence
- Integrity
- Innovation
- Fairness
- Care

GROWTH WITH RESPONSIBILITY

TCL is an example where there is all-round growth as the corporate governance is guided by win–win situation for all stakeholders. Thus, through its corporate governance trenched in ethical and fair business practices, it provides value to all those concerned such as customers, suppliers, shareholders, employees and society at large.

However, TCL does not want to remain complacent. Every year, TCL strives to improve its existing high-standard quality norms and systems. It has been awarded ISO-9001 registration for all its manufacturing plants. Because of corporate requirements, the company has also adopted the Tata Business Excellence Model which makes its processes more performance oriented and customer centric. Also, based on the Malcolm Baldrige National Quality Award model, TCL takes a holistic and comprehensive approach towards long-term sustainability of its business model. TCL also takes care of its employees through different welfare schemes. As a result, the employees drive the company's relentless march towards excellence and customer delight, and the management considers its employees as pillars of its growth and success. The company invests in them by providing opportunities for job enrichment, concentrated competency development, sharing of best practices and so on.

Safety is given paramount importance in TCL, and processes and systems have been defined to focus on safety, health and welfare of its staff. In addition, to protect environment, the company has committed itself to 'Responsible Care', a voluntary global forum in the chemical industry, where the company has to demonstrate and prove adherence to different standards in safety, health and environmental issues.

An example of TCL's principle of 'avoid, reduce and recycle' is its cement plant at Mithapur, which was set up solely to consume the solid waste generated during the manufacture of soda ash. The company has also developed the Mithapur salt works as a natural habitat for thousands of migratory birds. Its fertilizer unit at Babrala is the most energy-efficient plant in the Indian fertilizer industry.

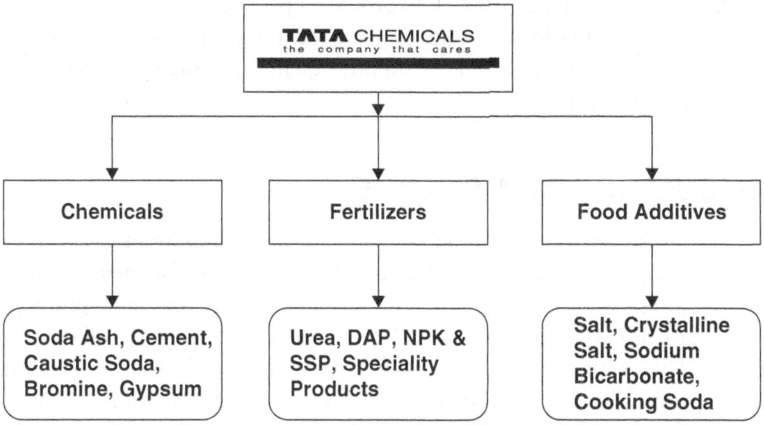

Figure 3.1 *Divisions at TCL*

ENRICHING LIFE

The Tata group has a principle by which, 'what comes from the people must go back to the people many times over'. Being part of the Tata group, TCL honours its legacy by following the standards and processes as enumerated in the Tata Chemicals Society for Rural Development (TCSRD). TCSRD was established in 1979 and is engaged in looking at the welfare of the society in and around chemical plants in the country. Its fundamental purpose is to foster development that is sustainable and integrated by taking care of the masses around the plants and factory in the country and does not restrict itself to Tata group alone. It helps in livelihood programmes, national resource management and building of health and educational infrastructure. The approach of TCSRD is to improve the lives of the rural communities through participation of the beneficiaries during the project design stage.

FERTLIZER SECTOR OF TCL

Tata Chemicals is a major player in the fertilizer market of our country. Tata Chemicals is a major manufacturer of urea, an important nitrogenous fertilizer, in India.

Tata Chemicals manufactures urea at its fertilizer plant in Babrala. The plant has an installed capacity of 8,64,000 tonnes per year, which constitutes nearly 12 per cent of the total urea produced by India's private sector.

The nature of the soil in many Indian regions is such that nitrogenous fertilizers are an important input for most crops. It is, thus, important that farmers have access to good urea at a low cost. To make fertilizers available to farmers at affordable prices and to encourage a balanced use, the Indian government regulates the sale price of fertilizers and provides a subsidy on urea and concessions on decontrolled phosphates and potassic fertilizers.

Tata Kisan Sansar (TKS)

TCL supplements such government initiatives by conducting programmes to educate farmers at the grassroots level about the proper use of urea manufactured by it. The company provides these services through the TKS.

TKS is a major initiative undertaken by TCL to provide a package of end-to-end services to farmers, including the use of modern technology to help increase yield, soil analysis and advice on NPK ratios, farm equipment leasing and credit facility. TCL supplies quality products to farmers through the TKS and through its huge network of distributors.

INDIAN AGRICULTURE AT A GLANCE

Agriculture accounts for 22 per cent of India's GDP, and, more importantly, about two-third of the country's population is dependent on agriculture and allied activities for their livelihood. Successive five year plans have stressed on self-sufficiency and self-reliance on food grain production, and concerted efforts towards this direction have resulted in a substantial increase in agricultural production and productivity. This is clear from the fact that from a very modest level of 52 million tonnes in 1951–52, food grain production increased to above 232.1 million metric tonnes in 2004–05. In India's success story of not only meeting the total requirement of food grains but also having their exportable surplus, the significant role played by chemical fertilizers is well recognized and established. Chemical fertilizers have played a vital role in the success of India's green revolution and consequent self-reliance in food grain production. The increase in fertilizer consumption has contributed significantly to a sustainable production of food grains in the country. The Indian government has been consistently pursuing policies conducive to increased availability and consumption of fertilizers in the country. The production of nitrogen (N) and phosphorus (P) fertilizers together has increased from mere 0.7 lakh metric tonnes in 1951–52 to about 184 lakh metric tonnes in nutrients terms in 2003–04. Since there are no commercially viable sources of potash (K) in the country, its entire requirement is met through import. The overall consumption of fertilizers in nutrient terms (N, P and K) currently is about 168 lakh metric tonnes per annum. Accordingly, consumption of fertilizers per hectare has increased from less than 1 kg in 1951–52 to 96.7 kg in 2004–05. As of now, the country has achieved near self-sufficiency in production capacity of urea, with the result that India could manage its requirement of these fertilizers through the indigenous industry, and imports of all fertilizers except Muriate of Potash (MOP) have presently been nominal.

TATA FERTILIZER

- Tata fertilizer is part of the Tata group, and it started its operations in 1994 at Babrala in the state of Uttar Pradesh, which is situated in the northern part of India.
- Urea is the main output from this unit, which is used as a fertilizer. The maximum capacity of the unit is 8,64,600 tonnes per annum. The installed capacity almost accounted for 13 per cent of total installed capacity in the country's private sector. Along with urea, this unit also produces ammonia, with an installed capacity of more than 1,500 tonnes per day.

STATERGIES ADOPTED FOR FERTILIZER BUSINESS

Tata Chemicals adopted the following strategies for marketing the fertilizers:

- Up-to-date technical information
- Effective distribution network
- Setup of fertilizer suppliers association
- Reduced prices of fertilizers

Up-to-date Technical Information

For up-to-date technical information, the following major steps are taken:

- Investments are done in regional testing capabilities for updating the technical information on a specific area.
- Technical reports on soil fertility are updated so that farmers can update the soil fertility status of their field.

Geographical Information System (GIS)

A *GIS* is an information system for capturing, storing, analyzing, managing and presenting data which are spatially referenced (linked to location).

In the strictest sense, it is any information system capable of integrating, storing, editing, analyzing, sharing and displaying geographically referenced information. In a more generic sense, GIS applications are tools that allow users to create interactive queries (user-created searches), analyze spatial information, edit data and maps, and present the results of all these operations. *Geographic information science* is the science underlying the geographic concepts, applications and systems, offered in degree and GIS certificate programs at many universities.

Collection of Data

The data is collected basically by *global positioning system* (GPS) and *remote sensing*.

GPS

The GPS is a navigation system which uses satellite-based technology. The GPS is based on a communication network which is possible because satellite-based navigation systems placed into orbit by the US Department of Defence. At the outset, GPS was used for military applications, but after a legislation was passed, the GPS was made available for civilian work. Since this is a satellite-based communication system, GPS works in any weather condition and at all times of the day. The system is available free of cost to the civilians and has found a great usage in developmental sectors such as urban planning.

How GPS Works

The satellites placed in the orbit (that develops communication network) circle the earth twice a day. The rotations around the earth are done in a very precise orbit, and while orbiting, these satellites transmit signal information to the earth station. At the earth station, GPS receivers use this information to calculate the user's exact location by calculating the time difference between the time it was transmitted and received by the earth station. This time difference is the distance between the GPS receiver and the satellites, which is used to determine the user's position and to display it on the earth station's electronic map.

GIS and Production Agriculture

At a grassroots level, GIS offers farmers various opportunities to increase production, reduce input costs and manage their land more efficiently. From handheld computer mapping in the field to the scientific analysis of production data at the farm manager's office, geography plays a role. These examples of

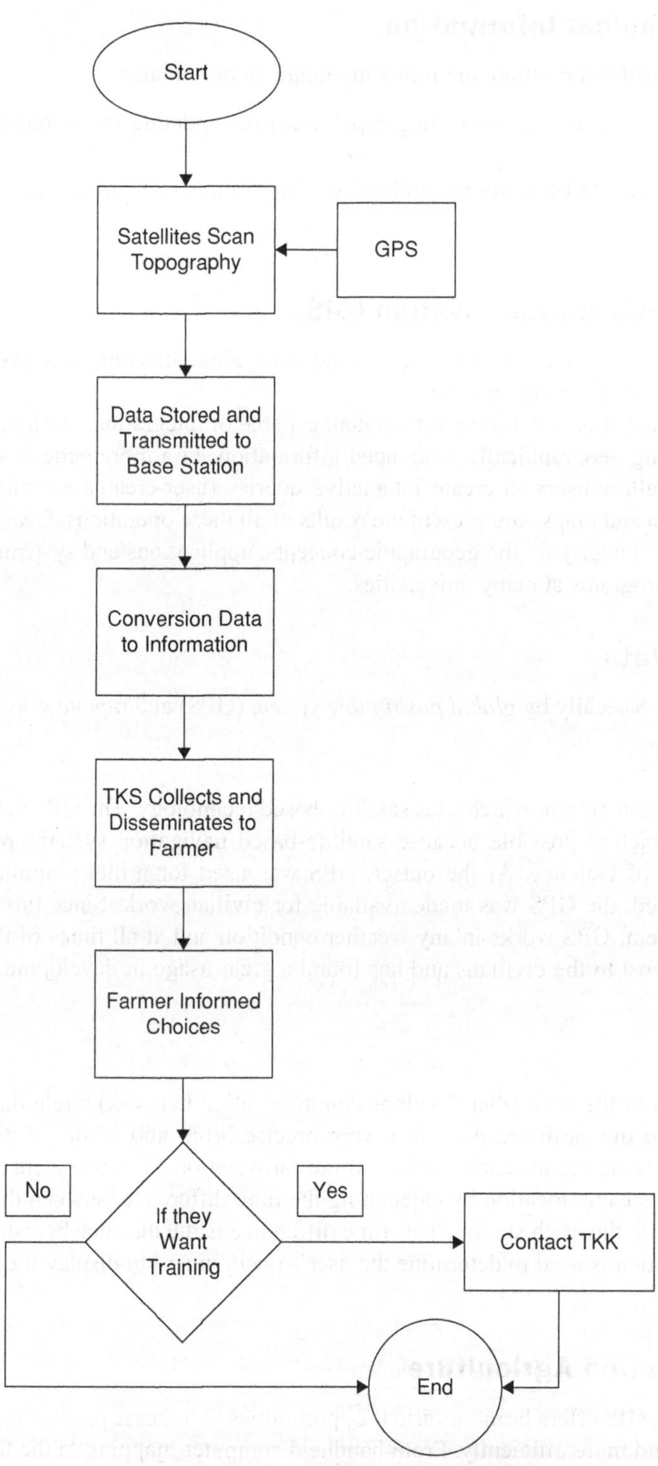

Figure 3.2 ***Functional Flowchart of GIS***

applications of GIS at the farm level are meant to provide users, both experienced and inexperienced, with some ideas for implementation.

How It Works in Rural India

GPS and geographic information system (GIS) are combined together to get information on developing and implementing precision agriculture. Through these systems, real-time data related to weather, field and geospatial data are collected and integrated with accurate position information so that farmers can use exact fertilizers with correct composition. GPS-based applications in precision farming are being used for farm planning, field mapping, soil sampling, tractor guidance, crop scouting, variable rate applications and yield mapping. This type of data collection helps farmers to work in all weather conditions which increase the productivity. Today, more precise application of pesticides, herbicides, and fertilizers, and better control of the dispersion of those chemicals are possible through precision agriculture, thus reducing expenses, producing a higher yield and creating a more environmentally friendly farm.

GPS helps in developing many tools that can help farmers and agribusiness to become more productive and efficient. By providing exact locations of fields, precision farming techniques can be employed. Many farmers have used GPS to improve their farming business by increasing yield from their fields. GPS also helps in mapping field boundaries, displaying roads and showing proximity to irrigation systems. It helps farmers to create farm maps with accurate acreage for each field area. It also shows if there are weeds and diseases in crops so that accurate medications can be applied. GPS allows farmers to accurately navigate to specific locations in the field, year after year, to collect soil samples and monitor crop conditions.

Agricultural advisers use GPS to provide solutions to crop and pest problems in the fields. They do not need to travel to the place and can work on several problems simultaneously. This becomes handy when parts of the crops are disease affected; the advisors can pinpoint the area with the quantity and the quality of pesticides that need to be applied. This reduces chemical drift and also chemical wastage.

GIS Functions in Tata Chemicals

The Tata group's precision farming concept uses GIS to manage and analyze data collected from different sources by various means, sophisticated and simple. The information, thus, collected includes census data, revenue data, socio-economic surveys, satellite imageries, soil-mapping data and market studies. These components form the basis of a precision farming project.

These data are converted to information and transferred to the central server and transmitted to the TKS. The TKS provides the farmers with the information on their field such as soil fertility, nutrient content and soil pattern.

Here, Figure 3.2 shows how the GIS is working in Uttar Pradesh, how GIS enabled the farmers to be aware of their field status, their socio-economic status, revenue, census, etc.

INFORMATION FLOW FOR MARKETING OF FERTILIZERS BY TATA CHEMICALS

Farmers in number of remote villages are the customers of Tata Chemicals. Thus, the major challenges ahead of the company while improving the market penetration and the customer relationship are as follows:

1. To reach the farmers in number of remote villages
2. To reach the farmers at a affordable cost for the business

Though these villages lack the Internet connectivity, the mobile phone density in Indian villages is around 20 per cent, in addition, the cost of connectivity per transaction is comparable to V-sat; thus, Tata Chemicals decided to use the telecommunication network, and they introduced the GoMobile Suite.

This tool basically uses the mobile phone network for processing sales orders and warehouse management. In the first step of the process, the field officers create an order using *goMobile Sales*. To create the order, the field officers choose a dealer, the product required by the dealer, the quantity and the delivery date. A new order is immediately created and transmitted to the central GoMobile server. Before placing the order, they can also view the dealer's credit limit, the list of orders placed and their status during the visit to the dealer. They can also check the credit and product availability and verify quota limits before creating the sales order.

After the field officers have placed the sales order, the dealers can view their order confirmation. The dealers can view their list of orders placed with Tata Chemicals. After confirming creation of their order, the dealers may create a payment for their order using GoMobile payments. The dealers are given a mobile portal in which they can enter payments, view outstanding payments, check status of the orders, etc. They can enter the payment details (DD No., Bank, Branch, City, Amount, etc.) against either outstanding or advance payments and send the details to the GoMobile central server.

The store managers can prepare reports containing orders and payments per dealer and use that information to prepare a delivery challan so that they can pick up the material from the store. The store managers can access different orders placed on each dealer and the amount of payments to be given to the suppliers/dealers for the same. Once the supplier/dealer arrives at the store with the paper-form DD and DDFL, the store managers can check the actual receipt against the order and record the physical receipt so that the payment can be processed in the Enterprise Resource Planning (ERP). The store managers can then create a delivery and a delivery challan to enable the dealers to collect the required material from the store.

Functions of Field Officers

- The field officers, during their visit to the dealers, can view their credit limit, the list of orders placed and their status.
- To create an order, the field officers choose a dealer, the product required by the dealer, the quantity and the delivery date.
- A new order is immediately created and transmitted to the central GoMobile server.
- The field officers can also do a credit check and a product availability check and verify quota limits before creating the credits.

Functions of Dealers

- The dealers are given a mobile portal in which they can enter payments, view outstanding payments, check status of order, etc.
- The dealers can view their list of orders placed with Tata Chemicals.
- They can enter the following payment details:

  1. DD Number
  2. Bank
  3. Branch
  4. City
  5. Amount

- Then, they send the details to the central GoMobile server.

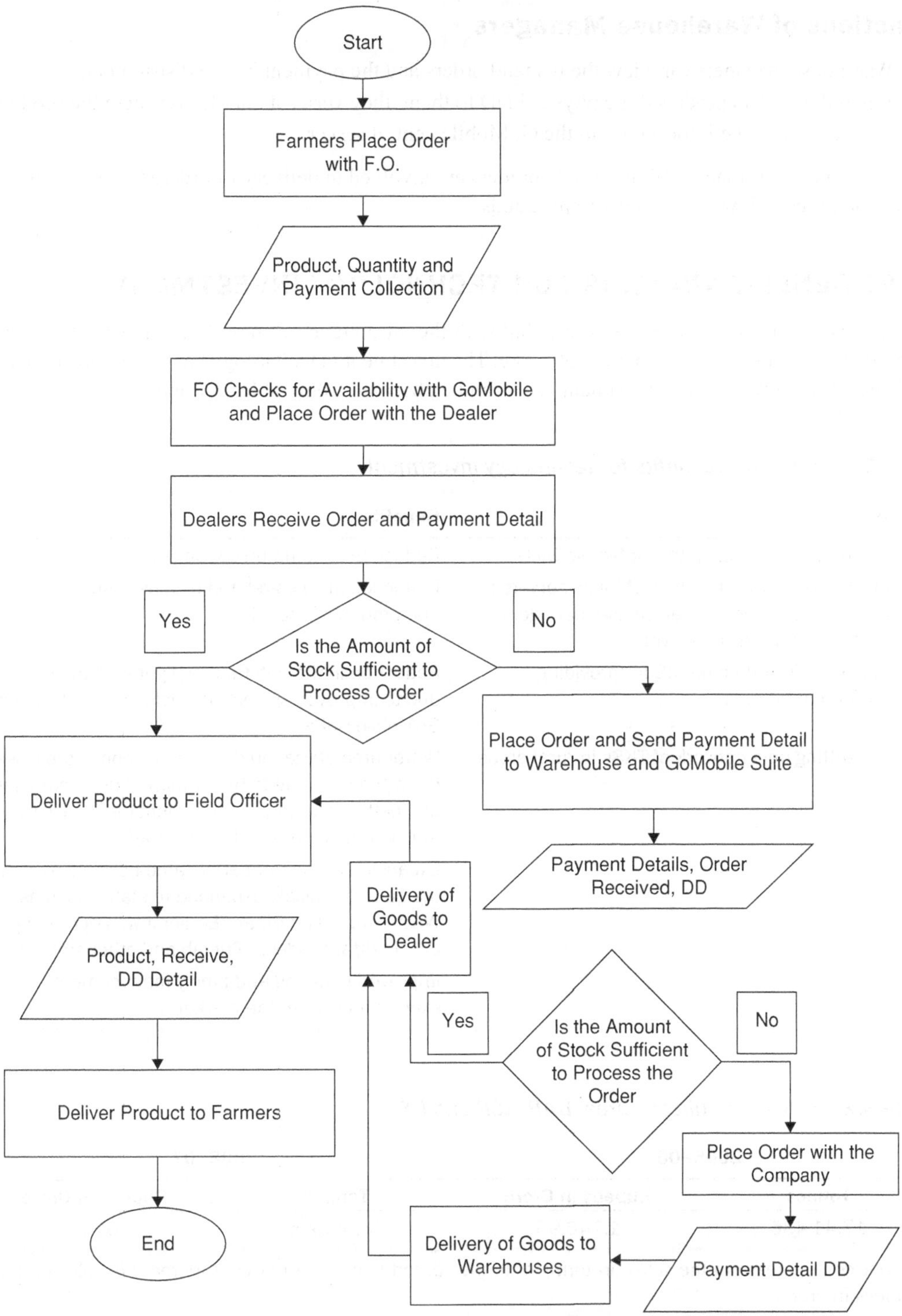

Figure 3.3 *Delivery of Goods*

Functions of Warehouse Managers

- Warehouse managers can view the demand orders and the payment by the distributors.
- When the dealers produced the physical DD to them, they verify it and deliver them the product.
- They also send the information to the GoMobile central server.

When an order is placed, all these stakeholders are involved in delivery of ordered goods. Figure 3.3 shows the process flow for the delivery of goods.

COST-BENEFIT ANALYSIS FOR TECHNOLOGY INVESTMENT

In 2003–04, business was worth 83 crore, but with the introduction of new MIS and establishment of TKS, in 2004–05 business was worth 150 crore. The investment in technology has cost implications, but the benefits far outweigh the investment. This can be observed from Tables 3.1 and 3.2.

Table 3.1 *Costs and benefits for technology investment*

Costs	Benefits
Cost incurred in setting up the GoMobile Suite	Reduction in communication costs
Cost incurred in providing the GoMobile servers to the dealers, field officers, warehouse managers for connecting to the central server	Reduction in sales-related expenses such as non-productive travel
Cost incurred in setting up GIS for providing information to farmers	Reduction in the outstanding figures of the dealers due to improved system of placing orders through GoMobile Suite
Cost of setting up a network of TKSs in rural areas	Better urea utilization due to reduction in the losses during storage due to better market understanding and better inventory management (as urea is very much prone to losses during storage)
	Expansion of the market became possible as now the Tata Chemicals expanded to states such as West Bengal and Bihar. (Earlier it was operating only in Uttar Pradesh, Punjab and other states.)
	Improved planning and timely management of expectations from the market

Table 3.2 *Sales of fertilizers: urea, DAP, SSP and NPK*

2005–06		2006–07	
Tonnes	**Rupees in Crore**	**Tonnes**	**Rupees in Crore**
17,41,436	1,746.93	18,50,695	2,010.45

6.27 per cent increase in the sales (in terms of tonnes of fertilizers). 15 per cent increase in sales (in terms of rupees in crore).

METRICS

- The metrics will be described in the form of a balanced score card.
- These metrics will provide a view of an organization's performance with respect to four perspectives. They are as follows:

Financial Perspective Metrics

It focuses on the strategy for growth, profitability and risk from the perspective of shareholders. The strategic objective of the company from the financial perspective is to achieve profitable growth and become globally competitive.

The financial perspective metrics includes the following:

1. *Return on investment*: It is calculated by the following formula:

$$\text{Return on investment} = \frac{\text{Net income}}{\text{Capital employed}}$$

2. *Return on marketing investment (ROMI)*: It can be calculated by the following formula:

$$\text{Return on marketing investment} = \frac{(\text{Increase in sales} - \text{marketing costs})}{\text{Marketing costs}}$$

In the case of Tata Chemicals, performance of the GoMobile Suite can be measured by this metrics. The customers of fertilizers are in many remote villages of India, thus, the fundamental challenges Tata Chemicals face in rural areas involve distance and the cost associated with overcoming that distance. We can analyze how the telecommunication technology has helped reduce the marketing cost and thus increase ROMI.

3. *Number of inventory days*: It can be calculated by the following formula:

$$\begin{aligned}\text{Number of inventory days} = {} & \text{The date of selling the fertilizer to farmers} \\ & - \text{the date of receiving the ordered fertilizer}\end{aligned}$$

The new system of placing orders through GoMobile Suite makes it possible to minimize the number of days the fertilizer stocked with the dealer. Hence, the performance of the process of placing the orders through GoMobile and selling fertilizers to franchisees can be measured by this metrics.

Customer Perspective Metrics

It focuses on the strategy for creating value from customers viewpoint. The strategic objective of the company from the customer perspective is to retain the share of existing customers in the sales and to increase the number of new customers.

The customer perspective metrics includes the following:

1. *Customer acquisition per period*: It can be calculated by the following formula:

$$\text{Customer acquisition per period} = \text{Number of new customers} / \text{Time period}$$

2. *Existing customers participation*: It is the percentage of sales made to existing customers and can be calculated by the following formula:

$$\text{Existing customer participation} = \frac{\text{Sales made to existing customers}}{\text{Total sales}}$$

Tata Chemicals established Tata Kisan Kendra to impart training and supply implements, to provide agronomical information to farmers and thereby to maintain customer relations.

The performance of this process can be measured by the above metrics. It will measure how far the newly introduced TKKs have been successful in increasing existing customer participation and customer acquisition.

Internal/Business Perspective

It focuses on the strategic priorities for the various business processes which create customer and shareholder satisfaction. The strategic objective of the company from the business perspective is to improve market share of niche products in which the company is a market leader.

The internal/business perspective metrics includes the following:

1. *Gain in market share*: It is the comparison of business's rate of sales in a specific market and the growth trend for that market. It can be calculated by the following formula:

$$\text{Market share} = \frac{\text{Total sales made by the company}}{\text{Total sales made by the competitors}}$$

In the case of Tata Chemicals, after introduction of the new business strategy, Tata Chemicals started selling its products through franchisees instead of wholesalers so that the franchisees concentrate on the sale of Tata's products only. The performance of the introduction of franchisees can be measured by the gain in market share.

2. *Brand awareness*: It can be measured with the help of market survey. It is indicated by the number of people questioned in the survey who know the company's brand. It can be calculated by the following formula:

$$\text{Brand awareness} = \frac{\text{Number of people surveyed who know the brand}}{\text{Total number of people surveyed}}$$

For this metrics, we need to carry out market survey, and the data is collected by the marketing department.

Learning and Growth Perspective

It focuses on the internal atmosphere of an organization. This perspective measures how the employees are performing in an organization and what is their level of satisfaction. Employee motivation and satisfaction can be measured by employee satisfaction index.

All these metrics required for different perspectives are summarized in Tables 3.3 and 3.4.

Table 3.3 *Metrics for an organization's performance*

S. No.	Metrics	Role	Periodicity
1	Customer acquisition per period	Field officer	Monthly during agricultural season
2	Existing customers participation	Field officer	Monthly during agricultural season
3	Market share gain	Field officer	Annually
4	Return on marketing investment	Marketing department	Annually
5	Employee satisfaction index	HR department	Quarterly
6	Brand awareness	Marketing department	Annually

Table 3.4 *Marketing balanced scorecard dashboard (refer the annexure)*

Perspective		Performance
Financial perspective metrics		
Customer perspective metrics		
Internal/business perspective metrics		
Learning and growth perspective metrics		
Total performance		
Strategy Tree and Scorecard Details		
Perspective	Goal	Description
Financial perspective metrics		
	ROI	Return on investment = net income/ capital employed
	ROMI	Return on marketing investment = (increase in sales – marketing costs)/marketing costs
	Total performance in group	**Financial perspective metrics**
Customer perspective metrics		
	Number of new customers	Customer acquisition per period
	Existing customers participation	Percentage of sales made to existing customers per period
	Total performance in group	**Customer perspective metrics**
Internal/business perspective metrics		
	Market share gain	Comparison of business's rate of sale in a specific market versus the growth trend for that market

(*Continued...*)

Table 3.4 (*...Continued*)

Perspective		Performance
	Brand awareness	The percentage of people questioned in a survey that know the company brand
	Total performance in group	**Internal/business perspective metrics**
Learning and growth perspective metrics		
	Employee motivation and satisfaction	Employee satisfaction index
	Total performance in group	**Learning and growth perspective metrics**
	The total performance	

COMPETITION ANALYSIS

1. *NFCL*: Nagarjuna Fertilizers and Chemicals Ltd. is a national level company, having its headquarters in Andhra Pradesh. It provides fertilizers as well as speciality products in the market. Presently, its speciality products, zinc sulphate monohydrate, zinc sulphate heptahydrate, calcium nitrate and boron, are available in the West Bengal market and not in Bihar. Earlier, it was also in Bihar. Its zinc sulphate monohydrate comes with a name of Maha Zinc containing 33 per cent Zn. It has a very less sale initially. So, the retailers are selling it by tagging it with urea, that is, if a farmer has to buy a bag of urea, he has to buy a small packet of Maha Zinc also.
2. *Sylvan Chemicals*: Sylvan Chemicals is also available in West Bengal. Its main products are zinc sulphate monohydrate, zinc sulphate heptahydrate, micronutrients and boron.
3. *Aries Agro Ltd.*: It is a Mumbai-based speciality product manufacturing company. Its speciality products are available with the brand name Agromin. Its foliar spray micronutrient containing iron, manganese, boron, copper, zinc and molybdenum is available in north Bihar. The soil application product of Agromin is available in Bihar and West Bengal, but Agromin in West Bengal does not contain molybdenum. Its products available in West Bengal are zinc sulphate monohydrate, micronutrients and boron.
4. *K. S. Agro Ltd.*: K. S. Agro is based in Andhra Pradesh, and its available products are zinc sulphate monohydrate, calcium nitrate, micronutrients and boron. It is available only in West Bengal.
5. *DSCL*: DCM Sriram Chemicals Ltd. is an old nationalized company which is famous with the brand name of Sriram in two states. Its available products are zinc sulphate monohydrate, zinc sulphate heptahydrate and boron. It is present in both West Bengal and Bihar. In West Bengal, it products are zinc sulphate heptahydrate and boron, but in Bihar, zinc sulphate heptahydrate is present. Boron is available in both the states.

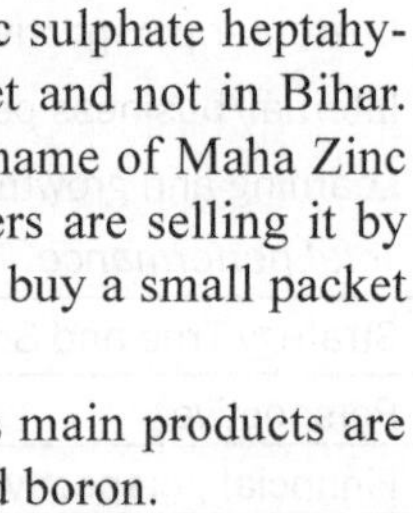

6. *Rallis*: Rallis is a Tata group company. Rallis has established a relationship with one of the world's largest producers of water-soluble fertilizers—M/s Yara International—to import speciality products. Its product boron with

the brand name 'Solubor' comes as a white-coloured nicely packaged product. Rallis has a marketing agreement with Borax, a UK-based company, who is the pioneer in boron nutrition. Solubor was released in 2005. It is also a water-soluble product and is applied in foliar spray form.

Another product is a micronutrient which comes with the brand name Tracel. Tata Tracel is scientifically blended multi-micronutrient mixtures specially designed for foliar applications. It comes with brand names Tracel-2, Tracel-3, etc. according to the mixture percentage. Tracel Foliar grades are water soluble, facilitating ready uptake of nutrients by plants. Tracel grades are compatible with most agrochemical formulations available in Rallis range, can be mixed and sprayed together.

Campaigns are launched to ensure that farmers are acquainted with a specific product depending on the region, type of soil and the crop being grown. Various indigenous means of promotion such as displaying hoardings, painting walls with fertilizer product details and decorating point of purchase outlets are also undertaken, especially during product campaigns and village fairs.

Tata Rallies is available in West Bengal only with the products micronutrient, boron and calcium nitrate. Its products are in a high demand in West Bengal.

7. *Multiplex*: Multiplex is supplying single micronutrients as well as multi-micronutrients containing all micronutrients. It is also supplying boron in the market. Its other products are specific to specific crops such as tobacco special, vegetable special. Multiplex has entered in the market of micronutrients in both powder and liquid forms for foliar spray and for soil application form also. Other than speciality products, other products of multiplex are organic manure, biofertilizers, biopesticides, plant bioactivators, wetting agents, plant growth promoter, pesticides, seeds and sprayers. Multiplex Allbore is a fine powder completely and immediately soluble in water containing 19 per cent boron.

Multiplex is present in both West Bengal and Bihar. In West Bengal, it is marketing only boron, but in Bihar, it is having a good market share and provides zinc sulphate monohydrate with the brand name High Zinc. Multiplex micronutrient is available in solid as well as in liquid form in Bihar. Boron is also marketed by Multiplex in Bihar and is in high demand.

8. *Dayal*: Dayal Group offers a comprehensive range of inputs from fertilizers, seeds, bio-products to animal feed and supplements. It is supplying zinc sulphate monohydrate, zinc sulphate heptahydrate, calcium nitrate and micronutrients in Bihar only. It is a famous brand among retailers in Bihar.
9. *Toto Care*: Toto Care provides boron in West Bengal. It is a famous brand among the retailers and farmers of Harishchandrapur in Malda district.
10. *Anchor Chemicals*: Anchor Chemicals is a Tarapur-based micronutrient company, which markets micronutrients in West Bengal only.
11. *Super Agro-India Ltd.*: This company supplies micronutrients, growth promoters, pesticides, fungicides and many other products. Its micronutrient is

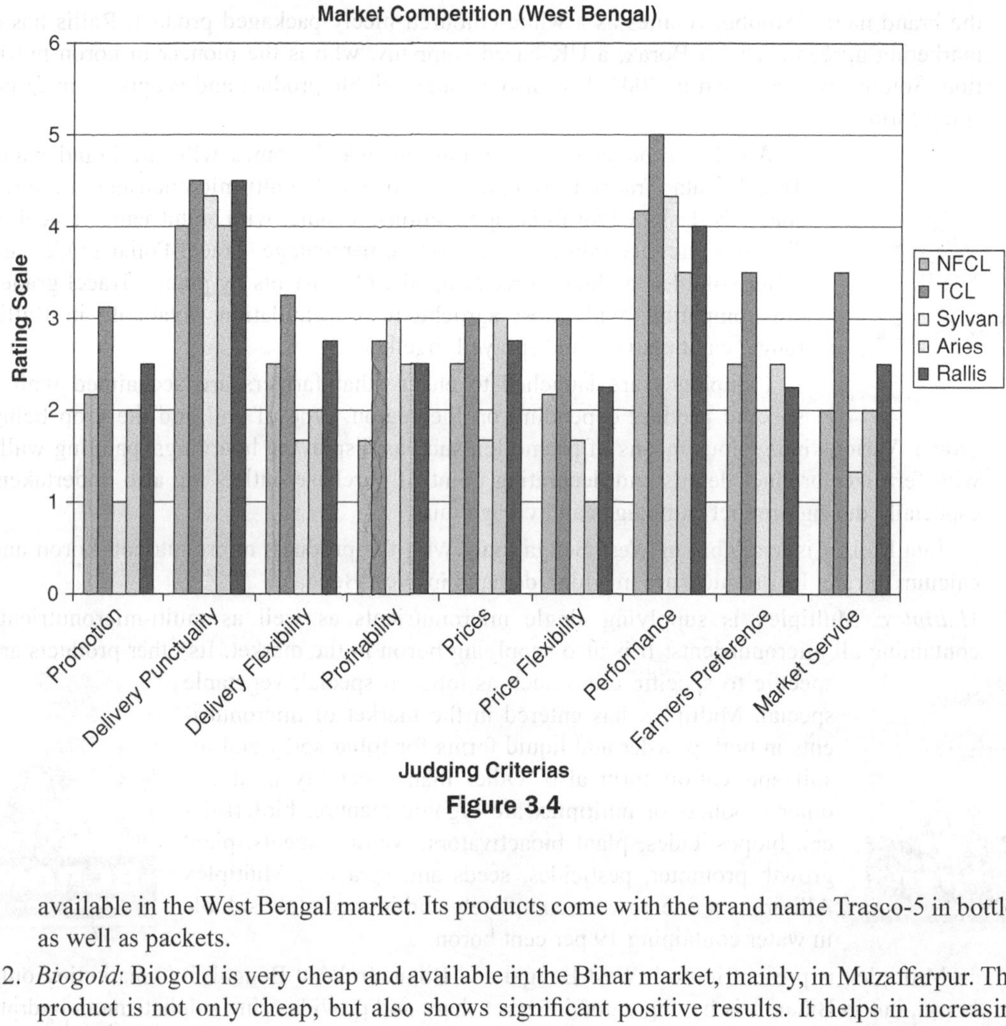

Figure 3.4

available in the West Bengal market. Its products come with the brand name Trasco-5 in bottles as well as packets.

12. *Biogold*: Biogold is very cheap and available in the Bihar market, mainly, in Muzaffarpur. This product is not only cheap, but also shows significant positive results. It helps in increasing the yield by solving problems of farmers, that is, helps in roots and soil attachment. Use of Biogold is leading to decrease in the sale of speciality products.

13. *Other companies*: There are many small or big companies existing in the market. Some of them are local also. There are some local companies in Bihar which are selling their products with the brand name Tata Paras. Relative positions of these competitors are shown in Figure 3.4.

SWOT ANALYSIS

Strengths

- A big fertilizer company which has got a respectful position among fertilizer customers
- Quality products

- Trust among the farmers in the quality of Tata fertilizers
- Good research and development processes
- Well-established marketing networks

Weaknesses

- Past track record of poor supply
- High dissatisfaction among customers due to fewer services and more problems with customer accounts
- Lack of awareness among the farmers on the benefits associated with the speciality products (promotional activity)
- Less number of people in the field
- Higher prices than other companies
- No incentives or schemes for customers
- No credit facility for dealers

Opportunities

- Presence of smaller number of good-quality brands
- Niche marketing for specific requirements for specific crops

Threats

- Supply and availability of low-grade and cheaper speciality products in the market and presence of local manufacturers using Tata Paras bag for selling their product are some of the threats.
- Large number of services are offered by different competitors.
- Success always depends on the natural factors such as rainfall. Lack of rain and flooded conditions will affect farmers as well as companies.

CONCLUSION

- By the intervention of new MIS, there is a three-fold revenue growth in the past three years with the TKS.
- In 2003–04, business was worth 83 crore. But with the introduction of new MIS and establishment of TKS, business in 2004–05 was worth 150 crore.
- There is better urea realization due to better market understanding.
- Better clarity in regulatory framework is emerging.

DISCUSSION QUESTIONS

1. How can you earn profit as well as serve the society?
2. How do you arrive at corporate objectives for such an organization?
3. What are the issues involved here? Are there conflicts among the stakeholders' objectives?
4. How can MIS help overcome these issues?

ANNEXURE

Metrics	How Will This Help to Improve Performance	Areas That Need Attention if the Value of the Metrics Is Decreasing (Suggestions)
Customer acquisition per period	This metrics helps to check how many new customers are enrolled.	If the TKK is not working well, increase the subsidies and offer.
Market share	Due to the use of GoMobile, we can maintain the inventory with dealers better so that customers do not have to opt for any other brand of fertilizers due to non-availability of Tata fertilizers during the peak agricultural season; thus, the market share is retained.	If the market share declines, it indicates that the customers are moving to the other brands, for which one reason could be unavailability of fertilizers with dealers; by using the database, we can check whether the problem is with field officers, dealers or warehouse managers. Another reason could be ineffective functioning of TKKs due to which the customers may not be remembering the brand of Tata fertilizers.
Brand awareness	As the field officer provides with scientific information and gives suggestions about suitability of fertilizers with the help of GIS, customers' trust in the company and its fertilizer brand is improved.	The functioning of TKKs needs to be improved so that customers start identifying the fertilizer by the brand name.
Existing customers participation	The MIS will help the company to know how many of the farmers actually become the dealers to buy Tata's products.	This will reduce the gap in communication between perception of the value received by the consumers and the actual value being proposed by the company.
Return on marketing investment	Investment done in fertilizer marketing through TKKs and TKSs is of no use if we are not able to convert the brand awareness about Tata fertilizers into actual sales: Through timely and sufficient supplies to the dealers, it is ensured that customers do not shift from Tata to some other brand due to unavailability of stock with the dealers.	Proper warehouse management and inventory control.

BIBLIOGRAPHY

1. T. K. Chanda, K. Sati, and C. Robotson. (2005). *Fertilizer Statistics 2004–05, the Fertilizer Association of India*. New Delhi: Rakmo Press Limited.
2. T. K. Chanda, K. Sati, and C. Robotson. (2004). *Fertilizer Statistics 2003–04, the Fertilizer Association of India*. New Delhi: Rakmo Press Limited.
3. M. Barman. (2005). *Fertilizer and Agriculture Statistics Eastern Region 2004–05, the Fertilization of India Eastern Region*. Kolkata: FAI Publications.
4. M. Barman. (2006). *Fertilizer and Agriculture Statistics Eastern Region 2005–06, the Fertilization of India Eastern Region*. Kolkata: FAI Publications.
5. The Fertilizer Association of India. (2006). *The Fertilizer (Control) Order 1985*. New Delhi: Rakmo Press Limited.
6. http://www.anchor-chemical.com/
7. http://www.ariesagro.com
8. http://www.tatachemicals.com
9. http://www.rallis.co.in/business/agri/fertilizers/solubor.asp
10. http://www.multiplexgroup.com/MultiMicronutrient.htm
11. http://www.dayalgroup.com/micro_nutrients.html
12. http://www.tatatkk.com/kisan_kendra.htm
13. http://www.tata.com/company/profile.aspx?sectid=ZE/HGJVcdzU=#ab
14. http://www.gis.com/
15. http://en.wikipedia.org/wiki/GIS

4

Case Study on Monsanto: Customized Global Marketing Strategy in India

INTRODUCTION

Monsanto Company (Monsanto) is a leading agro-based company in the United States, which is gradually speeding its network's expansion in different countries of the world. It mainly focuses on innovations and technologies to help farmers to produce more and more agricultural commodities in a sustainable manner to feed the world population. For this purpose, the company has set its vision as "to make the world a better place for future generations by providing value through the products and systems we offer to the farmers, which will result in increase in yield". Accordingly, the mission of the organization is "to deliver agricultural products and solutions to the farmers to meet the world's growing food need, to conserve natural resources by protecting the environment".

To be in line with its vision and mission statements, the organization has set its intermediary goals as follows: By 2030, Monsanto commits to help farmers to produce more and conserve more by

Developing improved seeds that help farmers' double yields from 2,000 levels for corn, soya bean and cotton with a $10 million grant pledged to improve wheat and rice yields.

Conserving resources by developing seeds that use one-third fewer key resources per unit of output than conventional seeds to grow crops, while working to lessen habitat loss and improve water quality.

Helping to improve the lives of all farmers who use Monsanto's products, including an additional 5 million people in resource-poor farm families by 2020.

HISTORY OF MONSANTO

Monsanto is a relatively new company. The company was founded in 1901 by John F Queenly. The original Monsanto produced and marketed agricultural chemicals, and in 1960 the agricultural division was established. Gradually, the company entered into molecular biology and biotechnology. The original Monsanto entered into a merger and changed its name to Pharmacia Corporation. In the year 2000, a new Monsanto company based on the previous agricultural division of Pharmacia was incorporated as a stand-alone subsidiary of the pharmaceutical company. The Monsanto of today focuses on agriculture and supporting farmers around the world in their mission to feed, clothe and fuel the growing world (*Source*: http://en.wikipedia.org/wiki/Monsanto).

ORGANOGRAM OF MONSANTO

> ***"As we continue the process of transforming Monsanto from a business based on chemistry to an agricultural global leader focused largely on seeds and traits, it's imperative that our business structure reflects the realities of how our business is changing," Grant,*** **CEO of Monsanto, said (Source: *Monsanto* Web site, April 2008).**

Executive Management of Monsanto in India

As far as Monsanto India Ltd. is concerned, the board of directors has seven members. Sekar Maharaja is the chairperson, whereas Amitabh Japery is the managing director.

The members of the company's board of directors with the company's other directors are given in Table 4.1.

Divisions of Monsanto in India

For efficient execution and control of all company operations, Monsanto has eight regional divisions in India. These regional divisions and their respective chief officers are shown in Table 4.2. These regional chief officers are the controlling heads of their respective divisions. The regional divisions are named according to the major river basins in India.

Operating Structure of Monsanto in India

Operating structure is the hierarchy-oriented structure that shows the order in which information and decision-making process flows in an organization. At the top level of Monsanto India Ltd. there is the chief executive officer, and at the lowest level there is the territory manager. Above the territory manager there is the regional coordinator, and above the latter there is the regional business manager. The zonal manager holds the position above the regional business manager. There are four zones, viz, eastern, western, southern and northern. For each zone, there is one zonal manager. All four zonal managers are under the managing director. The managing director is the position coming under the chief executive officer; Amitabh Japery is the managing director for Monsanto India Ltd. (see Tables 4.1 and 4.2, and Figure 4.1 for details).

There are four main departments, viz, business, human resources (HR), finance and marketing. The hierarchy of organizational structure is more or less the same for all four departments.

Table 4.1 *Monsanto India Ltd.—board of directors*

Serial Number	Name	Designation
1	Sekar Maharaja	Chairperson
2	Praveen Plodder	Director
3	R. C. Khanna	Director
4	H. C. Asher	Director
5	Brad Huseman	Director
6	Mark R Martino	Manager
7	Amitabh Japery	Managing Director

Table 4.2 *Regional divisions and their chief officers*

Serial Number	Regional Division	Chief Officer
1	Beas	Mrinmoy Choudhary
2	Ganga	Digonto Borah
3	Bhagirthi	Digonto Borah
4	Sabarmati	Somanath Ghatak
5	Narmada	Arif Mohammad
6	Brahmaputra	Bijit Sarmah
7	Godavari	Jitendra Joshi
8	Tungabhadra	Gajanan Werulakar
9	Cauvery	T. Rajmohan

Source: http://books.google.co.in/books? id=7Cq7nDrm5cEC&pg=PA576&lpg=PA576&dq=organisational+structure+of+monsanto&source=web&ots=PjxaFYTfdw&sig=L9W9yioSexSmXb5oYnYo3fGN6HM&hl=en&sa=X&oi=book_result&resnum=4&ct=result

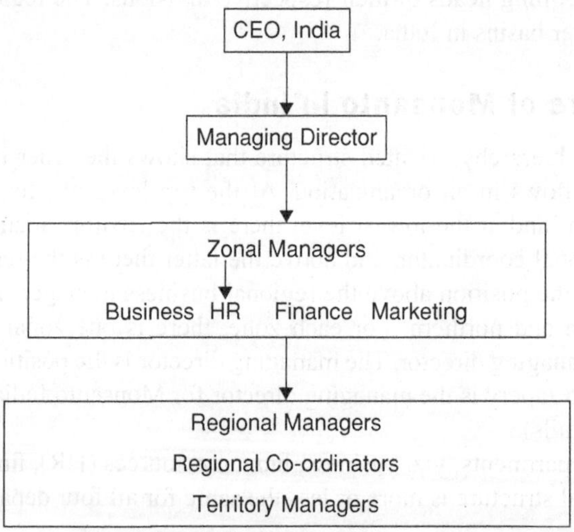

Figure 4.1 *Organizational Structure*

STAKEHOLDERS OF MONSANTO—A BRIEF REVIEW

The booming agricultural biotechnology industry in developing countries has opened up tremendous opportunities for many multinational corporations. But the entry of such companies into this lucrative market is not easy. The main reason is the challenges posed by the key stakeholders like media, environmental groups and regulatory authorities in such countries. Monsanto continues to engage with select stakeholders to gather information to make informed decisions and to share its practices with all stakeholders. At Monsanto, they are committed to building relationships based on integrity. Integrity, in alignment with their pledge, helps the company to earn and retain the trust of people with whom they do business. Monsanto is proud of its winning culture. It is based on several important norms:

- Taking ownership of the company's success
- Delivering products and technology of the highest quality
- Building strong relationships
- Creating a great place to work
- Conducting themselves with integrity

These are the work culture characteristics at Monsanto that helps it to develop a relationship with its stakeholders that grows stronger and better day by day.

STRENGTHS, WEAKNESSES, OPPORTUNITIES AND THREATS (SWOT) ANALYSIS

Company profile is the essential source for top-level company data and information. The company profile report examines a company's key business structure and operations, examines its history and products, and provides a summary analysis of its key revenue lines and strategy.

Monsanto is a global provider of agricultural products. The United States is Monsanto's major market. However, Monsanto also has substantial operations abroad, covering the regions of North America, South America, Europe, Asia, Australia and Africa. It is headquartered in St. Louis, Missouri, and employed 18,800 people as of August 2007. The company recorded revenues of $8,563 million in the fiscal year ending on August 2007, an increase of 17.4 per cent over the figure of 2006. The operating profit of the company was $1,418 million in fiscal year 2007, an increase of 21.1 per cent over the figure of 2006. The net profit was $993 million in fiscal year 2007, an increase of 44.1 per cent over the figure of 2006.

Strengths—to Build On

Brand equity—Monsanto is a global provider of agricultural products. The United States is Monsanto's major market.

Research and development (R&D)—Through investments in plant breeding and biotechnology, the company is working hard to deliver products that make farmers more productive and profitable.

HR policy—Monsanto is regularly honoured with awards recognizing the innovation, leadership and workplace satisfaction of its employees. This recognition generally reflects the feedback provided by the company's employees and others in the society.

Weaknesses—to Cover

Relationship with distributors—Since time immemorial, Monsanto has been popular for placing a very high brand value on serving its customer in the best possible way, although it has regular conflicts and disturbances with its distributors.

Lack of goodwill—In comparison with the number of years the company has been operational, it has not been able to build up a proportionally popular brand image in the market.

Legal issues—Monsanto over a long period of time has been regularly involved in legal issues regarding various operational problems.

Opportunities—to Capture

Untapped markets—Monsanto has immense market opportunities both in India and abroad, in terms of sophisticated seeds and other agricultural stuff.

Product-line diversity—Monsanto has diversified into various product lines, and through proper structure it can capture any required market.

Corporate social responsibility (CSR)—Over the years, Monsanto has gained market momentum in the area of CSR, but it has a long way to go.

Threats—to Defend Against

Competition
Antagonism
Controversies
Piracy

Source: http://www.pr-inside.com/monsanto-company-swot-analysis-r660829.htm

- Investment managers
- Venture capitalists
- Management consultants
- Research companies
- Other industry professionals

ENTERPRISE RESOURCE PLANNING (ERP) TAKES ROOT

Monsanto uses the business planning and control system (BPCS) package for its operations in the Asia–Pacific region (APAC), whereas it uses SAP for its operations in the rest of the world. This is done to reduce the cost of licence for implementing SAP in the APAC region. To make use of the benefits of ERP, both the packages have been integrated for the seamless transfer of information among packages.

R&D

Being an agricultural company, Monsanto focuses a lot on its R&D department for developing innovative technologies to ensure better farming and overall a better yield. It invests more than $2 million a day on developing such innovative technologies.

Some of the focus areas of Monsanto in this respect are as follows: *Delivering better seeds to farmers*—At Monsanto, the importance of seed in ensuring good overall agricultural productivity is understood very well. They know that it is the seed that is primarily going to determine the quantum and quality of agricultural produce. And thus, the company pays a lot of attention on the development of better-quality and high-yielding-variety (HYV) seeds.

Crops—At Monsanto, a lot of attention is paid to the following crops:

Corn—The company's understanding of the farming of corn helps it to do qualitative research to develop seeds with better yield and practices that enhance its total productivity.

Cotton—Apart from all other aspects of crops, a major stress is given to increase the durability of this crop.

Soya bean—Monsanto's research has helped it in developing seeds with better yield and of better quality and also to develop a high quality-rich in protein variety.

Fruits and vegetables—Monsanto understands the importance of fruits and vegetables in its customers' daily diet and the role these crops can play in the growth of the company. Thus it puts a lot of stress on, apart from other things, developing the end-market features of fruits and vegetables so as to attract customers.

(For more about Monsanto's R&D, please see http://www.monsanto.com/pdf/products/2008_monsanto_pipeline.pdf)

FUNCTIONAL INTEGRATION

For any organization, integration between different departments is a vital necessity. Finance, marketing, HR, operations and especially R&D (in the case of Monsanto) all play equally important roles in a company's growth and development. And it is this integration and its mode between the functional departments that differentiates an average company from an excellent one. In this respect, Monsanto is a leader. The design of its functional integration is such that it allows its different functional departments to act collectively, borrow ideas and share resources. This has been the key to its substantial growth. This integration is depicted in Figure 4.2.

Now, since Monsanto is a technology provider for the agricultural sector, to keep up with market trends and expectations it has to constantly work towards better products for its customers through innovative ideas and their applications, which are carried out by its R&D wing. Thus, the role of an R&D head becomes extremely important. He or she has to coordinate with various functional departments for various purposes, for example, with the marketing department for getting the latest market expectation insights or with the finance department for the budget allocation of R&D department as a whole and of individual projects. Thus, it becomes critical that the R&D department is managed well. This critical process can be explained diagrammatically, as shown in Figure. 4.3.

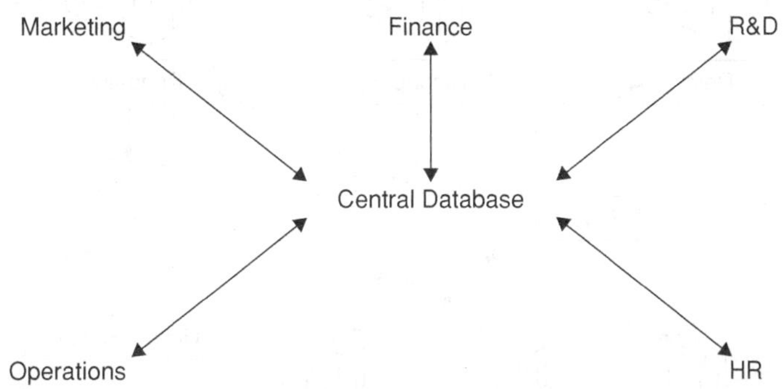

Figure 4.2 *Central Database Helps in Functional Integration*

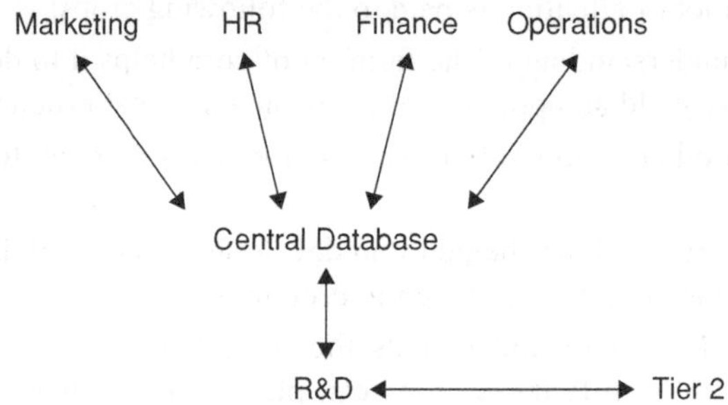

Figure 4.3 *Intra Departmental Processes*

INFORMATION SYSTEM ARCHITECTURE

The information system architecture of Monsanto in India has its roots in the computerization efforts undertaken by the company in 1995, when it started to computerize its operations in India and link them with the company's facilities in the United States and Singapore. It has three facilities in India, Mumbai (head office), Delhi (customer service centre) and Bengaluru (R&D hub), along with three production units at Silvassa and Elluru in Andhra Pradesh and Bellary in Karnataka.

To ensure proper transfer of information between these locations, the company has interlinked all the three locations through BPCS and the bandwidth of the links is dependent on the requirement at the respective locations. For example, Delhi needs only to use ERP data so it is connected with a 16 Kbps link; the manufacturing facilities need to access the ERP database as well as other databases, so they are all allotted 32 Kbps each; and the R&D centre at Bengaluru is linked with a 128-Kbps very small aperture terminal (VSAT) link and it is also linked to the US office with a 384-Kbps frame relay link along with an integrated services digital network (ISDN) backup. Proper provision is also made for any kind of disaster. An ISDN link is established from India to Singapore, which acts as a disaster recovery site, and then the ERP servers in Singapore take over. This entire framework is depicted in Figure 4.4.

(*Source*: Network Magazine, 'Case study on Monsanto's ERP implementation.')

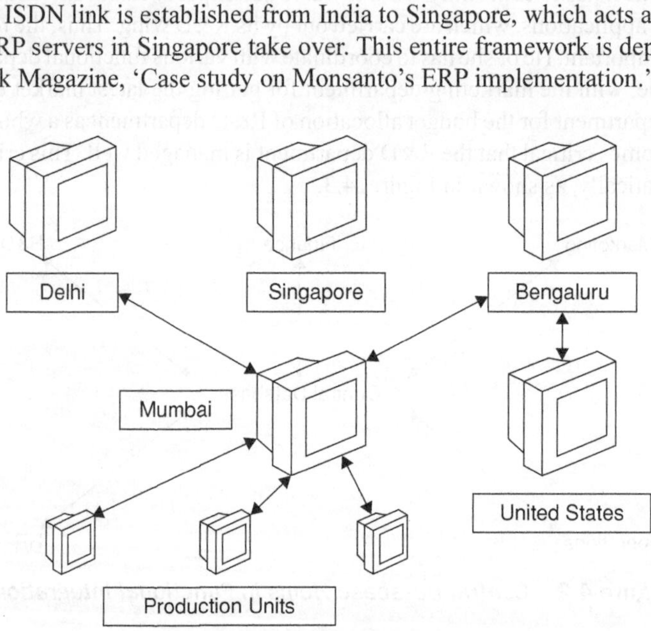

Figure 4.4 *Information Architecture*

MONSANTO's BUSINESS STRATEGY

Expansion in developing countries: Monsanto is looking at expanding its markets, especially in developing countries, so as to regain some of the ground that it has lost in the European and American markets.

Targeting the small farmer: Another way by which Monsanto is looking at expansion is by targeting the small farmer. Monsanto's customers largely comprise middle-income and rich farmers. Hence, it is now looking at developing a strong base at the small- and marginal-farmer level.

Increasing nutritional value for consumers: Monsanto knows that the best way to capture the market in developing countries is by increasing the nutritional value of products for consumers. It is quite obvious that a farmer eats the same food that he or she produces. So, the ideal method to market a product would be to ensure its nutritional value is high.

OPERATIONAL STRATEGY

Bring out customized and area-specific products: Monsanto's focus is on bringing out customized products that are developed specifically keeping in mind the characteristics of an area, such as soil types, climate and other factors.

Regain goodwill among farmers, especially in developing countries by providing technical assistance: This can be done by organizing special training courses for farmers in the use of modern methods of farming.

Launch a public relations exercise: As Monsanto's image has taken a beating in recent years, it needs to launch a massive public relations exercise in order to recapture its brand image.

Check piracy: Piracy must be checked by establishing direct relationships with farmers. One of the crucial issues faced by Monsanto is that after spending millions on R&D its product is pirated and sold at cheaper prices, leading to serious loss of revenue for the company. It can check this tendency by establishing direct relationships with farmers so as to increase brand loyalty.

R&D

The importance of research and development for companies in today's highly competitive business environment cannot be emphasized enough. This is especially true for an agri-biotech company like Monsanto. There are three principal benefits of R&D for Monsanto:

Financial perspective: Better products result in happier customers, leading to an increase in sales and better returns on investment (ROIs).

Customer perspective: Better customer relationships are the result of continuous improvement in the quality of products. This leads to a more satisfied client base and to better customer loyalty.

Internal perspective: A superior product leads to lesser storage costs due to its resistance to pests and negative environment effects. This leads to a reduction in operational costs.

Objectives of R&D for Monsanto

Developing seeds that are customized to the climatic conditions and soils of an area is one of the most important objectives of Monsanto. It leads to a wider market share for the company and to better brand building. Products of superior quality lead to higher customer satisfaction levels, which ensure customer loyalty.

Another objective of the company is to come out with easy-to-use products that require less technical knowledge; this would lead to better acceptance of the product among small and marginal farmers whose technical knowledge is limited.

Evaluating R&D Investments

Companies today invest astronomical sums in R&D. Monsanto, for example, invests 46 per cent of its profits in R&D. Hence, measuring and evaluating the performance of the R&D department is all the more significant today. However, R&D investments are difficult to evaluate. This is because the benefits can be seen only over a long period of time. Also, some of the benefits may be in the form of intangibles. Hence, the author has tried to identify the metrics that can help Monsanto evaluate its investments by using the balanced scorecard approach.

DEVELOPING R&D METRICS USING THE BALANCED SCORECARD APPROACH

The Annexure can be referred to for details. The strategy tree and scorecard details for Monsanto are given in Table 4.3. Metrics for evaluating the performance of the R&D department are given in Table 4.4, and metrics for individual projects are shown in Table 4.5.

Table 4.3 *Strategy tree and scorecard details*

Perspective	Goal	Weight (× 10)	Description	Performance (%)	Target Values (%)
Financial perspective		3		37.04	
	ROI	3	Revenue earned as a result of new products	30	100
	Profitability	6	Profits due to investments in R&D	60	10
Total performance in group			Financial perspective	37.04	
Customer perspective		3		36.19	
	Customer satisfaction	4	Number of customers satisfied with the new products	40	100
	Customer loyalty	2	Customers who are willing to buy the new products again	20	70
Total performance in group			Customer perspective	36.19	

Perspective	Goal	Weight (× 10)	Description	Performance (%)	Target Values (%)
Internal processes perspective		3		40.18	
	Efficiency	2	What is the efficiency of the R&D wing?	5	40
	Budget forecasting	3	Number of projects that are completed within the specified budget	30	100
	Expenditure forecasting	3	Accuracy of the expenditure forecast	3	8
Total performance in group			Internal processes perspective	40.18	
Education and growth perspective		2			
	Time (hours) reserved for innovations training	3	Time spent on training new scientists	3	5
	Training efficiency	3	Time taken for employees to become productive after receiving training	5	10

Table 4.4 *Metrics for evaluating the performance of R&D department*

Metrics	Formula	Role	Periodicity
Profitability (FP)	Revenue earned from new products Total revenue	Finance department	Annually
ROI (FP)	Total revenue from new products Total R&D funding	Finance department	Annually
Efficiency (IP)	Total number of successful launches Total number of projects undertaken	Operations department	Annually
On time and on budget (IP)	Number of projects completed on time and on budget Total number of projects undertaken	Operations department	Annually
Cost per scientist (L&G)	Total remuneration paid Total number of scientists	HR department	Annually

Note: FP—financial perspective, CP—customer perspective, IP—internal process, L&G—learning and growth perspective.

Table 4.5 *Metrics for individual projects*

Metrics	Formula	Role	Periodicity
Revenue (actual versus forecasted) (IP)	Forecasted value minus actual value	Finance department	Annually
Customer satisfaction (CP)	Total number of customers satisfied with the product Total number of customers polled	Marketing department	Annually
Budget (IP)	Expenditure forecasted value minus actual value	Finance department	Completion of the project
Customer loyalty (CP)	Total number of repeat customers for the product Total number of customers	Marketing department	Annually
ROI (FP)	Revenue earned from the product Total amount spent on the product	Finance department	Annually

FP—financial perspective, CP—customer perspective, IP—internal process, L&G—learning and growth perspective.

STRATEGY TREE

1. Financial perspective

   Maximize ROI through efficient selection of projects and reduced research costs.

   One of the most critical decisions that a company has to make is regarding which projects to undertake. This is a difficult task as this decision has to be made under considerable uncertainty. Hence, efficient selection of projects is vital.

   Maximize profitability through aggressive marketing and sales campaigns.

   After coming out with a new product, the company needs to work on promoting its sales. This has to be done through aggressive marketing and sales campaigns.

2. Customer perspective

   Deliver customized products requiring the least technical assistance to farmers. This essentially means delivering easy-to-use products.

   Reduce input costs for farmers. Reducing input costs leads to better returns for farmers, which leads to higher satisfaction levels and consequently more loyalty.

3. Internal Processes

   Weed out non-performing R&D teams. This is a critical issue. Measuring the effectiveness of employees is important because companies invest heavily in employee benefits and training.

   Accurate budget forecasting is crucial. Investments of astronomical magnitudes need accurate forecasting as the margin of error is very small.

4. Learning and growth

   Recruit new talent, comprising individuals who can think out of the box. In today's competitive environment, companies need to come up with new and innovative ideas all the time in order to capture the attention of the consumer; thus recruiting fresh talent is a must.

THE BENEFITS OF INFORMATION SYSTEM (IS) ENABLED MANAGEMENT TRANSFORMATION

The most measurable of all types of benefits are those involving reductions in management personnel. For example, at Monsanto plant nine of 15 accountants were no longer needed when accounting processes were made common and moved to the corporate level. Overall, the company eliminated 40 percent of its accounting staff by implementing an IS-enabled shared-services organization.

FUNCTIONAL BENEFITS OF FUNCTIONAL INTEGRATION

Operational Benefits

Enhanced inventory control—Better inventory management by identifying the ordering quantity.

Better quality tracking—There is an efficient feedback system that ensures proper quality tracking and control.

Reduced transaction costs—The required levels of inventory are known, which reduces the frequency of ordering it every time.

Research and Development Benefits

Better flow of knowledge—Knowledge sharing becomes easy and effective.

Coordination among research teams—Coordination of different resources becomes effective.

COST-BENEFIT ANALYSIS OF FUNCTIONAL INTEGRATION

History

The idea of CBA was first mentioned by Jules DuPont, a French engineer whose article on the subject published in 1848 is still worth reading. The British economist Alfred Marshall can be credited with some formal concepts that are the foundation of CBA. But the practical development of CBA was an outcome of the Federal Navigation Act of 1936. This act mentioned that the US Corps of Engineers carry out projects for the improvement of the waterway system only when the total benefits of a project exceed the costs of that project. Thus, the Corps of Engineers created systematic methods for measuring such benefits and costs. The engineers in the corps did this without much assistance from economics or accounting professionals. Only in the 1950s did economists try to provide a rigorous, consistent set of methods for measuring benefits and costs and for deciding whether a project is worthwhile.

Example of a CBA

A company that would like to install the SAP R/3 ERP package to improve its business might use a CBA to make up its mind. Points on the minus (cost) side would be

- The price of the software
- The cost of consultants to install and implement the software
- The cost of training required for users of the software

However, points on the plus (benefits) side would be

- Improved business processes (leading to an annual cost decrease)

- Due to better available information, the company will be able to make better decisions (leading to additional cash flows), and
- Increased staff morale, due to the use of these modern tools to support the business.

(*Source*: http://www.12manage.com/methods_cost-benefit_analysis.html)

Mistakes and Problems with CBA

A frequently made mistake in the CBA method is the use of non-discounted amounts for calculating costs and benefits. A method like net present value (NPV), payback period or internal rate of return (IRR) is strongly recommended, because all these methods account for the time value of money. Another frequently occurring problem with CBA is that typically the costs are tangible, hard and financial, whereas the benefits are not only hard and tangible but also soft and intangible. Caution should be taken here against people who claim that "if you cannot measure, it does not exist OR it has no value". Especially in very strategic investments, frequently the intangible benefits clearly outweigh the financial benefits. Risk must often be considered as a factor when making a decision.

EVALUATION OF TANGIBLES

Net Present Value (NPV)

NPV or net present worth (NPW) is defined as the total present value (PV) of a time series of cash flows. It is a standard method for using the time value of money to appraise long-term projects. Used for capital budgeting, and widely used in economics, NPV measures the excess or shortfall of cash flows, in PV terms, once financing charges are met.

Each cash inflow/outflow is discounted back to its PV. Then they are summed. Therefore, NPV is the sum of all terms

$$\frac{R_t}{(1+i)^t}$$

where

t—the time of the cash flow

i—the discount rate (the rate of return that could be earned on an investment in the financial markets with similar risk.)

R_t—the net cash flow (the amount of cash, inflow minus outflow) at time t (for educational purposes, C0 is usually placed to the left of the sum to emphasize its role as the initial investment).

What NPV Means

NPV is an indicator of how much value an investment or project adds to the value of a firm. NPV is calculated using a formula, as shown in Table 4.6. NPV is used to find the feasibility of implementing a project. Table 4.6 shows the decision possibilities when using NPV.

Payback Period

Payback period in business and economics refers to the period of time required for the return on an investment to 'repay' the original investment. It intuitively measures how long something takes to 'pay for itself'; projects with shorter payback periods are obviously preferable to those with longer payback

Table 4.6 *Decision possibilities when using NPV*

If ...	It means ...	Then ...
NPV > 0	The investment would add value to the firm	The project may be accepted
NPV < 0	The investment would subtract value from the firm	The project should be rejected
NPV = 0	The investment would neither add value to nor subtract value from the firm	This project adds no monetary value. Decision should be based on other criteria, for example, strategic positioning or other factors not explicitly included in the calculation.

(***Source***: http://en.wikipedia.org/wiki/Net_present_value)

However, NPV = 0 does not mean that a project is only expected to break even, in the sense of undiscounted profit or loss (earnings). It will show net positive cash flow and earnings over its life.

periods (all else being equal). Project managers use payback period due to its ease of use despite its recognized limitations, which are described in the following paragraph. The expression is also widely used in other types of investment areas, often with respect to energy efficiency technologies, maintenance and upgrades or other changes.

Payback period as a tool of analysis is often used because it is easy to apply and easy to understand for most individuals regardless of academic training or field of endeavour. When used with care or for comparing similar investments, it can be quite useful. As a stand-alone tool to compare an investment with 'doing nothing', payback period has no explicit criteria for decision making (except, perhaps, that the payback period should be less than infinity):

$$\text{Payback} = \text{Days / Weeks / Months} \times \text{Initial investment / Total cash received}$$

(*Source*: http://en.wikipedia.org/wiki/Payback_period)

MODEL FOR EVALUATION OF INTANGIBLES

The Hypothetical Case of Star Ltd

(Case adapted from proceedings of the 34th Hawaii International Conference on System Sciences, 2001)

The company's annual appraisal showed that customer satisfaction levels had gone down by 21 per cent with customers and 15 per cent with suppliers. The management realizing that diminishing satisfaction levels would eventually have an impact on sales ranked satisfaction improvement as a key goal during system evaluation. A method pretty similar to the quantification technique was used, and improved customer/user satisfaction was identified as a key system deliverable. Customer satisfaction existed as a metric within Star Ltd. with data collected on an annual basis. The information systems department of Star Ltd. compiled a list of customer-reported system deficiencies from the last satisfaction survey they had conducted, for the purpose of converting satisfaction from an intangible factor to a measurable factor. It was followed by a close analysis of the situation, that is, analysis of the performance of various items in the current system and the changes expected to be made post-installation of the ERP system. A baseline was established to help the managers to project the level of satisfaction improvement once the proposed system was in place. Managers of Star Ltd. consulted customers and projected that the proposed ERP system could improve customer satisfaction by 5 per cent initially and by approximately 2 per cent a year thereafter (assuming expectations were met). The next major task in this analysis was to predict the economic value of an increase in customer satisfaction. This step was also accomplished through several interviews and surveys with the customers and suppliers of Star Ltd.

Managers in the sales and marketing department undertook the surveys and interviews with customers and suppliers as they were the ones who were the most familiar to customers. The results of several interviews suggested that for each 5 per cent improvement in customer satisfaction, Star Ltd. could expect a 1 per cent gain in market share. The results, although non-scientific, indicated that market share increases would result in significant benefits for the company. The final step of this process was to evaluate the potential cash flow resulting from market share gains. Based on the cash flow resulting from the customer market share improvements, the CBA was redone and the results appeared as shown in Table 4.7.

SAMPLE ITEMS FOR CUSTOMER SATISFACTION SURVEY

Table 4.7 *Sample items for customer satisfaction survey*

Item	Current System	ERP System
Enter pricing data	5–80 days	5 minutes
Committed ship date	1 day	Real time
Schedule orders	Overnight	Real time
Credit check	15–20 minutes	Real time
Enter order	30 minutes	5 minutes
Inquiry and response	15–20 minutes	Real time

CBA (TANGIBLES AND INTANGIBLES)

Table 4.8 *The first CBA conducted for Star Ltd.*

Productivity	Inventory	IT Operations	User Satisfaction	Implementation Cost	Total*
18.8	49.1	23.4	228.7	73.4	228.9

NPV in million rupees has been considered in the table.
*Additional factors have been considered.

Seeing the threat to its market share and revenues, Star Ltd. undertook a major organization-restructuring exercise. As part of this effort, the systems division of the firm was asked to justify in economic terms a large investment in an ERP solution. In the first CBA (shown in Table 4.8), the management used estimates of productivity savings, inventory savings and savings resulting from more effective information systems operations to calculate the NPV for the project. The NPV of productivity improvements and inventory reductions resulting from new system implementation were estimated at Rs 18.8 million and Rs 49.1 million, respectively, over the 10-year time-horizon utilized. The NPV for cost savings from IT operations was estimated to be Rs 23.4 million. The NPV for the project was estimated to be Rs 28.1 million, and all NPV calculations assumed a 20 per cent hurdle rate. Table A1 shows that the internal rate of return for this project was estimated to be 39.2 per cent. With these estimates, the ERP Implementation project meets the hurdle rate criteria set by the management of Star Ltd. In a subsequent CBA, many of the same figures' cost and benefit figures were utilized; however, the intangible items of customer satisfaction were also included. The assumption made by the Star Ltd. management was that implementing the ERP system would have a significant and positive impact on customer satisfaction and would thereby improve market share. This view had been justified by the data gathered earlier through customer interviews. The NPV resulting from increasing the customer satisfaction was estimated to be Rs 228.7 million. This caused the new NPV of the project when customer satisfaction was included to be valued at Rs 228.9 million (see Table 4.8). Upon including the intangible of customer satisfaction, the ERP implementation project was found significantly more beneficial for improving the organization bottom line.

As a result of the evaluation and analysis, the information systems department of Star Ltd. was given the approval to implement the ERP package. The implementation of the new system, including replacement of legacy hardware and software, was conducted on time and on budget. During its first year of operation, the ERP system contributed over Rs 225 million in savings and productivity improvements. The results of CBA and intangible analysis were the factors that convinced Star Ltd. to make the decision to implement the system. Without the aforementioned numerical results, the senior management would not have agreed to go ahead with the project regardless of anticipated benefits. This emphasizes the importance of inclusion of intangible benefits in CBA and their quantification.

RECOMMENDATIONS

Courses of Action

- To merge with companies having strong financial resources
- To have interrelationships
- To enter into acquisitions

Monsanto's swelling new product pipelines is an expensive endeavour and so the firm has to merge with companies that can provide it the resources and at the same time maximize its potential pharmaceutical and agricultural biotechnology pipelines. They invest $2 million a day to develop better seeds to help farmers to reduce input and increase production.

In the past year and a half, Monsanto has made concerted efforts to help augment conservation of traditional and sustainable agriculture. They recognize that the world is at the tipping point in terms of food production demands, population increase and limited resources. Seventy per cent of all fresh water is currently used for agriculture, and by 2050 we are projected to have 9 billion people on our planet. Global climate change is yet another obstacle to overcome. Monsanto's claims to sustainable practice is defined only when it means increased production to meet everyone's needs, more efficient use of natural resources and provision of a better quality of life for farmers and their families. This acknowledgment is a major step for a global corporation. The Monsanto pledge expands the firm's commitments to include doubling seed production by 2030, establishing a $10 million grant for research to increase wheat and rice yields, developing seeds that will reduce resources by 30 per cent by 2030 and helping 5 million additional farmer families in resource-poor locations by 2020. Although they are not focused on limiting their contributions exclusively to the organic or sustainable philosophy, they are taking on the responsibility of carefully developing new technology and science to move towards a more environmentally conscious corporation.

Monsanto is able to make a large impact by working with other businesses and farmers to develop ideas and expand their products. Hugh Grant acknowledges that the company experiences success only when farmers are successful. This connection with success leads to a dedication for agriculture and forces the corporation to continuously conduct new research and develop applications to match the changing challenges in the field. They also work closely with the youth to develop new opportunities through providing scholarships, internships and donations to the younger generation.

There is some controversy and negative publicity associated with Monsanto. The company has been known to sue farmers who reused their seeds illegally. Defendants have complained about 'unfair' legal cases of a lone famer against a giant corporation. But the company addresses this by explaining and legitimizing its commitment to patents; it explains that it has always been explicitly clear with farmers on this matter. Another controversy is the firm's research and monetary expenses towards corn ethanol production. Monsanto recognizes the global food crisis, but it also recognizes the growing cost of oil. The firm has responded by continuously modifying its research and products to meet both food and energy needs. It is also questioned about its push towards genetically modified (GM) crops. While many have moral objections to genetically engineered crops (e.g., the movement against BT brinjal), the reality is there is no doubt that GM crops have increased the yields of some crops. The central focus of Monsanto is on increasing yields and it continuously works with different countries and farmers to address these concerns.

DISCUSSION QUESTIONS

1. What is the market potential of agricultural products in India?
2. What are the challenges that a multinational company faces while marketing its products to farmers?
3. How will a management information system help in overcoming these challenges?

BIBLIOGRAPHY

1. http://www.monsantoindia.com/monsanto/layout/default.asp, 2008.
2. http://economictimes.indiatimes.com/Interviews/Monsanto-attempts-new-model-to-take-on-free-farming/articleshow/5320779.cms, 2008.
3. http://economictimes.indiatimes.com/news/news-by-company/earnings/earnings-news/Monsanto-India-posts-Rs-845-cr-loss-in-March-quarter/articleshow/5935063.cms, 2008.
4. Humphreys, Gary (2001). *Project Management Using Earned Value.* Humphreys and Associates. ISBN 0-9708614-0-0.
5. Philipson, Erik and Sven Antvik (2009). *Earned Value Management.* Elanders Sverige AB. ISBN 978-91-977394-5-0.
6. Project Management Institute (2005). *Practice Standard for Earned Value Management.* Project Management Institute. ISBN 1-930699-42-5.
7. Solomon, Paul and Ralph Young (2006). *Performance-Based Earned Value.* Wiley-IEEE Computer Society. ISBN 978-0-471-72188-8.

8. Stratton, Ray (2006). *The Earned Value Maturity Model.* Management Concepts. ISBN 1-56726-180-9.
9. U.S. Air Force Materiel Command (1994). "Guide to Analysis of Contractor Cost Data". AFMCPAM 65–501.

ANNEXURE

Table A1 *Internal rate of return*

Perspective	Performance (%)
Financial perspective	69.00
Customer perspective	75.00
Marketing perspective	75.00
	75.00
Total performance	
Scorecard includes four categories and 12 indicators	

Help	
—	You can change the values in the 'Weight' column, the value must be between 0 and 10; Value '10' means that the perspective or goal is the most valuable.
—	You can change the values in the 'Performance' column;

Strategy tree and scorecard details:

Perspective	Goal	Weight (× 10)	Description	Performance (%)	Target Values (%)	Maximum Performance	Real Performance
Financial perspective				69.00			
	ROI	8	Revenue earned from new products as a percentage of total cost incurred		100	0	0

(*Continued*...)

Table A1 (...*Continued*)

Perspective	Goal	Weight (× 10)	Description	Performance (%)	Target Values (%)	Maximum Performance	Real Performance
Total performance in group		9	**Financial perspective**	**69.00**		75	69
Customer perspective				75.00			
	Customer satisfaction	9	Percentage of customers satisfied with the new product		100	0	0
	Customer loyalty	7	Percentage of customers willing to do business again		100	0	0
Total performance in group		8	**Customer perspective**	**75.00**		69	85
Marketing perspective		2		75.00			
	Sales	9	Sales due to new products as a percentage of total sales		100	0.18	0
Total performance in group		8	**Marketing perspective**	**75.00**		144.18	154
	Total performance in	**Balanced scorecard**		75.00			
Powered by	Balanced Scorecard Designer (http://www.strategy2act.com/#index.htm)						

WHAT IS EVA?

Economic Value Addition (EVA™) is a successful performance metric used by investors to analyse the performance of a company.

To many, the EVA metric (also known as 'economic profit') is too complex to understand. EVA is a measure of how much a firm is adding to the wealth of its shareholders. It takes into account how much the shareholders are expecting, at least to compensate for the risk taken by them in investing in the firm. There is no real profit made otherwise. Zero EVA is also an achievement, which signifies the firm has just met the shareholders' expectations. EVA is a mileage tracker that helps drug companies to know whether they are heading in the correct direction towards enhanced performance or are going off the track. Maximizing shareholders' value has always been the first concern of all industries and the agriculture industry is no exception. EVA provides a snapshot of the performance of various departments to departmental heads who can find out on their own whether they are creating or destroying the value of a firm's shareholders. EVA helps in the smart allocation of capital.

Companies interested in enhancing the wealth of their shareholders should try to weave the concept of EVA into their systems in the following fashion:

- Formulate final objectives: A concern should be aware of its long-term financial objectives and the performance destination it wants to reach. This can be done from
    - Flow view: This lays down the route to be followed by the concern to reach its destination.
    - Stock view: The target here is the milestone. For example, if a company is at performance level 'A', it will attempt to reach a level of '2A'.
- Recognize the various sources of contribution: The concern should be able to estimate the contributions from various products. It should also know the changes to be made in its organizational structure.
- Distribution of wealth to the managers and shareholders: The managers should reach an understanding with the shareholders on goals and performance levels. The next decision the managers have to make is regarding the outcome of overperformance/underperformance.
- Decision making: The management must follow value-based principles to improve their decision making so as to strike a balance between long-term decisions that affect NPV and operational decisions.
- Providing training: The entire change management program requires considerable training on the part of the mangers for its successful implementation.

The future of an industry depends on its ability to diversify its risks, the extent to which it is able to build its marketing network, its forward and backward integration capabilities and its mergers and acquisitions.

EVA COMPUTATION

1. *NOPAT*:

   NOPAT is the difference between net operating profit before interest (PBIT) and tax:

   $$\text{So, PBIT} - \text{Tax} = \text{NOPAT}$$

2. *Cost of capital (CC)*:

   $$\text{CC} = \text{WACC} \times \text{CE}$$

WACC—weighted average cost of capital
CE—capital employed

3. *WACC*:

$$\text{WACC} = K_d \times (\text{Dept}/\text{Dept} + \text{Equity}) + K_e \times (\text{Equality}/\text{Debt} + \text{Equality})$$

K_d—cost of debt
K_e—cost of equity

$$K_d = I(1 - T)$$

I—interest rate
T—tax rate

$$K_e = R_f + \beta(R_m - R_f)$$

R_f—risk-free interest rate
R_m—rate of return from markets
β—Systematic risk

Table A2 *EVA calculation for Monsanto for 2007*

PBIT (in million dollars)	1,376.0000
Tax (in million dollars)	383.0000
NOPAT	993.0000
Interest rate (*I*;%)	5.2200
Tax rate (*T*;%)	8.0200
K_d (%)	4.8000
R_f (%)	7.8500
R_m (%)	15.8900
β	1.3429
K_e (%)	18.6500
Debt (in million dollars)	1,150.0000
Equity (in million dollars)	7,505.0000
WACC (%)	16.6600
Capital employed (in million dollars)	8,655.0000
Cost of capital (in million ollars)	1,441.9230
EVA (in million dollars)	−448.9230

Table A3 *Net operating profit before interest and after tax*

NOPAT:

NOPAT is net operating profit before interest and after tax.

So, PBIT − Tax = NOPAT

Cost of capital (CC):

CC = WACC × CE

WACC—weighted average cost of capital

CE—capital employed

WACC:

WACC = K_d × (Debt/Debt + Equity) + K_e × (Equity/Debt + Equity)

K_d—cost of debt

K_e—cost of equity

$K_d = I(1 - T)$

I—interest rate

T—tax rate

$K_e = R_f + \beta(R_m - R_f)$

R_f—risk-free interest rate.

R_m—rate of return from markets

β—systematic risk

(β is the relative price movements of the stock vis-à-vis the market.)

5

Case Study on DCM Shriram Consolidated Ltd: An Early Adopter of MIS

INTRODUCTION TO DCM SHRIRAM CONSOLIDATED LIMITED (DSCL)

Delhi Cloth and General Mills Company (DCM) Limited was founded by Lala Shri Ram in 1889, and it has come a long way since it was founded. The company operates in chlorovinyl and agricultural sectors. The company believes that the best way to make use of every input of energy is through vertical integration. The Hariyali division of the company was awarded the ACE—Best Customer Award for the successful implementation of SAP IS retail package. The company is also known for maintaining high standards of safety for its workforce, and its Kota complex won the prestigious British Sword of Honour in 2006 for implementing and practising the best safety standards.

To maintain its competitive edge, DSCL thrives to strengthen its agri- and energy-intensive businesses and offers value-added and knowledge-based products and services in the areas of its operations. The company strongly believes that to be successful in the long run, the business should connect to the society as well as all stakeholders. It takes care of not only its employees but also the society at large. It employs state-of-the-art technology to reduce environmental pollution. It has made significant contributions to the society in the fields of environment, healthcare, family planning, education, cultural heritage, rural development and in promoting livelihood at grass root level. Its chloralkali facility at Bharuch, Gujarat, has been recognized with an SA 8000:2001 certification by RINA (*Registro Italiano Navale*), making it one among the few companies in India to get this recognition. The achievements of the company can be summarized as follows:

- The Hariyali division of the company was awarded the ACE—Best Customer Award for the successful implementation of SAP IS retail package.
- All its main locations/products have ISO 9000 and ISO 14000 certifications and OHSAS 18001: 1999 system of occupational health and safety certifications. The Kota complex of the company

was recognized in 2006 with the prestigious 'British Sword of Honour' for implementing and practising the best safety standards.

HISTORICAL MILESTONES

The company was founded by Shri Ram Lalaji. Shriram was born into a family of Agarwal banias of modest means; in the productive 79 years of his life, Shriram built an industrial empire comprising industries manufacturing a vast variety of goods like textiles, sugar, alcohol, heavy chemicals, *vanaspati*, pottery, fans, sewing machines, electric motors and capacitors. The industrial legacy that he left behind was valued at Rs 600 million at the time of his death. Reared in a milieu that considered deft nepotism, black marketing and tax evasion a must for success in business, Shriram set for himself rigid standards of morality in his dealings with the public and government and made no compromises in order to earn more money or gain a favour. Although he himself was deprived of opportunities for higher education, he understood how important higher education is in building the future of a nation. As a result, he helped to finance a network of schools, colleges, industrial institutes and research laboratories. He was also the founder chairman of Industrial Finance Corporation and the chairman of Sindri Fertilizers, the first national venture in the public sector in free India.

Although Shriram lacked formal education, he read extensively. His reading included religious scriptures, Sanskrit classics, Urdu and Persian poetry, and some English biographies. He assiduously promoted men of learning and culture. Most of all, he admired scientists on whom he pinned his hopes for the salvation of his country. One of his lovable eccentricities was that he used to carry out experiments to produce new varieties of food in his own room and then subject his none too robust digestive system to his new recipes.

DCM has been following a growth strategy by aligning its business processes with its vision and mission. Over a period of time, it expanded to different related areas, sometimes by merging its existing business divisions and sometimes by acquiring units that can take the firm further in achieving its vision. As of today, the main business units of DSCL comprise *agribusinesses*, such as sugar, urea, agri inputs, Shriram Bioseeds, *Hariyali Kisaan Bazaar*; *energy-intensive businesses*, such as chemicals, polyvinylchloride (PVC) resins, cement; *value-added businesses*, such as Fenesta™ Building Systems, polyvinylchloride (PVC) compounds, energy services; and *other businesses*, such as textiles.

DSCL'S BOARD OF DIRECTORS

The names and designations of the members of DSCL's board of directors are given in Table 5.1.

Table 5.1 *Names and designations of directors*

Serial Number	Name	Designation
1	Ajay S. Shriram	Chairman and senior managing director
2	Vikram S. Shriram	Vice chairman and managing director

(***Continued...***)

Table 5.1 (...*Continued*)

Serial Number	Name	Designation
3	Rajiv Sinha	Deputy managing director
4	Ajit S. Shriram	Director (sugar)
5	S. S. Baijal	Director
6	Arun Bharat Ram	Director
7	Pradeep Dinodia	Director
8	Vimal Bhandari	Director
9	Sunil Kant Munjal	Director
10	D. Sengupta	Director
11	S. C. Bhargava (LIC Nominee)	Director
12	N. J. Singh	Whole-time Director–EHS (Environment, Health and Safety).

CORPORATE VISION OF DSCL

Corporate vision of an organization is a short, succinct and inspiring statement of what the organization intends to become and achieve at some point in the future, and is often stated in competitive terms. Vision refers to a category of intentions that are broad, all-inclusive and forward-thinking. It is the image that a business must have of its goals before it sets out to achieve them. It describes aspirations for the future, without specifying the means that will be used to achieve those desired ends. The vision of DSCL is to become the most trusted household name in the farming community.

MISSION STATEMENT OF DSCL

DSCL's mission statement is a reflection of its endeavours to achieve its vision. The statement reflects the company's approach of targeting all-round holistic improvement rather than profit alone. DSCL understands that to be successful, it has to have a win-win formula for customers, employees and shareholders through innovation and by providing new services. For customers, the mission statement states that the company needs to provide customer satisfaction by surpassing expectations and delivering superior products. For employees, it adopts a route of continuously improving and upgrading the skills and competencies of its people by helping them to realize their potential. It also encourages a spirit of teamwork among employees by making all the departments work closely as a cohesive, well-knit team with a spirit of openness and collaboration.

DSCL AGRIBUSINESS

Agri-input marketing is the core business of DSCL. The reason is that the company generates around 75 to 80 per cent of its revenue from its agri-input marketing division. The main function of this division is the marketing of seeds, pesticides and fertilizers. The company has manufacturing facilities at Kota in Rajasthan; Bharuch in Gujarat; and Ajabpur, Rubapur, Hariawan and Loni in Uttar Pradesh. Its hybrid seed operations are at Hyderabad (Andhra Pradesh), Vietnam, the Philippines and Thailand. The company also has window fabrication units at Bhiwadi in Rajasthan, Bengaluru, Mumbai, Hyderabad and Chennai.

Components of the DSCL Agribusiness

The components of DSCL's agribusiness are as follows:

Sugar: DSCL has four sugar production facilities, one each at Ajbapur, Rupapur, Hariawan and Loni in central Uttar Pradesh. The sugar cane procured from growers around the company's factories is the primary input for the company's sugar operations. Over 2,00,000 farmers supply cane to the factories. In order to facilitate the procurement of sugar cane, the company has set up over 250 cane centres at its sugar mills. This has significantly reduced the time taken in getting cane to the manufacturing facilities. The average distance covered by growers is around 5–7 km, and within 48–72 hours after harvesting sugar cane reaches the factories.

Urea: The company is among the first urea manufacturers in the country, with production starting way back in the 1960s. The urea plant has a production capacity of 3,79,000 TPA (Tonnes Per Annum), which includes a capacity of about 700 TPA of ammonia—ammonia is an ingredient in the urea manufacturing process. Over the last four decades of operations, the urea brand 'Shriram' has developed a strong presence in the rural market and is identified with premium-quality products.

Agri inputs: DSCL's agri-input business produces urea fertilizer and is engaged in the marketing of a range of other fertilizers, pesticides and other agriculture-related products. The agribusiness is leveraging modern management practices to realize significant value:

- A strong 'Shriram' brand equity.
- Over three decades of direct relationship with the farming community with the supply of agri inputs and the provision of education, training and community development programs.
- Operations spanning the north, west and south of India.
- An infrastructure of over 30 sales offices, 12 distribution warehouses, 200 wholesale outlets and 4,800 retail outlets.
- Shriram BioSeed Genetics India Ltd of Hyderabad, Andhra Pradesh, produces high-quality hybrid seeds.

Shriram Bioseed: DSCL has a 100 per cent subsidiary named Shriram Bioseed Genetics India Limited, which produces hybrid seeds. These seeds are exported to Vietnam, the Philippines and Thailand, and the company proposes to expand the export of such seeds to other locations in the Asia–Pacific region. At present, the company deals in corn, bajra (pearl millet), jowar, paddy, BT cotton, vegetables and sunflower seeds.

Hariyali Kisaan Bazaar: It is a rural retail initiative undertaken by DSCL to create a rural hub that makes agricultural and consumer products (of all manufacturers) and agri services available to farmers in a fair, transparent and convenient format. Currently, there are over 50 such bazaars; the company plans to increase them to 300 by December 2008.

STAKEHOLDERS OF DSCL AND THEIR OBJECTIVES

The following are the major stakeholders of DSCL:

1. The major objective of *distributors/direct dealers and retailers* is to maximize their profit margin and enable easy liquidation of inventory. The main issues and challenges that lie ahead of them are limited space, the demand and supply gap, and seasonal variations with varying pressure from market forces.
2. *Farmers* are also one of the major stakeholders of DSCL. DSCL works for farmers with the following major objectives in mind: The company tries to give maximum satisfaction to the farmers in exchange for their hard-earned money and the company maximizes their returns by giving them quality products. But while delivering these products, the company faces the major challenge of ensuring timely deliveries.
3. The other stakeholders for which DSCL is responsible includes the *company and its employees*. The major objectives for them include profitability, deeper penetration into rural markets and increasing the total market share with flexible procurement. The challenges faced when fulfilling these objectives are those corruption associated with distribution of company products and greater market coverage.
4. And the last stakeholder is *government*, which monitors the company's quality products and price levels. Government follows the system of fair trade practices.

BUSINESS OBJECTIVES OF DSCL

The company's philosophy regards agribusiness as a key growth driver for achieving business success. It believes agricultural sector is a high potential area, where the expertise and strengths accumulated by the company over the decades, makes it possible to add considerable value. This approach also helps to capitalize on emerging opportunities. *The company aims to cater to all the needs of farmers, develop extensive networks and expand its market share*. The agribusiness offerings of the company comprise agricultural inputs, which are both manufactured and merchandised by the company. The company wants to maximize the sales from both the manufacture and merchandising of these offerings. The company's objective is to move towards providing total solutions to farmers for which DSCL has undertaken initiatives in rural retailing, which holds immense promise in terms of untapped opportunities in saleability and growth potential.

The company wants to extend its offerings to other products and services (product diversification). Currently, the company offers multiple products and services to the rural and farming communities, including agri inputs, diesel and petrol (under an alliance with Bharat Petroleum Corporation Limited [BPCL]), consumer goods, durables, apparels, insurance, agronomy advisories, credit and contract farming. *The company desires a radical expansion in the field of rural retailing* with retail outlets all over the country. From about three-thousand outlets five years ago the company has already scaled its operations to 6,000, and it further aims to achieve a larger market share by the end of 2010. To develop a robust and extensive distribution network for providing online agronomy services to farmers, Shriram *Krishi Vikas Kendra*s have been established across the country with the objective of increasing farmer profitability by providing them with effective agronomy services.

BALANCED SCORECARD AND THE DERIVATION OF OPERATIONAL OBJECTIVES AND STRATEGIES

A balanced scorecard is a multi-dimensional framework for describing, implementing and managing strategies at all levels of an enterprise by linking objectives, initiatives and measures to an organizational strategy. The scorecard provides an enterprise view of an organization's overall performance by integrating financial measures and other key performance indicators around organizational growth, customer perspective, internal business processes and learning and innovation.

The balanced scorecard compares measures of past performance (lagging indicators) with measures of the drivers of future performance (leading indicators). The objectives and measures of the scorecard are derived from the organization's vision, mission and business objectives. There are four perspectives in a balanced scorecard:

1. *Financial perspective* focuses on the strategy for growth, profitability and risk from the perspective of the shareholder.
2. *Customer perspective* focuses on the strategy for creating value and differentiation from the customer's point of view.
3. *Internal/operational perspective* focuses on the strategic priorities of various business processes to ensure customer and shareholder satisfaction.
4. *Learning and growth perspective* focuses on the strategic priorities to create a climate that supports organizational change, innovation and growth.

Steps to Implement the Balanced Scorecard to Drive Performance

1. Build consensus around strategies.
2. Synthesize the strategic objectives.
3. Prepare a strategic map.
4. Select performance measures.
5. Select strategic initiatives.
6. Prepare an implementation plan.
7. Cascade the balanced scorecard.
8. Align the human resource to the balanced scorecard.
9. Set up a strategic feedback and review system.

Derivation of Operational Objectives Using Balanced Scorecard for DSCL

The operational objectives for DSCL are shown in Table 5.2.

Table 5.2 *Operational objectives*

Serial Number	Strategic Objectives	Performance Measures	Weightage (%)
Financial perspective			**40**
F.1	Return on investment	Profitability status	30

(*Continued...*)

Table 5.2 *(...Continued)*

Serial Number	Strategic Objectives	Performance Measures	Weightage (%)
F.2	Return on marketing investment	Proportion of marketing costs in the total cost of production	20
F.3	Cost of sales	Total cost incurred by the company	20
F.4	Sales per employee	Employee contribution towards net sales	20
F.5	Claims percentage	Pilferage incurred during transportation	10
Customer perspective			**20**
C.1	Number of new customers	Customers acquired during a time period	25
C.2	Customer loyalty	Brand awareness and loyalty of farmers towards DSCL products	30
C.3	Dissatisfaction management	Effectiveness in operations	25
C.4	Conversion rate	Visitors turning into prospective customers	20
Internal process/ operational perspective			**30**
O.1	Inventory turnover rate	Assessment of how fast inventories are replenished	30
O.2	Effectiveness of distribution channels	Defects in distribution channels	20
O.3	Stock position	Material consumed during the period	20
O.4	Transit time	Time taken for the material to reach the end users	10
O.5	Resource utilization	Optimum utilization of the allocated budget	20
Learning and growth perspective			**10**
G.1	Percentage increase in market share	Measures market penetration and market coverage	40
G.2	Percentage growth	Intra-company growth and inter-company growth	30
G.3	Success rate	Measures operational and business excellence	30

Design of Status Reports

Business objectives lead to the formulation of operational strategies. The operational strategies were derived using the balanced scorecard techniques under the four perspectives discussed in the preceding section. The various perspectives of the balanced scorecard are measured using metrics, which are shown in Table 5.3.

Table 5.3 *Metrics defined to measure operational objectives*

Serial Number	Strategic Objectives	Formulae
Financial perspective		
F.1	Return on investment	Net income/capital employed
F.2	Return on marketing investment	Increase in sales—marketing costs
F.3	Cost of sales	Factory cost + administrative overheads + selling and distribution overheads
F.4	Sales per employee	Net sales/total number of employees
F.5	Claims percentage	(Total loss and damage claims/total transportation costs) multiplied by 100
Customer perspective		
C.1	Number of new customers	Customers in the current period – customers during the last year
C.2	Customer loyalty	Tendency of a customer to choose a DSCL product/total products in the market
C.3	Dissatisfaction management	Number of complaints after execution of an order/previous number of complaints
C.4	Conversion rate	Visitors who take the desired actions (purchase)/total number of customers
Internal process/ operational perspective		
O.1	Inventory turnover rate	Cost of materials consumed during the period/average stock held during the period
O.2	Effectiveness of distribution channels	Defects in distribution channels (checkpoints)/total number of checkpoints
O.3	Stock position	Inventory in the beginning + purchases during the year – sales during the year
O.4	Transit time	Number of days (hours) from the time a shipment leaves the organization to the time it arrives at the desired location versus the transit time quoted by the carrier
O.5	Resource utilization	Budget spent/total budget allocated

(***Continued...***)

Table 5.3 (*...Continued*)

Serial Number	Strategic Objectives	Formulae
Learning and growth perspective		
G.1	Percentage increase in market share	Comparison of business rate in a specific market/the trend of the market
G.2	Percentage growth	*Intra*: (current year's share – previous year's share/previous year's share) × 100 *Inter*: share of DSCL/total market share of all the competitors taken together
G.3	Success rate	Number of successful projects/number of projects held by the company

ARCHITECTURAL DESIGN OF INFORMATION SYSTEMS

A critical analysis of the pyramidal structure of management information system (MIS) reveals the fact that decision making in an organization takes place at three levels, viz, the top management is involved in strategic planning, the middle management is involved in operational planning and the lower-level management is involved in transactional planning. The pyramidal structure of MIS gives us the clear picture about the effective delegation of jobs in an organizational hierarchy.

The information system of DSCL includes

1. *Information flow*
2. *Product flow*

Information Flow in DSCL

The information flow in case of DSCL is a two-way process. Since the focus is on agri-input marketing of DSCL, the line function of the company must be understood, which is as follows: The company sends information regarding various policies and schemes to the state marketing officer or SMO. The SMO prepares the strategic plan relating to different markets and sends it to the divisional marketing officer or DMO, and the DMO, keeping the aforementioned things in mind, prepares an operational plan and directs it to the MO or the sales marketing executive. The marketing officer (MO)/SMO executes the operational plan using field assistants and the sales force. Field assistants act as the face of the company to customers; they collect information from the customer, who are farmers in this case, about the demand for agri inputs and other requirements. They also give technical and functional inputs about the use of fertilizers, pesticides and other agri inputs to the farmers; further, the field assistants send the information about the demand of various products and agri inputs to the MO. Likewise, the information passes through various levels, viz, District Sales Office (DSO) and Zonal Sales Office (ZSO), and finally reaches the company's head office.

Product Flow in DSCL

DSCL as a company does not manufacture agri inputs; rather it only markets the products. The reason for doing so is as follows: If any foreign player needs to market its product, it has to establish a manufacturing unit in the desired country and thereafter look after the marketing the distribution of the products, which would involve a lot of cost. Therefore, it tries to market its products via entities like DSCL. DSCL imports fertilizers and other agri inputs from countries like Germany and Denmark and with the help of carry forward agents (by giving them some margin) sends them to distributors and retailers (purchase points) who direct them to farmers or the end consumers. The company also uses the 'direct dealer strategy' whereby a dealer directly sells the company products to the end users or the retailers. The advantage of using direct dealers is that the company is able to have a single point of contact between the end users and itself and at the same time establish a check on the corruption and pilferage that can take place in the supply chain. At the same time, the disadvantage of having a direct dealer is that market coverage becomes limited since the direct dealer is unable to cater to the entire market; the dealer is also not able to give functional as well as technical inputs about the use of the catered agricultural products to the farmers. Therefore, the company uses both direct dealers and carry forward agents to deliver its products to the end users.

PERIODICITY AND ROLE OF THE ACTIVITIES DESIGNED IN THE INFORMATION SYSTEM

The activities of the DSCL agri division can be studied under transactional, operational and strategic heads. This is done by the lower, middle and top managements, respectively.

1. The sales information, customer satisfaction index and word-of-mouth impact are studied by field assistants using the sales force on a daily basis.
2. After the compiled data is sent by the field assistant, sales marketing executives carry out data analysis and systematic evaluation to generate useful information within a period of 14 days.
3. After the sales marketing executive compiles the data, it is sent to the divisional marketing officer who finds out the actual sales, number of visits and their effectiveness, and the net profit generated from the operation. The data is then sent to the SMO in a period of one month.
4. The SMO, after receiving the data from the lower levels, compiles the data to generate business plans and their strategic implementation, which are then sent to the company within a period of one month.

Tools Used in Database Management

Similar and related data stored under a single head so that it can be accessed by many users for different purposes at a given time forms the database. DSCL uses the tools and techniques of database management systems and also of relational database management systems. It also uses data security tools like password authentication software. The company has networked all its locations on a wide area network (WAN) and has implemented a SAP R/3 enterprise resource package (ERP) across the company. Other key IT-enabling initiatives are customer relationship management (CRM) and business information warehousing (BIW).

SAMPLE STATUS REPORT

The sample status report shown in Table 5.4 gives details of the various parameters used in designing the metrics.

Table 5.4 *Sample status report*

Serial Number	Particulars
1	Sales
2	Net income
3	Marketing costs
4	Number of complaints after executing the project
5	Current year market share
6	Budget spent
7	Budget allocated
8	Number of projects held by the company
9	Number of days/hours for a shipment to reach its destination
10	Inventory replenishment time
11	Numbers of visitors who turned into prospective buyers
12	Total number of visitors
13	Capital employed
14	Total transportation cost
15	Total loss/damage during transportation
16	Market share of previous year
17	Number of successful projects
18	Opening stock and closing stock
19	Factory cost, selling and distribution costs
20	Total number of checkpoints

CONCLUSION

The field of MIS can deliver a great many benefits to enterprises in every industry. Expert organizations such as the Institute of MIS, Southborough, MA, along with peer-reviewed journals such as *MIS Quarterly* continue to find and report new ways of using the MIS to achieve business objectives. After analyzing the MIS of DSCL, the following can be concluded:

Core competencies: Every market-leading enterprise will have at least one core competency, that is, a function it performs better than its competition. By building an exceptional MIS into the enterprise, it is possible to be one jump ahead of competition. MISs provide the tools necessary to gain a better understanding of the market as well as of the enterprise itself.

Increase effectiveness of supply chain: Better monitoring and controlling improves and streamlines business processes. With the availability of correct and timely information on process performance, there comes the ability to improve the management of the supply chain, including everything from the sourcing of materials to the manufacture and distribution of the finished product.

Market dynamics: As the performance of business processes improve, the ability to react to changes in market conditions also improves. With timely and faster status reporting, the enterprise can react more quickly to its environment, enabling it to be one jump ahead of competition and provide better service and get a larger piece of the pie.

DISCUSSION QUESTIONS

1. How has safety been ensured in DSCL plants?
2. What are the different areas of business DSCL is engaged in?
3. What are the business objectives for DSCL?
4. Who are the shareholders in this organization? Are there conflicts among the stakeholders' objectives?
5. How will a Balanced Scorecard help design corporate strategy for DSCL? How do you monitor alignment of business objectives with strategy through MIS?

BIBLIOGRAPHY

1. http://www.dscl.com, 2008.
2. http://www.karmayog.org/csr1to500/csr1to500_19754.htm, 2008.
3. http://www.scribd.com/doc/25773039/Comparative-Analysis-on-Dscl, 2008.

6

Case Study on the Hub and Spoke Model of HDFC Bank for Agriculture and Microfinance Business

INTRODUCTION TO AGRIBUSINESS AND MICROFINANCE

Agricultural growth is crucial for alleviating rural poverty. Availability of institutional credit to more farmers and of appropriate quantity and quality of agricultural credit to farmers are crucial for realizing the full potential of agriculture as a profitable activity. Recognizing the crucial role of credit, the Tenth Five-Year Plan (2002–07) envisages a substantial jump in credit flows to agriculture to Rs 7,36,750 crore in the plan period as compared to the credit flow of Rs 2,29,956 crore achieved in the Ninth Five-Year Plan period. Credit flow to agriculture sector from all formal sources amounted to Rs 70,810 crore in 2002–03 and to Rs 86,981 crore in 2003–04, much below the levels envisaged in the tenth plan. Concerned over the slow growth of agricultural credit, Government of India announced a comprehensive policy on 1 June 2004. The policy envisaged 30 per cent increase in credit to the agriculture sector in 2004–05 over an estimated credit flow of Rs 80,000 crore in 2003–04. The implementation of the policy has been entrusted to private sector banks (PSBs), regional rural banks (RRBs) and cooperative banks. The policy indicated that each rural and semi-urban branch of commercial banks, on an average, would take up at least two to three new investment projects in the area of plantation and horticulture, fisheries, organic farming, agro-processing, livestock, micro-irrigation, sprinkler irrigation, watershed management, village pond development and other agricultural activities. National Bank for Agriculture and Rural Development (NABARD) has been asked to advise district-level technical committees to review the scales of finance to meet the realistic credit needs of farmers, especially for capital-intensive agricultural operations.

The Indian budget for 2004–05, presented in the parliament on 8 July 2004, proposed the doubling of credit to agriculture in three years and announced further measures to achieve the targeted growth in agricultural credit. These measures include holding the sponsor bank of each RRB squarely responsible for the performance of an RRB under its control and initiating an incentive scheme under which RRBs adopting new governance standards and abiding by prudential regulations qualify for receiving funds from the government for their restructuring. The budget proposed the setting up of a task force to examine the reforms required in cooperative banking system, including the appropriate regulatory regime to be established. The task force has submitted its draft report since 2005. The draft report was put on the Web sites of the Reserve Bank of India (RBI) and the Ministry of Finance in 11 January 2005 for inviting comments. The report is likely to be finalized shortly after taking into account the feedback received.

As indicated in its mid-term review of November 2003, RBI constituted the Advisory Committee on Flow of Credit to Agriculture and Related Activities from the Banking System (Chairman: V. S. Vyas). The advisory committee submitted its interim report in April 2004 and its final report in June 2004 (Box 3.2.3.51). Based on the recommendations contained in the interim report of the Vyas Committee, RBI in its annual policy statement for 2004–05 announced a number of measures to improve credit delivery to agriculture. These included treating loans to storage units designed to store agricultural products, irrespective of location, as indirect credit to agriculture; treating investment by banks in securitized assets representing direct (indirect) lending to agriculture; and waiver of margin/security requirement for agricultural loans up to Rs 50,000 and in the case of agribusiness and agri clinics for loans up to Rs 5 lakh. In addition, RBI also aligned repayment dates with dates of harvesting of crops by treating loans granted for short-duration crops as non-performing assets (NPAs) if instalment of principal or interest thereon remains unpaid for two crop seasons beyond the due date. Loans granted for long-duration crops are treated as NPAs only if the instalment of principal or interest thereon remains unpaid for one crop season beyond the due date. As recommended by the Vyas Committee, RBI announced that microfinance institutions (MFIs) would not be permitted to accept public deposits unless they comply with the extant regulatory framework. The recommendation relating to service area approach (SAA) was accepted and an announcement to this effect was made in the RBI's mid-term review of annual policy statement for 2004–05. During 2007–08, most of the PSBs, cooperative banks and RRBs have reduced the rate of interest on farm loans up to Rs 50,000 to 9.0 per cent and in some cases to 8.5 per cent. This has enabled farmers to derive the benefit of falling interest rates and to improve their margins on farming and allied operations. Also, as a measure to minimize the incidence of underfinancing, the scale of finance for crop loans and unit costs of farm investments have been further revised and made more realistic in the current year. Furthermore, to mitigate the risk from drought conditions, banks have either postponed the recovery of loans or converted short-term credit to medium-term credit with appropriate rescheduling in repayment in the drought-affected areas. The norms of financing in the *Rabi* season have been liberalized taking into account the likely shortfall in *Kharif* output on account of deficient rainfall.

The 'Farm Credit Package' announced in June 2004 stipulated the doubling of the flow of institutional credit for agriculture in the ensuing three years. The target of 30 per cent growth in agricultural credit in 2004–05 was surpassed by the actual growth of 44 per cent in overall credit by all agencies to Rs 1,25,309 crore in 2004–05. Based on this encouraging performance, the target for institutional credit for agriculture and allied activities for 2005–06 was raised to Rs 1,41,000 crore, which again was surpassed by the actual achievement of Rs 1,80,486 crore (provisional). The target for such credit for 2006–07 was fixed at Rs 1,75,000 crore, of which 85 per cent (Rs 1,49,343 crore) was achieved by 31 December 2006.

COMPANY PROFILE OF HDFC

The Company

The Housing Development Finance Corporation (HDFC) Limited was among the first in India to receive an 'in principle' approval from RBI to set up a bank in the private sector, as part of RBI's liberalization of the Indian banking industry in 1994. The bank was incorporated in August 1994 under the name HDFC Bank Limited, with its registered office in Mumbai, Maharashtra. HDFC Bank commenced its operations as a scheduled commercial bank in January 1995.

Currently, HDFC Bank has 758 branches, has 1,716 automatic teller machines (ATMs) and covers 325 cities in India, and all the branches of the bank are linked to one another on an online real-time basis. The bank offers many innovative products and services to individuals, corporations, trusts, governments, partnerships, financial institutions, mutual funds and insurance companies. It is a pathbreaker in the Indian banking sector. In 2007, HDFC Bank acquired Centurion Bank of Punjab, making its total number of branches more than 1,000. The official license was given to the branches of Centurion Bank of Punjab to continue working as HDFC Bank's branches on 23 May 2008. Over the decade of its operations, HDFC Bank has been recognized, rated and awarded by a number of organizations.

Ratings for HDFC Bank

The Bank has its deposit programmes rated by two rating agencies—Credit Analysis & Research Limited (CARE) and Fitch Ratings India Private Limited. The Bank's fixed deposit programme has been rated CARE AAA (FD) [Triple A] by CARE, which represents instruments considered to be 'of the best quality, carrying negligible investment risk'. CARE has also rated the Bank's certificate of deposit (CD) programme PR 1+, which represents 'superior capacity for repayment of short-term promissory obligations'. Fitch Ratings India Pvt. Ltd. (a 100% subsidiary of Fitch Inc.) has assigned its tAAA (ind) rating to the Bank's deposit programme, with the outlook on the rating as 'stable'. This rating indicates 'highest credit quality' where 'protection factors are very high'.

The Bank also has its long-term unsecured, subordinated (tier II) bonds rated by CARE and Fitch Ratings India and its tier-I perpetual bonds and upper tier-II bonds rated by CARE and CRISIL Ltd. CARE has assigned the rating of CARE AAA for the subordinated tier-II bonds, whereas Fitch Ratings India has assigned the rating AAA(ind) with the outlook on the rating as 'stable'. CARE has also assigned CARE AAA [Triple A] for the Bank's perpetual bond and upper tier-II bond issues. CRISIL has assigned the rating AAA/Stable for the Bank's perpetual debt programme and upper tier-II bond issue. In each of the aforementioned cases, the ratings awarded are the highest assigned by the rating agencies for those instruments.

Code of Corporate Governance

HDFC Bank believes in adopting and adhering to the best recognized corporate governance practices and in continuously benchmarking itself against each such practice. The Bank understands and respects its fiduciary role and responsibility to shareholders and strives hard to meet their expectations. The Bank believes that the best board practices, transparent disclosures and shareholder empowerment are necessary for creating shareholder value. The Bank has infused the philosophy of corporate governance into all its activities. The philosophy of corporate governance is an important tool for shareholder protection and maximization of their long-term values. The cardinal principles such as independence, accountability, responsibility, transparency, fair and timely disclosures and credibility serve as the means for implementing the philosophy of corporate governance, in both letter and spirit.

BUSINESS SEGMENTS OF HDFC

HDFC Bank offers a wide range of commercial and transactional banking services and treasury products to wholesale and retail customers. The bank has three key business segments: wholesale banking services, retail banking services and treasury.

Wholesale Banking Services

The Bank's target market ranges from large blue-chip manufacturing companies in the Indian corporate sector to small and midsized corporations and agriculture-based businesses. For its customers, the Bank provides a wide range of commercial and transactional banking services, including working capital finance, trade services, transactional services and cash management. HDFC Bank is also a leading provider of structured solutions, which combine cash management services with vendor and distributor finance for facilitating superior supply chain management for its corporate customers. Due to its superior product delivery/service levels and strong customer orientation, the Bank has made significant inroads into the banking consortia of a number of leading Indian corporations, including multinationals, companies from domestic business houses and prime public sector companies. It is recognized as a leading provider of cash management and transactional banking solutions to corporate customers, mutual funds, stock exchange members and banks.

Retail Banking Services

The objective of a retail bank is to provide its target market customers a full range of financial products and banking services, giving the customers a one-stop window for all their banking requirements. The products are backed by world-class service and they are delivered to customers through the growing branch network, as well as through alternative delivery channels like ATMs, phone banking, Internet banking and mobile banking.

The HDFC Bank's preferred programme for high net worth individuals, HDFC Bank Platinum Plus and the Bank's Investment Advisory Services programmes have been designed keeping in mind the needs of customers who seek distinct financial solutions, information and advice on various investment avenues. The Bank also has a wide array of retail loan products including automobile loans, loans against marketable securities, personal loans and loans for two-wheelers. It is also a leading provider of depository participant (DP) services for retail customers, providing customers the facility to hold their investments in the electronic form.

HDFC Bank was the first bank in India to launch an international debit card in association with Visa International of California (Visa electron), and the Bank issues the Mastercard Maestro debit card as well. The Bank launched its credit card business in late 2001. By March 2008, the bank had a total card base (debit and credit cards) of 9.1 million. The Bank is also one of the leading players in the 'merchant acquiring' business with over 61,000 point-of-sale (POS) terminals for debit/credit cards acceptance at merchant establishments. The Bank is well positioned as a leader in various Internet-based business-to-consumer (B2C) opportunities including a wide range of Internet banking services for fixed deposits, loans, bill payments, etc.

Treasury

Within this business, the bank has three main product areas: foreign exchange and derivatives, local currency money market and debt securities, and equities. With the liberalization of financial markets in India, corporations need more sophisticated risk management information, advice and product structures. These provisions and fine pricing on various treasury products are provided through the Bank's treasury team. To comply with statutory reserve requirements, the Bank is required to hold 25 per cent of its deposits in government securities. The treasury business is responsible for managing the returns and market risk on this investment portfolio.

MISSION AND STRATEGY OF HDFC

The mission of HDFC Bank is to be 'a world-class Indian bank', benchmarking themselves against international standards and best practices in terms of product offerings, technology, service levels, risk management, and audit and compliance. The objective is to build sound customer franchises across distinct businesses so that the Bank is a preferred provider of banking services for target retail and wholesale customer segments and to achieve a healthy growth in profitability, which is consistent with the Bank's risk appetite. HDFC Bank is committed to meet this objective while ensuring the highest levels of ethical standards, professional integrity, corporate governance and regulatory compliance. HDFC Bank's business philosophy is based on four core values: operational excellence, customer focus, product leadership and people.

The *business strategy* of HDFC emphasizes the following:

- Increase their market share in India's expanding banking and financial services industry by following a disciplined growth strategy focusing on balancing quality and volume growth while delivering high-quality customer service
- Leverage the technology platform and open scalable systems to deliver more products to more customers and to control operating costs
- Maintain high standards of asset quality through disciplined credit risk management
- Develop innovative products and services that attract the Bank's targeted customers and address the inefficiencies in the Indian financial sector
- Continue to develop products and services that reduce the cost of funds
- Focus on healthy growth of earnings with low volatility

ORGANIZATIONAL HIERARCHY OF HDFC

Jagdish Capoor took over as the Bank's chairman in July 2001. Prior to this, Capoor was a deputy governor of the RBI. The Managing Director of HDFC Bank Aditya Puri has been a professional banker for over 25 years, and before joining HDFC Bank in 1994 he was heading Citibank's operations in Malaysia (see Figure 6.1 for the organizational hierarchy of HDFC).

The Bank's board of directors comprises eminent individuals with a wealth of experience in public policy, administration, banking industry and commercial banking. Senior executives representing HDFC are also on the board of directors. Senior banking professionals with substantial experience in India and abroad head various businesses and functions and report to the managing director. From the professional expertise of the management team and the Bank's overall focus on recruiting and retaining the best talent in the industry, it is clear that the Bank believes its people a significant competitive strength.

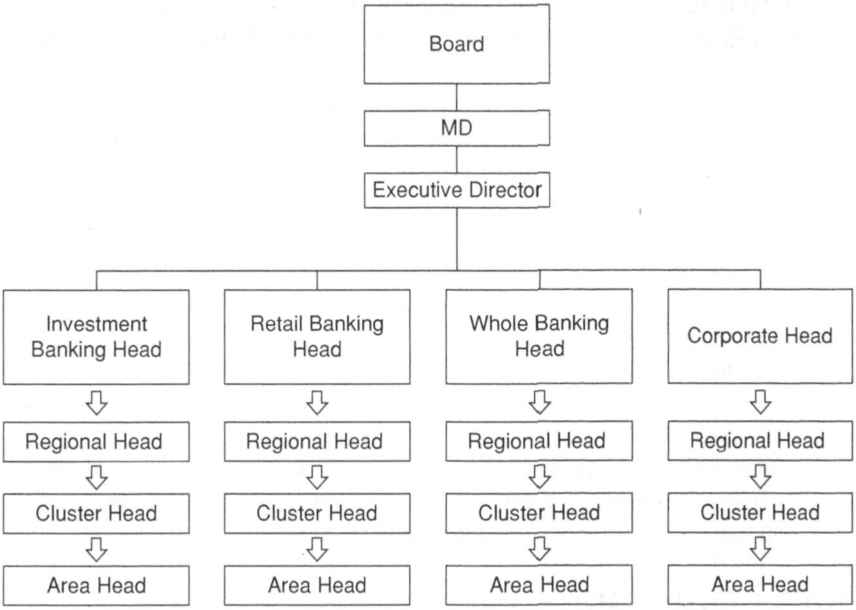

Figure 6.1 *Organizational Hierarchy of HDFC Bank*

AGRIBUSINESS AND MICROFINANCE BUSINESS

HDFC Bank, as a leading Indian private sector bank, is fully committed to ensuring that the benefits of world-class banking reach all sectors of the country, particularly to rural areas and to the agriculture sector. The Bank provides need-based agricultural loans of varying tenors to all creditworthy clients engaged in farming of staple as well as cash crops, horticulture, plantations, poultry business, animal husbandry, dairying, seeds, warehousing, etc. The Bank also finances the supplies of a wide range of agri inputs like seeds, fertilizers, pesticides, micronutrients and micro-irrigation tools. The Bank identifies transportation and storage and processing of food and other agricultural commodities as thrust areas and is offering working capital and term loans of varying tenors to eligible processors, based on not only their financials but also the strengths of underlying commodities. In this manner, the Bank facilitates the food chain from the 'farm gate to the food plate'. The Bank is expanding its rural presence rapidly in order to deliver these products effectively at the doorsteps of their valued customers at affordable prices.

The Bank has relationships with 110 microfinance institutions and has extended credit facilities, whereby 1.61 million households have become the beneficiaries of financial inclusion. In addition, the Bank under the direct self-help group (SHG) linkage programme has credit-linked and financed over 32,000 SHGs with roughly half a million households benefiting from this initiative. HDFC Bank has been continuously making efforts as well as exploring various opportunities for ensuring greater financial inclusion and increasing its outreach to the rural and underbanked areas of the country. The Bank has taken several initiatives, which include the following:

- Financing SHGs through the services of non-governmental organizations (NGOs) as intermediaries to provide financial and banking services to the weaker and underprivileged sections of the population

- Working with MFIs across India to provide credit support to deserving beneficiaries
- Reaching out to rural areas and distributing retail asset products through cooperative banks and societies
- Entering into tie-ups with post offices in Punjab, Karnataka and Andhra Pradesh using the 'business facilitator' (BF) model with a view to increasing the distribution outreach to rural and semi-urban customers mainly for retail loan products
- Providing small ticket warehouse receipt–based finance against warehouse receipts issued by central warehousing corporations and the State Warehousing Corporation, which has helped farmers to achieve better prices for their produce, reduce wastages and avoid distress sales
- Opening branches at *Mandi* (market) locations like Ganganagar in Rajasthan and Unjha in Gujarat so as to ensure availability of credit to farmers
- Providing finance to self-employed individuals, small entrepreneurs, shopkeepers, small-scale service establishments, factory workers and workers in small-scale/medium-scale manufacturing and processing units, particularly in rural and semi-urban areas
- Besides the aforementioned initiatives, the bank also provides loans against gold jewellery at various locations across the country primarily to meet the short-term loan requirements of the common masses that had hitherto been serviced by local moneylenders

KISAN GOLD CARD (KGC)

As mentioned in the Introduction section, among the various product offerings of HDFC Bank for the farmer KGC is a key IT-enabled offering bringing convenience, flexibility and ease in accessing funds. The farmer can use the card to withdraw cash from the ATMs of all banks anywhere in the country.

Multiple Functions of KGC

There are three different functions of KGC:

- The term loan
- The farm equipments/tractor loan
- Traders' cash credit

HDFC Bank designed the KGC envisaging a convenient and hassle-free granting of loans to farmers for meeting their production and investment requirements. Other banks do give these loans, but with its technology edge HDFC conceived a real plastic for the farmers for giving them the convenience to bank anywhere and anytime without being restricted to a 10 a.m. to 2 p.m. banking culture. The card, launched in association with Visa Inc., can also be used at all POS terminals globally. The facilities provided by KGC are

- Drawing of cash from ATMs (domestic consumption)
- Agricultural needs:

  Crop production: Purchase of agricultural equipments/implements
  Irrigation: Construction of farm-related buildings
  Post harvest: Investments in agriculture-related activities
  Dairy and piggery
  Bee keeping
  Pisciculture

- Personal accident insurance cover, worth Rs 2 lakh
- Debit/credit card

Features of KGC

Eligibility criteria: A farmer who owns land is eligible for KGC.

Documentation: Documentation is based on crop production requirements.

Withdrawal limit: Daily withdrawal limit using the card is Rs 15,000 from ATMs and Rs 25,000 for use in merchant outlets.

Credit limit: Credit limit is based on the requirement of farmers.

Association: KGC has an association with Visa Inc.

Validity and renewability: The card is sanctioned for three years and can be renewed.

IT AND MANAGEMENT INFORMATION SYSTEM (MIS) IN HDFC BANK

IT Intervention

This section highlights HDFC Bank's innovative IT-enabled strategic initiatives developed with a view to bring to rural India the same hassle-free banking services that hitherto were being provided only to the urban customer in metropolitan cities and big cities. The Bank's Hub and Spoke model, which was adopted to bring world-class banking services to underbanked and unbanked rural India, is a case in point.

Under the Hub & Spoke model (see Figure 6.2), a 'hub' is a location having HDFC Bank branch presence and a 'spoke' is the target rural location typically located at a distance 30–40 km from the hub branch. Customers at the spoke locations maintain their savings accounts with the hub branch, but they are able to transact in these bank accounts through the business correspondents (BCs) located at these spokes. The Bank has tied up with several such BCs, mostly credit societies and cooperative banks, who act on its behalf in accepting deposits as well as facilitating withdrawals of small value cash at their counters. The crucial technology enabler in this arrangement is the POS/electronic data capture (EDC) machine installed at these BC counters, which make the transactions possible in an easy and hassle-free manner.

Today, through the aforementioned innovative yet simple technology-enabled arrangement, debit-card holders of Unnati savings account—HDFC Bank's recently launched savings bank account that caters specifically to the rural population—can access their bank accounts through BCs. The transactions are effected easily by swiping the cards at the POS/EDC terminals established at the BC counters. At the time of swiping their cards, customers are required to feed in their pin number, known only to them, which adds a measure of safety to the transaction. Needless to say, customers can also access their accounts directly from HDFC Bank branches or through the ATMs situated at hub locations. This arrangement has given the Bank's rural customers cash transaction capability at locations far away from the bank branches or ATMs.

Unnati savings account is thus a unique new-age product whose other salient features include mobile banking, phone banking and Internet banking, which enable the customers to remotely query their accounts. Customers can also very conveniently carry out e-booking of railway tickets and e-recharging of mobile phones.

HDFC Bank is now looking at rural markets as the next business opportunity and is offering a complete bouquet of modern, high-tech products to the farming community to cater to its current as well

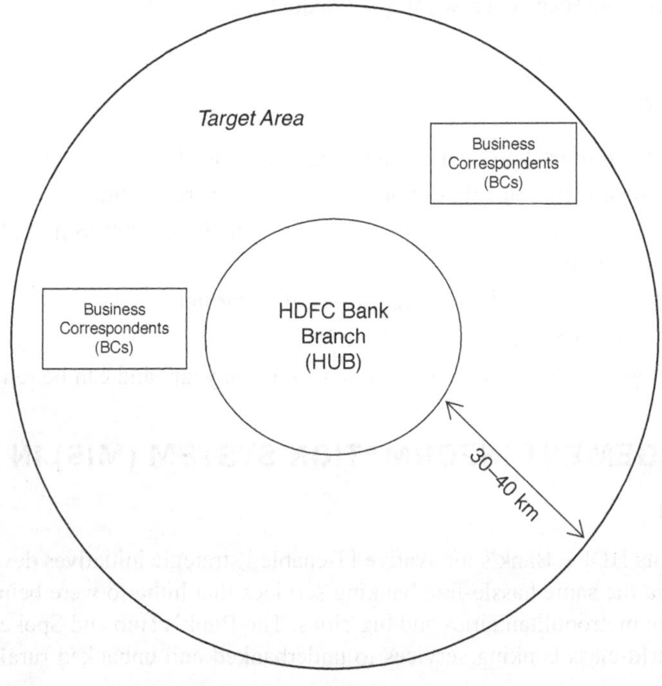

Figure 6.2 *Channels for Lending*

as future banking/financial needs. Among the various product offerings for the farmer, KGC is a key IT-enabled offering bringing convenience, flexibility and ease in accessing funds. The farmer can use the card to withdraw cash from ATMs of all banks anywhere in the country.

'No Frills' savings account is yet another product meant for the not-so-affluent rural customer. It has features like zero-balance requirement, issue of free ATM card and the allowance of an adequate number of free transactions every month. Finally, the Bank's microfinance unit is currently working out a solution to facilitate account operations of SHGs with the Bank at non-branch locations by possibly providing hand-held devices to BCs. This arrangement, once implemented, is expected to benefit SHGs comprising mostly poor women from rural areas who are generally located in underbanked locations and to bring them under financial inclusion.

Role-based Security

The bank provides following security to sensitive financial data for its customers: login security, IPIN (Internet banking password) security, session security, digital certificates, virtual keyboard, InstaAlert service, different security solutions and security teams.

Login Security

Access to a customer's Internet Banking account is granted using a customer ID and an IPIN that are known only to the customer. Without providing a valid IPIN corresponding to a customer ID, access to a customer account cannot be gained by anyone. The customer's NetBanking service is revoked if it is not used by the customer for more than 180 days for security.

IPIN Security

IPIN is randomly generated by the banking system and is directly printed on tamper-proof media such that it is not accessible by anyone other than the customer.

Customers are forced to change their IPINs upon first login such that they are assured the IPINs have not been compromised before delivery. IPINs are stored by the Bank by using encryption technology such that they are not accessible to anyone including the system administrator.

Session Security

Access to their own accounts are provided through a secure Web page that encrypts the session between the customer's computer and the Web page using 128-bit encryption so that the communication between customers' computers and the Web page cannot be intercepted by anyone over the Internet. For protection against misuse, HDFC Bank systems time out their customer login sessions to NetBanking accounts upon prolonged inactivity.

Digital Certificates

The Web page of HDFC Bank's Internet banking server is identified by means of a digital certificate provided by Verisign, Bangalore, to assure its customers that they are on the correct site and to protect them from revealing their confidential account information on some fake Web site.

Virtual Keyboard

Customers can use the feature of virtual keyboard while logging into their NetBanking accounts. This protects the users' IPINs from being compromised by keylogger software installed on untrusted/shared computers, for example, those used in cybercafés.

InstaAlert Service

The Bank has an InstaAlert service to send SMS/e-mail alerts to its customers upon registration for defined transaction denominations and upon addition of beneficiaries for carrying out third-party transactions.

Security Solutions

All banking systems are secured using state-of-the-art security solutions that are acknowledged world-wide, viz, firewalls, intrusion detection systems, intrusion prevention systems and anti-malware systems, to extend secure banking services to their customers.

Security Teams

The Bank has robust processes, skilled people and competent service providers who monitor round-the-clock the security of its systems.

BUSINESS SOLUTIONS

As one of India's largest financial institutions, HDFC Bank relies on data protection and storage management solutions Symantec, Mumbai, to help ensure its data and business-critical applications

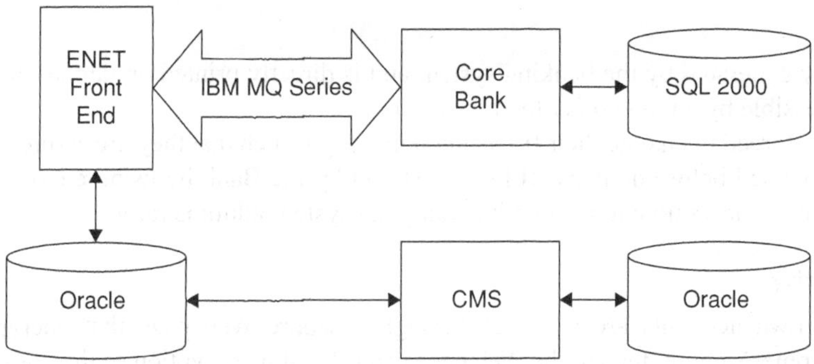

Figure 6.3 *Flow of Transactions*

are available round the clock. With data growing at a clip of 50 per cent annually, the flexibility and automation features included in VERITAS Storage Foundation software from Symantec help HDFC Bank to keep up with the demand while controlling costs and improving staff productivity by 10 per cent. With VERITAS NetBackup software, HDFC is able to speed up its backup process, which translates to a 50 per cent improvement in data centre staff productivity, and minimize the time for which data is unavailable. When the various operational efficiency gains are tallied, it is found that HDFC Bank has realized a 98 per cent return on investment since the software solution was implemented in 2003 (see Figure 6.3).

INTEGRATED INFORMATION SYSTEM

The information flow in HDFC Bank is shown in Figure 6.4. The agribusiness and rural business division of HDFC bank has two major parts:

- Business team with a national head and the credit decision
- Marketing team with a national head

The business team further has two important models:

- KGC
- MFI

KGC itself has three functions of lending loans:

- Term loan
- Farmers' equipment/tractor loan
- Traders' cash credit

There is the sales team and the product team to take care of the KGC model, and there are regional heads, state heads and cluster heads for the areas. The relationship manager is contacted by the cluster head and then we have the executives or the contract employees for every area. In the MFI model, there is wholesale lending and retail lending: The Bank does direct lending for MFIs as such and through BCs in the name of retail lending. The process is then carried over to the credit decision and the marketing team who take care of the portfolio quality, timely repayment and financial viability of the loan applicants.

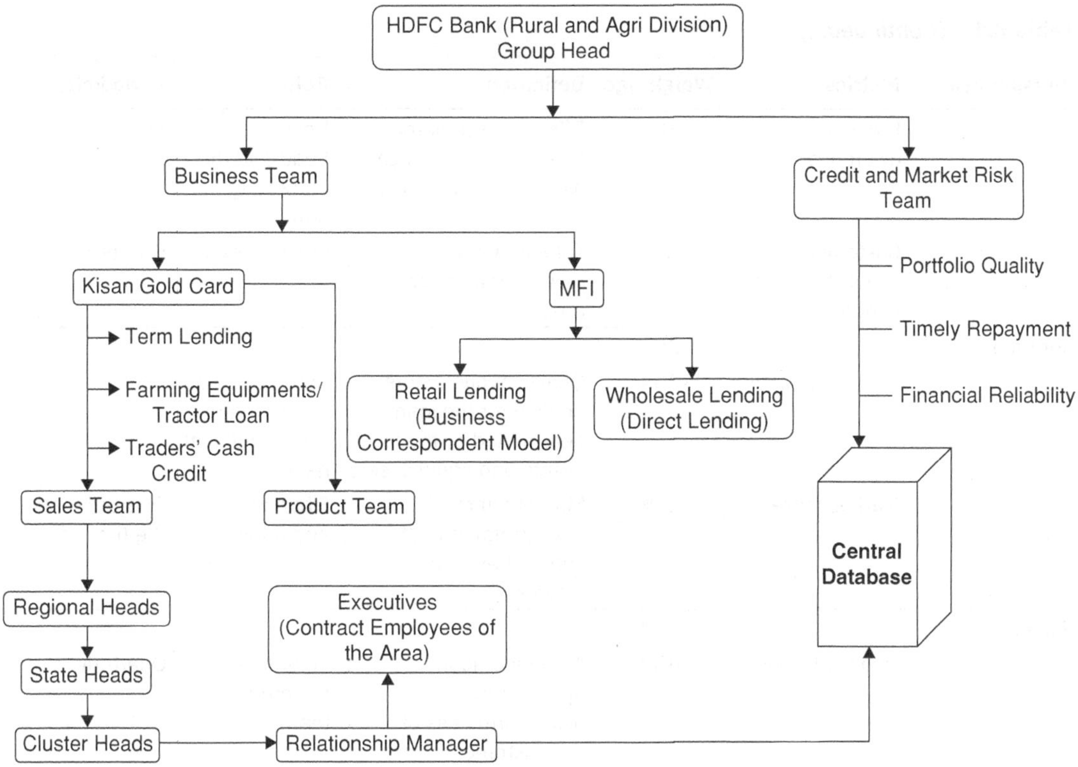

Figure 6.4 *Information Systems in HDFC Bank*

TEMPLATE OF BALANCE SCORECARD

Table 6.1 shows how a balanced scorecard has been used to arrive at a strategy for different perspectives. (Please refer to ANNEXURE for the balanced scorecard for HDFC agribusiness and MFI.)

Table 6.1 *Strategy for different perspectives*

Perspective	Metrics	Weightage	Definition	Role	Periodicity
Customer		40%			
	Willingness to apply for the card	15%	As per the questionnaire	Executives or the contract employees	Monthly
	Frequency of usage of the card	20%	Number of times the card has been swiped	Relationship managers	Monthly
	Conversion rate	10%	Number of people who applied/number of people approached by the sales team	Relationship manager with the executives	Half yearly

(Continued...)

Table 6.1 (*Continued...*)

Perspective	Metrics	Weightage	Definition	Role	Periodicity
	Product awareness	30%	Effectiveness of the awareness campaign, as found by executives	Regional head and the marketing team	Monthly
	Customer acquisition per period	25%	Total number of new customers per quarter	Cluster head	Quarterly
Internal		**20%**			
	Portfolio quality	70%	Quality of customers applied for the loan = determined by the fixed assets and liquid assets	Credit decision and marketing team—regional head	Monthly
	Market share	30%	Market share of HDFC/total market share of existing players	Finance and audit team—auditor	Quarterly—at the time of financial report
Financial		**30%**			
	Financial viability	40%	Amount of loan applied for/ assetworthiness of the customer	Finance and the credit teams	Quarterly
	Loan period	40%	Number of months for which the loan is applied/12	Credit team—the entire team	Yearly
	Increase in sales	20%	(Sales in current year - sales in previous year)/ sales in previous year	Sales team—regional head	Quarterly—at the time of financial report
Learning/ growth		**10%**			
	Employee motivation and satisfaction	100%	Bonuses offered - attrition rate	Human resource team—talent management	Quarterly

RECENT DEVELOPMENTS AND THE FUTURE

Merger with Centurion Bank of Punjab: In 2007, HDFC Bank acquired Centurion Bank of Punjab, making its total number of branches more than 1,000. However, the official license was given to Centurion Bank of Punjab branches to continue working as HDFC Bank branches on 23 May 2008. With this merger, HDFC Bank overtook ICICI Bank in terms of branch network (there are 955 branches for ICICI in India).

HDFC to open over 100 rural branches in the next fiscal, 26 August 2008:

To penetrate the rural market, India's third largest bank HDFC has chalked out new measures to expand its network to the rural areas of the country with the aim of enabling farmers and SHGs to access banking and finance products. New branches in rural areas would be equivalent to the core banking facilities that HDFC provides to customers in metropolitan cities. During the next fiscal, HDFC Bank is planning to open more than 200 branches across the country. Of these, it will open more than 100 branches in rural areas.

CONCLUSION

If technology permits, then KGC can be further used by the government for the efficient functioning of its development schemes like NREGS (National Rural Employment Guarantee Scheme), JRY (Jawahar Rozgar Yojana), SGSY (Swarnjayanti Gram Swarozgar Yojana), IAY (Indira Awas Yojana), etc. It is also possible that KGC can be used as an identity card for the farmer/rural inhabitant and as a digital information carrier for the government officials. With the use of KGC, government will be able to recognize the eligible and deserving people who should be allowed to avail themselves of the development schemes. In this manner, the number of defaulters will reduce and might come down to zero. This single card will make it hassle free for farmers to avail themselves of the schemes and their benefits, because with the card's help farmers will not have to go through a complicated documentation process that takes a whole lot of time to complete. With such a use of KGC, targeted, efficient and hassle-free efforts towards development can thus be accomplished.

DISCUSSION QUESTIONS

1. Describe the business processes in HDFC?
2. How would an MIS help HDFC in aligning its corporate objectives with operational transactions?
3. How does an MIS help to improve business potential for the agriculture and microfinance division of HDFC?

BIBLIOGRAPHY

1. http://www.hdfcbank.com, 2008.
2. http://www.banknetindia.com, 2008.
3. http://www.nabard.org, 2008.
4. http://drishteefoundation.org/new/pdf/DF-ANNUAL%20REPORT2005-06.pdf, 2008.

7

Case Study on ICICI Lombard

INSURANCE: AN INDUSTRY OVERVIEW

Insurance is used to 'insure' against any loss. In a way, this is a risk mitigation plan against any contingency loss. While insuring, the risk is equitably transferred from one entity to another. This transfer is not free and the entity to which the risk is transferred charges a premium to the entity that transfers the risk. The entity that charges a premium for transferring the risk to itself is called the insurer. The period and degree of risk coverage depends on the charged premium.

Historically, the insurance concept gained momentum in 1666, when the Great Fire of London devoured 13,200 houses. It was a calamity; as an aftermath of the disaster, Nicolas Barbon catered to the insurance concept and opened an office in London. Later in 1680, he started the first ever insurance company, where he started insuring buildings against fire. The insurance coverage at the time was to transfer risk related to brick and framework of a building to the insurance company in the event of fire. With the passage of time, the coverage of insurance has grown many folds and now covers many risks apart from fire. Today, in India insurance sector along with banking industry adds up to 7 per cent of the country's gross domestic product (GDP). In spite of all this, penetration of the insurance sector in the country is very poor. Nearly 80 per cent of the Indian population do not have life and health insurance cover. This is an indicator that the growth potential for insurance sector is immense in India.

Principles of insurance: Commercially, insurable risks typically share seven common characteristics:

1. A large number of homogeneous exposure units
2. Definite loss
3. Calculable loss
4. Accidental loss
5. Large loss

6. Affordable premium
7. Limited risk of catastrophically large losses

Types of insurance: The following are the various types of insurance:

1. Disability
2. Casualty
3. Life
4. Property
5. Liability
6. Credit
7. Vehicle insurance
8. Health
9. Other types

Insurance companies: Insurance companies may be classified into two groups:

- *Life* insurance companies, which sell life insurance, annuities and pensions products.
- *Non-life*, *general* or *property/casualty* insurance companies, which sell other types of insurance: They provide payments depending on the loss from a particular financial event. General insurance typically comprises any insurance that is not determined to be life insurance. The company of our focus for discussing management information system (MIS) is a general insurance company called ICICI Lombard.

ICICI LOMBARD: COMPANY OVERVIEW

- *Vision*: To be the market leader in the field of private general insurance
- *Mission*: To bring innovative insurance solutions to customers' doorstep

Following the passing of Insurance Regulatory and Development Authority Act in 1999 and the issuance of licenses to private players in the sector in 2000, the insurance industry scenario was all set to change dramatically. The market looked promising with a net premium income of Rs 9,300 crore, and it was growing at 11.4 per cent. The penetration of the insurance sector was as low as 0.54 per cent and thus offered significant opportunity and space for multiple players. In 2001, the ICICI Group entered the private general insurance sector by forming a partnership with Fairfax Holdings of Canada to establish ICICI Lombard.

The insurance industry during the period had just been liberalized and a number of private players were starting to invest in the domain. Till that time, the market had only four public players who, over the years, had built up a strong customer base at the national level. They had strong relationships with the people and every salary-earning person in the country had an insurance policy from one or the other of these players. Hence, the private players had to innovate and come up with innovative products to attract customers. The government, thankfully, had provided a level playing field for all players, which allowed companies like ICICI Lombard to be more customer friendly. This helped in creating new markets and categories with distinctive features and other areas of opportunity for growth. However, the Indian market owing to its vastness and diversity posed unique and varied risks to private players compared to the markets of developed countries. There was a need to understand the dynamics of Indian consumers as the dynamics in the sub-continent are quite different than at other places, viz. the USA. To address these challenges, ICICI Lombard adopted a segment-by-segment plan. It prioritized its strategy on target customers as it had to first create awareness among potential customers about itself and build credibility among them. As part of its strategy, ICICI Lombard initially focused on the corporate segment and built up a balanced and profitable portfolio across industries. It also collaborated with Lombard to take advantage of technology to provide standardized levels of service to customers at a fast pace.

Dedicated relationship managers who were the single point of contact for both business development and claims servicing assured a single-window access to the company. Reinsurance arrangements with reputed international reinsurers provided the contingency capital that was required to assume large risks. An employee mix of experienced insurance professionals and individuals from a diverse range of industries from financial services to consumer goods led to an aggressive and innovative approach to market development. This was combined with the practical knowledge of category risks. A geographic information system (GIS)-enabled risk accumulation tool allowed the company to monitor geographical risk on a real-time basis. Having achieved market leadership in the corporate segment among the private players in the field, ICICI Lombard established the 'Bancassurance' model (Bank Insurance model) as a significant and viable generator of revenues, working closely with its partners and offering innovative retail risk products such as Loan Care (to cover loan defaults) and Weather Index Insurance (to cover weather risks). Within two-and-a-half years of entering the market, the company was strongly positioned as the largest private general insurance company with a total gross written premium of Rs 506.7 crore. During the fiscal year 2003–04, the company expanded its presence to 63 locations from 35 offices in the previous year.

ICICI Lombard General Insurance achieved a market share of 29.8 per cent among private sector general insurance companies and an overall market share of 11.9 per cent during the fiscal year 2008. The gross return premium grew by 11.4 per cent from Rs 30.3 billion in the fiscal year 2007 to Rs 33.45 billion in the fiscal year 2008. The company is growing at a steady pace and has carved a niche for itself in the general insurance segment.

Human Resources (HR) Strategy

One of the major stakeholders for a successful organization is its employees, and ICICI Lombard adopts a progressive and dynamic HR policy throughout the organization. Through several workshops, employees are trained in ethics, values and the reason for which the company exists. This creates a consistency in thought process and similarity in attitude while dealing with customers. The business goals are well divided among different business sections and a proper performance appraisal process has been put in place. The performance appraisal process believes in adopting company values at all levels, which is driven by result orientation, adaptability to change, and humility and respect for both subordinates and peers. The company believes that investment in human capital is critical for achieving and sustaining growth.

The work culture is performance driven and there is result orientation with emphasis on employee satisfaction and retention. Ever since the insurance industry has opened up, large-scale poaching of employees is in vogue; hence, ICICI Lombard invests in its employees to reduce attrition rate. Job rotation is also considered to improve job satisfaction; as a result, one has the opportunity to work in different areas like underwriting, sales, product management, operations and customer service. Different training programmes such as product training, functional training and soft skill improvement are conducted to increase the required skill levels.

As part of its growth strategy, the company is strengthening its multiple levels of distribution channels; it has employed employees for aggressive marketing of its new products. It also has plans to achieve reach and penetration by targeting varied segments including large, small and medium enterprises; government enterprises; retail businesses; Bancassurance; and Internet sales. Technology has been used strategically at all levels for cost-effective product distribution, for increased operational efficiencies, as a risk mitigation tool, to reduce customer response times, for faster claims servicing and to ensure that quality processes are standardized throughout the company.

Characteristic Features of ICICI Lombard

The following are the characteristic features of ICICI Lombard:

- Simple and fast documentation
- Lightning-fast claims settlement
- Instant online policy issuance
- Comprehensive product line
- High security offered through 128-bit encryption in the case of online data exchange

Achievements of ICICI Lombard

The following are the achievements of the company:

- First general insurance company in India to become ISO 9001:2000 certified
- Assigned the iAAA rating by Investment Information and Credit Rating Agency (ICRA), indicating the highest claims-paying ability
- Achieved financial breakeven in the first full year of operations
- Achieved underwriting breakeven in the second year of operations
- First company to provide digitally signed documents through an online interface
- Achieved underwriting breakeven in the second year of operations
- Adjudged the 'General Insurance Company of the Year' at the 11th Asia Insurance Industry Awards 2007
- Adjudged the most Customer Responsive Company in the insurance category at the *Economic Times* Avaya GlobalConnect Customer Responsiveness Awards 2006
- Awarded the Best Housing Insurance award in Smart Living Awards by 360 Degrees, a Times of India Group subsidiary, in 2006
- Awarded the Gold Shield for 'Excellence in Financial Reporting' by the Institute of Chartered Accountants of India (ICAI) for the year 2006
- Adjudged among the top three companies in the 'Insurance Website of the Year' category at the 9th Asia Insurance Industry Awards function in 2005

OBJECTIVES OF STAKEHOLDERS

- Employees:

  Increasing market share

  Increasing premium revenue

Retaining and increasing customer base
Creating brand value

- Shareholders: maximizing shareholder value
- Sales, agents and brokers: publicizing the company's services
- Customers:

Added value in return for premium
Greater customer satisfaction

SERVICES OFFERED BY ICICI LOMBARD

ICICI Lombard offers a wide range of services covering various areas of insurance and different segments of customers. Its services can be classified under four broad categories:

1. Personal products: These are of the following types:
    1. Health insurance: The company offers protection in cases of unexpected medical emergencies. In the case of a sudden illness or an accident, the health insurance policy takes care of the hospitalization, medical and other costs incurred.
    2. Home insurance
    3. Motor insurance: This is a comprehensive policy that covers not only third-party liability but also damage to the vehicle and accidental injury.
    4. Overseas travel insurance
    5. Domestic travel insurance
    6. Student medical insurance
2. Business products: These services are aimed at businesses of all kinds and sizes. The insurance products are as follows:
    1. Fire insurance
    2. Marine insurance
    3. Industrial insurance
    4. Corporate insurance
    5. Liability insurance
    6. Credit insurance
3. Non-resident Indian (NRI) services: These services are the same as those offered in personal products, but the focus here is on NRIs. A service specially offered in this category is parents' overseas travel.
4. Rural insurance: At ICICI Lombard, investing in rural markets is seen as a major social responsibility. The protection provided to the rural class is specified and customized according to the class's needs. Through a multiple channel system, it not only provides agricultural protection but also health, motor and other covers. The services unique to this category are tractor and weather insurance.

CHANNELS USED TO TAP CUSTOMERS

The company follows a multiple channel approach to tap customers. The main objectives of such channels are

To create value beyond the 'product'

To convert potential customer to clients

To spread awareness about the company and its products

Depending on the effectiveness, the following channels are used for sales, service and other allied activities:

Physical: Sales force, agents and brokers are the driving force behind the company's business. They are the points of contact with the end customer, and they share the company's vision of bringing innovative insurance solutions to customers' doorsteps.

Direct: The company's sales force—sales executives and sales officers—form the company's backbone and are the most powerful assets behind its growth.

Indirect

Brokers: Insurance broking plays a vital role in the distribution of insurance solutions. Through this channel, the company plans to reach out to a wider customer base to increase its market share. Customers look forward to insurance brokers for expert advice on customized insurance solutions.

Agents: Agents are the face of the company and are critical to its growth. The company has individuals and corporate enterprises as its agents.

Online: ICICI Lombard has developed a Web-based system to meet all the pre- and post-policy transactions and the MIS needs of its customers. The online initiative supports online policy sales, which is directly linked to the payment gateway server for online payments. The company uses the Web integration process with its channel partners to streamline its sales process; increase revenues; and reduce costs, delays and buyer dissatisfaction.

The main features of online insurance are

- Do-it-yourself architecture
- Fast, convenient and easy to use
- Ability to buy/renew policies
- 24/7 access to all of an individual's policy details
- Provision of regular premium-renewal reminders
- Single view of all insurance policies held by an individual
- Availability of 'online manager', a tool to manage an individual's entire insurance portfolio
- Instant issuance of digitally signed policies
- Use of the most advanced technology and state-of-the art infrastructure
- Online claim intimation and status tracking

Bancassurance Channel

This is a channel used by insurance companies by integrating different insurance and banking operations. It is a strategy adopted by banks or insurance companies aiming to operate in the financial services market in a more or less integrated manner. The strategy has been used in international markets by many insurance companies to distribute insurance products, and the same is used by ICICI Lombard in India. The company uses this strategy at more than 50 locations in India, where dedicated teams of product managers, sales managers and sales executives successfully link different financial services and the distribution of those financial products. As a result, ICICI Bank offers insurance products to its own customers using the same customer database. ICICI Bank is the number one private retail bank in India and has a huge customer base. Because of the Bankassurance strategy, ICICI Lombard had a huge customer base at the inception stage.

Telesales Channel

A strategy used by ICICI Lombard has been the Telesales channel. This channel has been used effectively by ICICI Lombard to sell, cross-sell and up-sell various products and services to customers. Telesales has been used to shorten the sales cycle and increase revenues and profitability. Using the existing customer database from ICICI Bank, the channel taps customers through telephone calls that are followed up by direct sales. The channel also uses institutional and relationship sales, transactional sales, segment-/account-specific targeted sales, event-based activities, ongoing communication to build trust and generate repeat purchase, and teleservicing.

ORGANIZATIONAL STRUCTURE

The organizational structure of ICICI Lombard is as follows: It is headed by Sandeep Bakshi, who is the managing director cum chief executive officer of the company. Visakha Mule is the executive director of the company. She is followed by Rakesh Jain as the retail head. The whole organizational function can be divided into four different heads:

1. Sales
2. Claims
3. Underwriting
4. Marketing

The four functional areas are headed by four different business heads. Under each business head, there is a geo head or zonal head. A zone may consist of a single state or a number of states. Each state is headed by a state head. Previously, the post of geo head was not present. A branch manager heads each branch office. He or she is followed by many sales managers. A number of unit sales officers are headed by a sales manager. Sales officers are the points of contact for customers.

Figure 7.1 gives a graphic description of the organizational structure of ICICI Lombard. The sales section is taken as an example to give the structure of the subordinate levels. The other three sections have a similar structure with some minor changes depending on the nature of their activity.

CORPORATE STRATEGY OF ICICI LOMBARD

Fixing the Premium Amount

The premium amount for a particular product is fixed by the underwriter team. For example, vehicle premium has three parts:

1. Owned damage
2. Third-party damage
3. Sales tax

Out of the aforementioned three parts, sales tax is fixed by the sales tax department. The third-party damage amount is fixed by the Insurance Regulatory Authority of India (IRDA). Before January 2007, the owned damage amount was also fixed by IRDA. But after January 2007, the respective insurance company has been handed over this prerogative. The underwriter team on behalf of the company fixes the amount for owned damage. Owned damage is fixed by the underwriter team after taking into consideration the risk involved in that particular product. To know the situational factors involved,

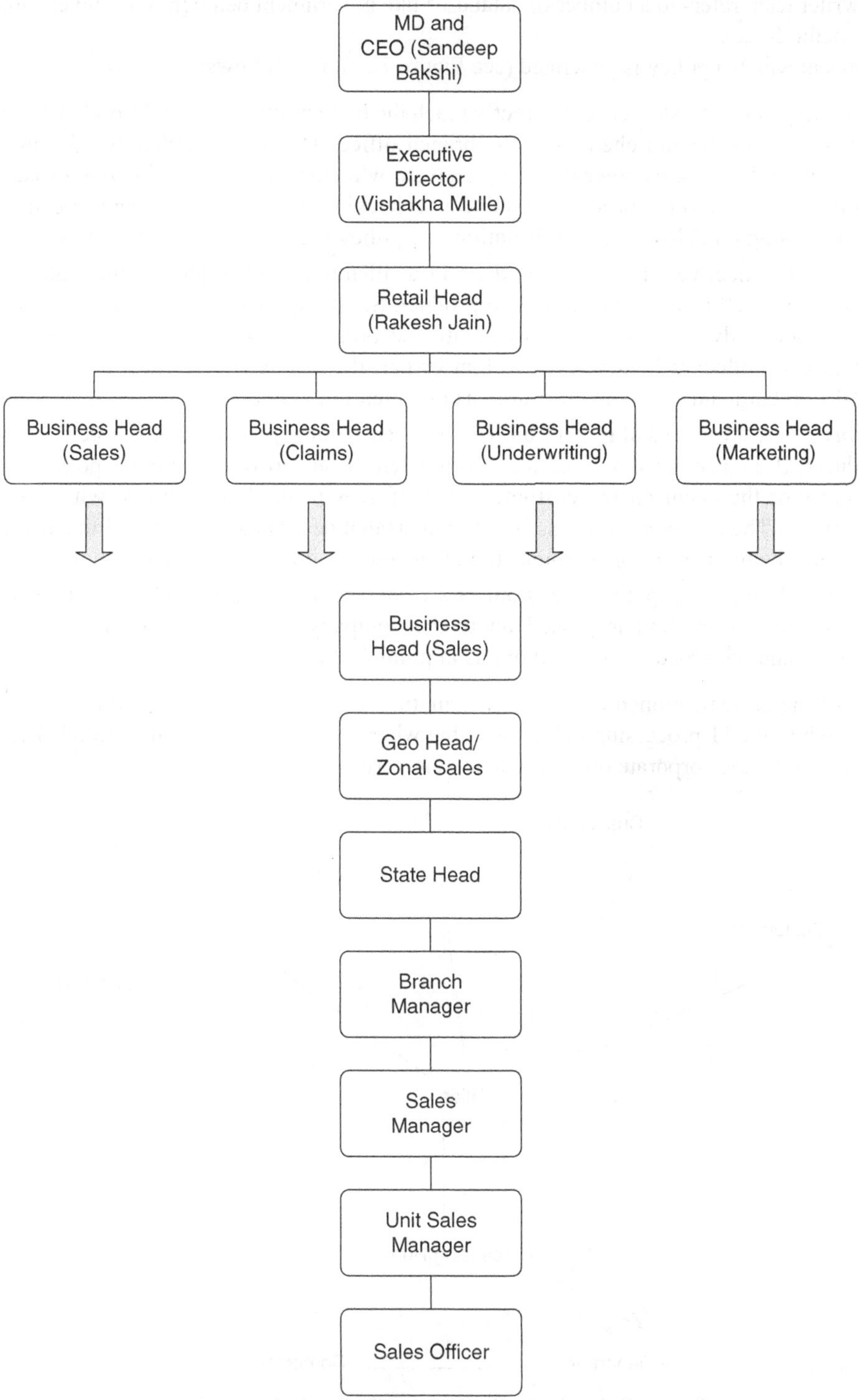

Figure 7.1 *Organizational Structure of ICICI Lombard*

the underwriter team refers to a number of databases like government demographic and economic data, statistical methods, etc.

The ways in which a policy is generated (see Figure 7.2) are as follows:

1. *Direct approach*: Customers can directly reach the branch office of ICICI Lombard and submit relevant documents and cheques in the branch office. The office verifies the documents and checks with the bank whether the cheque given by a customer is valid in which case it sends all the documents to the processing hub for rechecking the documents electronically. Then if the processing hub also gives confirmation, the policy is generated and given to the customer.
2. *Brokers*: Prospective customers could be in a dilemma about selecting the right insurance company as well as the right insurance product. So, prospective customers go to the brokers to get expert advice. After interacting with the broker when a customer thinks that ICICI Lombard's product is better suited to him or her, the customer reaches the branch office of ICICI Lombard and the same procedure as that mentioned in point 1 of this list is followed.
3. *Agents*: There are agents of ICICI Lombard who reach out to people and promote the company's products. If a customer is willing to avail himself or herself of a particular policy, either the customer or the agent on the customer's behalf goes to the branch office with the relevant documents. The remaining process is the same as that described in point 1 of this list, the only difference being that the agent comes to the customer's doorstep with the policy.
4. *Telesales*: In this case, potential customers are contacted over phone. When a customer shows interest, the information is passed on to the company's agent. The agent approaches the customer and the process is carried out as in point 3 of this list.

In each of the aforementioned cases, the information about the transaction is transferred from the processing hub to the IT processing hub in Mumbai where all the data are finally stored. The data can then be accessed by the corporate office for analyzing performance.

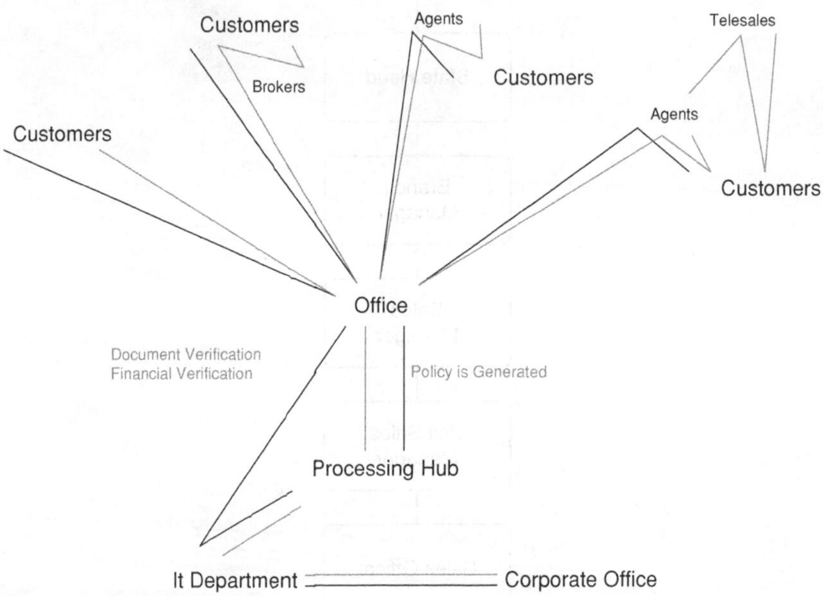

Figure 7.2 *Ways in Which a Policy Is Generated*

Knowing Your Customer

All things said and done, the simple truth is that customers will not buy a product if they do not feel its need. So, a company has to understand its customers' needs if it wants to succeed. Thus, knowing and understanding customers' needs is the core of every successful business. Once this is known, the information can be used to persuade potential and existing customers that buying from a particular company is in their best interests. For this purpose, ICICI Lombard follows the 'eight W and two H' approach.

The Eight W and Two H Approach

The approach specifies the things a company needs to know about its potential and existing customers:

- *Who they are*: The first step is to identify the customer. Who is her or she? What are his or her needs? What are his or her likes or dislikes? Knowing the customer profile is extremely important, whether the customer is an individual or another business group.
- *What they do*: If a company sells directly to individuals, it is worth knowing their occupations and interests. If the firm sells to other businesses, it helps to have an understanding of what their business is trying to achieve.
- *Why they buy*: Knowledge about the intentions behind a customer's purchase makes it easier to match their needs to the products a company is offering.
- *When they buy*: Approaching customers just at the time they want to buy massively increases the chances of a successful deal.
- *What makes them feel good about buying*: It is essential to know what makes the customers feel good to increase customer satisfaction by living up to their expectations.
- *What they expect of you*: The first step in living up to customers' expectations is to know what they expect. For example, if a company's customers expect reliable delivery and the company does not disappoint them, it stands to gain repeat business.
- *What they think about you*: The biggest asset for anyone is one's image or goodwill of others. Do a company's customers feel the company is reliable enough? Do they trust the company? Have the company been able to strike a healthy relationship with them? All these factors affect a sale greatly.
- *What they think about your competitors*: Knowing how a company's customers view its competitors enables the company to stand a much better chance of staying ahead of its rivals.
- *How they buy*: It is important that target customers are comfortable with the mode of purchase. Knowing how they prefer to buy—online or face-to-face meeting with an agent—enables a company to choose the right channel. Moreover, it is vital to know what mode of payment they are more comfortable with—cash, credit cards or cheques.
- *How much money they have*: A company can be more successful if it can match what it is offering to what its customer can afford. It is important to ascertain the customer's budget and then make offers accordingly.

BALANCED SCORECARD

For the *balanced scorecard of ICICI Lombard*, please refer to ANNEXURE, Table A1. In ICICI Lombard, the balanced scorecard perspective includes mainly three parameters, viz, employee performance, employee satisfaction index (ESI) and learning progress. For these three parameters, appropriate weightage is given, performance measure is estimated and target value is fixed.

Business process perspective: This perspective deals with processes related to ICICI Lombard's settling of customer claims and sale of its products through various channels like agent, banks, brokers, the Internet, etc. The two most important parameters considered for ICICI Lombard are average claim settlement time and percentage of claims out of total claims settled in stipulated time. ICICI Lombard assigns appropriate weightage to these parameters.

Customers' perspective: ICICI Lombard mainly uses customer satisfaction index as a future trend for business.

Financial perspective: This perspective has traditionally been considered the most important perspective in business. Under financial perspective, ICICI Lombard uses parameters such as claims on various parameters which can be measured as follows:

Total performance in insurance claims management =

$$\frac{[(\text{Financial perspective} \times \text{Weightage}) + (\text{Business processing perspective} \times \text{Weightage}) + (\text{Learning and growth perspective} \times \text{Weightage}) + (\text{Customers' perspective} \times \text{Weightage})]}{(\text{Sum of the respective weightages})}$$

BENEFITS OF MIS

- Time taken in each step of work flow is drastically reduced due to the use of *Premia* and *Genesis Pathfinder*.
- *Genesis Pathfinder* helps to quote, issue and manage policies and critical insurance functions from the Internet as well as the intranet.
- *Online Manager* enables customers and brokers to process business transactions independently (in less than 10 minutes).
- Improved speed and accuracy of claims processing is provided by Taslima (integrating Collaborative Portal Server (CPS) and Customer Relationship Management (CRM)).
- Citrix Metaframe enables faster rollouts of applications.

DISCUSSION QUESTIONS

1. What is the role of insurance companies in the development sector?
2. What is the potential of insurance sector in India after privatization?
3. What are the business processes in use in ICICI Lombard, and what are the challenges faced by the company?
4. What are the ways in which MIS can help to overcome the challenges mentioned in Question 3?

BIBLIOGRAPHY

1. www.icicilombard.com, 2008.
2. www.en.wikepedia.org, 2008.
3. www.lawgazette.org.sg, 2008.
4. www.balancedscorecard.org, 2008.

ANNEXURE

Table A1 *Balanced scorecard for ICICI Lombard*

Insurance claims Management scorecard

Insurance claim management is one of the key elements required for enhancing the public image of the company and to get through the stiff competition present in the insurance sector. Key Performance Indicators (KPI) help in effectively evaluating the performance of the company and in aligning business goals with individual performance

Perspectives	**Performance**
Financial perspective	
Business processing perspective	
Learning and growth perspective	
Customers' perspective	
Total performance	
Scorecard includes four categories and 16 indicators	

Help

The values in 'Weight' column must be between zero and 10

A value 10 means that the corresponding perspective or goal is the most valuable one

Strategy tree and scorecard details:

Perspective	**Goal**	**Weight (×10)**	**Description**	**Performance (%)**	**Measure Units**	**Target Values**
Financial perspective		3				
	Return on capital employed	4	It means amount generated on capital invested			
	Market share by sales	3	The ratio of revenue generated to total industry revenue		%	
	Legal cost incurred as a percentage of total cost	3	It is the percentage of legal cost to total cost		%	
Total performance in group			**Financial perspective**			
Business processing perspective		3				
	Percentage sales through various channels	3	It gives the weightage of every channel		%	

(***Contintued…***)

Table A1 (*...Continued*)

Perspective	Goal	Weight (× 10)	Description	Performance (%)	Measure Units	Target Values
	Claim settlement time	4	It refers to average time taken in the settlement of claims		days	
	Percentage settlement of claims	3	(Total claims settled/ Total claims received) × 100		%	
Total performance in group			**Business processing perspective**			
Learning and growth perspective		2				
	Employee performance	3	It indicates an employee's efficiency		%	
	ESI	3	It measures organizational commitment		%	
	Learning progress	4	The resulting increase in knowledge or capability before and after training		%	
Total performance in group			**Learning and growth perspective**			
Customers' perspective		2				
	Percentage decrease in customer complaints	3	It means percentage decrease in the number of customer complaints received regarding claim management activities		%	
	Customer satisfaction index	4	It shows customers' response to services		%	
	Percentage reduction in average claim processing time	3	(Decrease in claims settlement time/ Last year's claim settlement time) × 100		%	
Total performance in group			**Customers' perspective**			
	Total performance in insurance claims management scorecard Total performance in insurance claims management = ((Financial perspective × Weight) + (Business processing perspective × Weight) + (Learning and growth perspective × Weight) + (Customer's perspective × Weight))/(Sum of the respective weights)					

Table A2 *Sample MIS report*

Serial Number	Metrics	Formulae	Roles	Periodicity
1	Return on capital employed	(Operating profits)/(Total assets – Current liabilities)	Financial executive	Annually
2	Market share by sales	Total revenue generated/Total revenue generated in this industry	Marketing executive	Annually
3	Legal cost incurred as a percentage of total cost	Legal cost/Total cost	Financial officer	Annually
4	Percentage sales through various channels	(Sales by a particular channel/ Sales of the company) × 100	Marketing officer	Monthly
5	Claim settlement time	Time difference between settlement and receipt of claim	Claim settle-ment officer	Real-time basis
6	Percentage settlement of claims	(Total claims settled/Total claims received) × 100	Claim settle-ment officer	Real-time basis
7	Employee performance	(Target achieved/Target given) × 100	Marketing officer	Monthly
8	ESI	(See Table A3 for the questionnaire)	HR manager	Half yearly
9	Learning progress	Performance after training – Performance before training	HR manager	Annually
10	Percentage decrease in customer complaints	Decrease in complaints between last year and this year/Number of last year's complaints	Customer support officer	Weekly
11	Customer satisfaction index	Number of complaints addressed/ Number of complaints received	Customer support officer	Weekly
12	Percentage reduction in average claim processing time	(Decrease in claims settlement time/ Last year's claim settlement time) × 100	Claim settle-ment officer	Yearly

Table A3 *Employee satisfaction index*

	Criteria (out of 10)	Employee A	Employee B	Employee C	Employee D	Employee E
1	Communication					
2	Recognition					
3	Convenience					
4	Challenge					
5	Personal growth					
6	Recreation					
7	Job security					
8	Compensation					
	Total (out of 80)					
	Individual ESI = Total/80 × 10					
	Grand ESI = (Total individual ESI/Total number of employees) × 10					

8

Case Study on Reliance Life Insurance: Use of Information System as a Strategic Management Tool

INTRODUCTION

Insurance is often defined as a device (social and financial) that ensures safety of economic value of life and other valuables. Under a plan for insurance, a large number of people associate themselves by sharing risks attached to individuals. The risks against which insurance can be made include fire, death, accidents and burglary. Any risk contingent upon these may be insured against a premium commensurate with the risk involved. Therefore, collective bearing of risk may be termed as insurance.

Insurance is a contract wherein in lieu of payment of a premium by the insured the insurers pay for the financial losses incurred by the insured as a consequence of the occurrence of unpredictable events. The term 'risk' implies the possibility of adverse consequences resulting from any accidental happenings that produce a financial loss.

Insurance is sometimes also conceived of as a pool wherein a large number of people subjected to a similar risk contribute to a common fund out of which the losses incurred by the unfortunate few, due to unforeseen accidental events, are compensated for. The basis of insurance is that a risk is shared by a large group of individuals. The losses of an individual are distributed over a vast group of individuals.

Life Insurance

When a person buys a life insurance, a contract is signed between the person getting insured (policy owner) and the insurer. As per the contract, a premium is paid at regular intervals by the policy owner (the insured) so that risks related to life (such as death because of accidents or ill health) are transferred to the insurer. In the event of death, the insured's nominees get the total sum that is assured by the insurer during the signing of the contract.

INDIAN LIFE INSURANCE INDUSTRY

In 1999, the insurance sector was opened to private participation and Insurance Regulatory and Development Authority (IRDA) was formed. Prior to this, Life Insurance Corporation (LIC) of India used to dominate the market and the market was totally a sellers' market. But after the market opened up and because of the presence of 16 competing companies offering innovative services, the market transformed into a buyers' market. Strong performance by LIC, ICICI Prudential and State Bank of India (SBI) Life helped the 16-player-strong life insurance industry to mop up Rs 2,982 crore in April 2010 compared with Rs 1,996 crore collected in the same month last year, according to the data compiled by IRDA.

However, some life insurers such as Bajaj Allianz, ING Vysya Life and Reliance Life saw a decline in premium collections during the period under review. The country's largest life insurer LIC saw new premiums grow by 57 per cent to Rs 2,134 crore in April 2010 by selling 15,89,684 policies against Rs 1,355 crore a year ago. It had a market share of 71.56 per cent in April. The 15 private players together saw their business grow by 32 per cent to Rs 848 crore with a market share of 28.44 per cent.

- Investment policies—The main objective is to facilitate the growth of capital by regular or single premiums. Common forms of investment policies (in the United States) are whole life, universal life and variable life policies.

Characteristics of the Indian Insurance Industry

Before we go through case facts, let us understand insurance domain as it is prevalent in India. The indian insurance market has the following noticeable points:

- More than a century in India
- Large mobilization of savings next only to banks
- Significant participant in capital markets
- Constitutes 15 per cent of gross domestic savings
- Assets under management—more than Rs 4,00,000 crore
- Invested in infrastructure Rs 40,000 crore
- *Employment*: employs close to 2,00,000 people; retail customers: 92 per cent
- *Agency force*: 1.5 million
- *Policies in force*: Nearly 20 crore
- *Offices*: Nearly 3,000 offices across India and growing
- *Growth*:
    - Penetration grew from 1.2 to 2.2 per cent of gross domestic product (GDP)
    - Insurance density grew from Rs 280 to Rs 600 (per capita premium)
    - Premium grew from Rs 28,000 crore to Rs 63,000 crore

In the insurance industry, to know the maturity level of the organization, two metrics are used for measurement. They are:

1. Life insurance density: Life insurance density is measured as total annual premium payments divided by population. It is constructed as premium in local currency divided by the purchasing power parity conversion factor, obtained from the world development indicators and the population.
2. Life insurance penetration: Life insurance penetration is defined as a ratio of the total premium paid as the percentage of GDP. Life insurance penetration in India was 3 per cent in 2006 to 2007. The impetus for growth has come from both public and private insurers.

Table 8.1 *Top insurance players*

Insurers	Premium (in crore rupees)
ICICI Prudential	271.00
Bajaj Allianz	124.00
SBI Life	90.00
HDFC Standard	70.00
Max New York Life	69.00
Tata AIG	48.00
Aviva	39.00
Reliance Life	33.00
Birla Sun Life	28.00
Kotak Mahindra Old Mutual	26.00
ING Vysya	22.00
MetLife	19.00
Shriram Life	4.50
Sahara Life	1.70
Bharti Axa Life	0.72

Both these parameters (that is, life insurance density and life insurance premium) are very small in magnitude in India and with the introduction of private players there is a huge scope for the growth of life insurance industry in India. Table 8.1 shows the performance of the top 15 players in the industry (other than LIC) during 2006–07.

ICICI Prudential topped the private players' chart with its premium income rising by 84.5 per cent to Rs 271 crore, and it held 9.08 per cent share of the market.

RELIANCE LIFE INSURANCE (RLI)

RLI is an associate company of Reliance Capital Limited, which is a part of Reliance—Anil Dhirubhai Ambani Group. Figure 8.1 presents the growth of RLI for the years 2007 and 2008.

The characteristics of RLI are as follows:

- One of the fastest gainers of *market share* in new business premium among the private players with an incremental market share of *4.1 per cent* in the financial year 2007–08—recorded growth from 3.9 per cent in April 2007 to 8 per cent in February 2008 (*Source*: Insurance Regulatory and Development Authority (IRDA), Figure 8.1)
- Continues to be *one among the fast-growing private life insurance companies in the country* with a year-over-year growth of *195 per cent in new business premium* as of March 2008
- A company that crossed *1.7 million policies in just two years* into its operation, post the takeover of AMP Sanmar business
- Initiated *Express Life*, a unique *over-the-counter* sales process for unit-linked insurance policies (ULIPS) in the industry
- Accomplished a large distribution ramp-up in the industry in a short span of time by opening *600 branches in 10 months*, taking the overall branch network to more than 740 branches
- Continues to be one of the two life insurance companies in India that have been certified *ISO 9001:2000* for all their processes

Figure 8.1 ***RLI—Growth***

- Awarded the *Jamnalal Bajaj Uchit Vyavahar Puraskar 2007—Ceritificate of Merit* in the financial services category by the Council for Fair Business Practices (CFBP)

VISION, MISSION AND GOALS

The *vision* of the company is

Empowering everyone to live their dreams.

The *mission* of RLI is to

Create unmatched value for everyone through dependable, effective, transparent and profitable life insurance and pension plans.

The *corporate goals* of the company are as follows:

- *RLI would strive hard to achieve the three goals mentioned as follows*:
  - *Emerge as a transnational life insurer of global scale and standard*
  - *Create the best value for customers, shareholders and all stakeholders*
  - *Achieve impeccable reputation and credentials through best business practices*

The vision of RLI is to enable everyone to realize their dreams—be it a safe post-retirement life, a dream house or a secure future for one's children. RLI helps customers to fulfil their dreams. The mission of RLI is to fulfil the dreams of its customers by providing them with products that satisfy their needs.

STAKEHOLDERS AND THEIR OBJECTIVES

Figure 8.2 shows different stakeholders in insurance domain and their objectives.

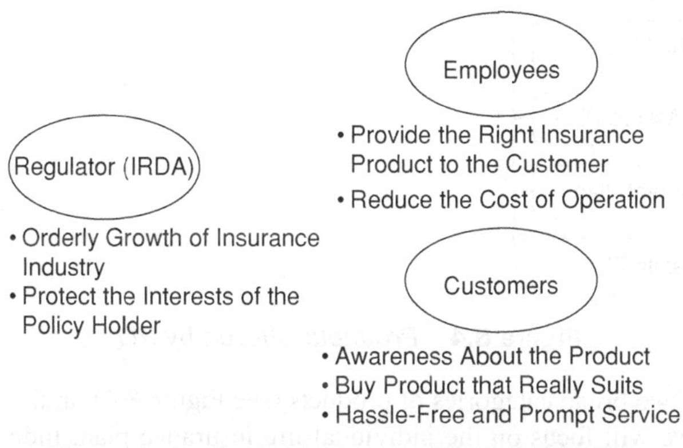

Figure 8.2 ***Stakeholders and their Objectives***

STAGE OF THE ORGANIZATION

Figure 8.3 shows organization maturity over its life time.

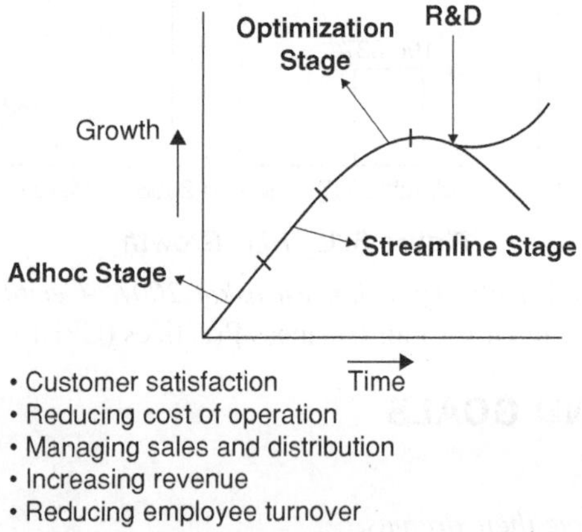

Figure 8.3 ***Organization Maturity Over Life Span***

PRODUCTS OFFERED BY RLI

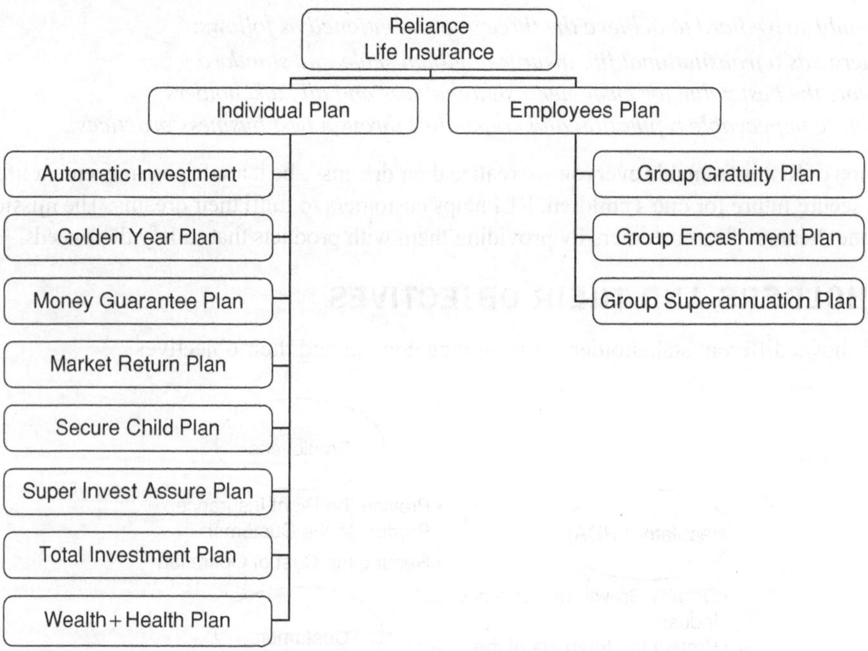

Figure 8.4 ***Products Offered by RLI***

Reliance Insurance has two broad categories of products (see Figure 8.4): individual insurance product and group insurance. We will focus on the individual life insurance plan. Individual life insurance is sub-divided into the categories shown in Table 8.2.

Table 8.2 *Sub-divisions of individual life insurance*

Protection plans
To protect a family choosing a limited-period plan or a lifetime protection plan, depending on its needs.
Savings and investment plans
Reliance savings and investment plans help customers to set aside some money to achieve specific goals in life, which means that they can enjoy life and provide for a family's daily needs.
Retirement plans
Invest in Reliance retirement plans and save money to enjoy life even after retirement. Customers will never have to depend on another person or make any compromises to maintain their current lifestyle ...
Child plans
To save systematically and secure a child's future needs.

Reliance has many products under its savings and investment plan category, which is in fact the highest selling segment of RLI. Products under this category are discussed in the following section.

Savings and Investment Plans from Reliance

- *Reliance Super InvestAssure Plan*: Reliance Super InvestAssure is a complete plan that addresses vital needs like flexibility, security, investment return and financial planning with all its key benefits.
- *Total Investment Plan I—Insurance*: Reliance TIPS Series I Insurance is a unit-linked investment + insurance plan that helps customers to meet all their financial needs without the complexity of managing multiple products.
- *Reliance Wealth + Health Plan*: Invest in the Reliance Wealth Health Plan and balance your health needs and wealth needs without compromising either health or wealth.
- *Reliance Automatic Investment Plan*: The Reliance Automatic Investment Plan is an enhanced unit-linked plan that allows customers to choose the right investment mix to reap maximum benefits. It also provides enhanced life cover.
- *Reliance Money Guarantee Plan*: To reap the benefits of a rising market and to protect themselves from market decline, customers can invest in the unit-linked Reliance Money Guarantee plan, which gives the perfect balance between protection and savings.
- *Reliance Cash Flow Plan*: One can invest in the Reliance Cash Flow Plan and reap the dual benefits of a life insurance plan and that of easy liquidity through lump sum cash, which means customers can get a percentage of the sum assured at periodic intervals.
- *Reliance Market Return Plan*: The Reliance Market Return Plan gives insurance protection and allows customers to benefit from investment growth. The plan has a tenure spanning the customer's entire life and meets the changing requirements customers may have from time to time.
- *Reliance Endowment Plan*: The Reliance Endowment Plan gives customers financial independence by allowing them to decide the amount of sum assured based on their current financial position and expected future expenses.
- *Reliance Special Endowment Plan*: Imagine an endowment plan that protects customers for a certain period even after customers have received lump sum—this is exactly what the Reliance Special Endowment Plan offers a customer along with other added benefits.

- *Reliance Whole Life Plan*: Investing in the Reliance Whole Life Plan gives the families of customers a lifetime of timely financial support. This will help customers to enjoy their lives to the fullest.
- *Reliance Golden Years Plan*: The Reliance Golden Years Plan helps customers to save systematically and generate the much-needed corpus to help them enjoy life after retirement.
- *Reliance Golden Years Plan Value*: Investing in the Reliance Golden Years Plan Value helps customers to realize all their post-retirement dreams. The plan helps customers to generate the amount they will need for the future.
- *Reliance Golden Years Plan Plus*: Investing in the special Reliance Golden Years Plan Plus not only helps customers to build the corpus they need after retirement but also collects a basic minimum amount in case something were to happen before they realize their dreams.
- *Reliance Connect 2 Life Plan*: The Reliance Connect 2 Life Plan gives customers the option to upgrade their life cover to keep pace with their changing lifestyle. With the growth in a customer's income, the life cover of his or her family also grows.

ISSUES AND CHALLENGES FACED BY RLI

RLI is a relatively new entrant in the insurance sector. To attract customers, RLI targets the urban youth segment. The younger generation prefers life insurance as a saving as well as investment option. As a result, most of the products in RLI's portfolio are ULIPs. The customer expectancy of value addition in terms of equity-linked gain and collateralization of policy for loans requires collaboration with multiple agencies. New opportunities in pension funds and stringent regulatory compliance present opportunities as well as challenges to RLI. These challenges and issues are summarized as follows:

- Business challenges and issues for industry
- Technical challenges and issues

Business Challenges and Issues for Industry

- Negative underwriting of (property and casualty)—claims' cost continues to rise
- Price increase in select markets, in response to loss of trends, litigation and state regulators
- Disproportionate manual operation and high paperwork
- Increasing global competition
- Pressure of regulatory compliance
- Increasing customer expectation
- Efficient and effective service—changing requirements
- Requirements to provide high benefi ts at low prices
- Compelling product changes
- Unfavourable trends in investment returns
- Slow penetration of new products and competitive time to go to market
- Issues in channel management

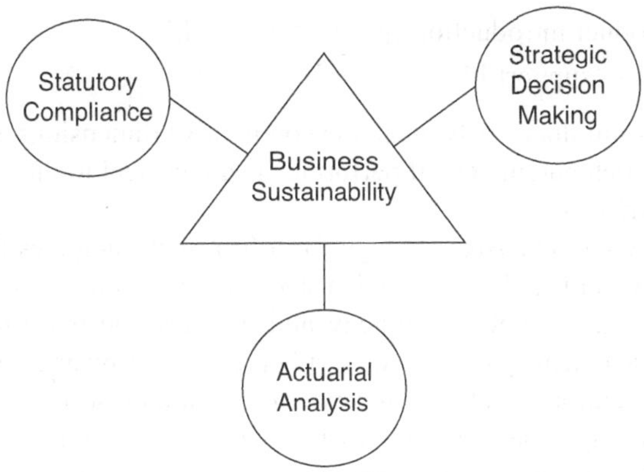

Figure 8.5 *Issues and Challenges*

Technical and Organizational Issues and Challenges

- Disparate system—heterogeneous platforms
- Working in 'siloed' systems, use of multiple data models and lack of 'documentation'
- Difficulty, delay and requirement of enormous efforts in providing strategic information and regulatory compliance ... many still 'excel' dominance.
- Existence of multiple versions of the truth
- Creating an enterprise-wide common customer view (including third-party- and intermediary-collected data)
- Using customer information (including analytics) and business intelligence to personalize the experience and interaction of customers
- Ensuring that all channels have access to centralized customer information in real time
- Centralizing content repository and sales information/systems
- Limiting access to centralized information, based on job role
- Using technologies to trigger events or notifications and route actions based on business rules and intelligence (Figure 8.4 summarizes all the aforementioned issues and challenges.)

OPERATIONS STRATEGY OF RLI

The major dimensions that form the competitive position of the company include the following:

1. Cost—'make it cheap'
2. Product quality and reliability—'make it good'
3. Delivery speed—'make it fast'
4. Delivery reliability—'deliver it when promised'
5. Coping with the changes in demand—'change its volume'

6. Flexibility and new product introduction speed—'change it'
7. Other product criterion—'support it'

An operation cannot excel simultaneously on all the competitive dimensions. Consequently, a firm's management has to decide which parameters of performance are critical to the firm's success and then concentrate on these characteristics.

The task of developing a comprehensive strategy for a firm that integrates the finance, marketing and operations functions is complex. Robert Kaplan and David developed a framework called the balanced scorecard to derive the operations strategy and measure the performance of a firm. It is a strategic planning and management system used worldwide to align business activities to the vision and strategy of an organization, improve internal and external communication and monitor the organization's performance against strategic goals. It provides a framework that not only measures performance but also helps planners to identify what should be done and measured. It enables an organization to clarify its vision and strategy and translate them into action.

The four perspectives in the balanced scorecard are financial, customer, internal, and learning and growth perspectives.

The operational strategy for RLI is as follows:

1. Increase the number of customers by providing more innovative products based on the needs of different customers and by increasing customer awareness.
2. Reduce the operational cost by training advisors, providing new product details through the Internet and increasing the number of active advisors.
3. Improve customer satisfaction by reducing policy issue and claim time by 50 per cent.

Financial Perspective

Financial objectives include developing new sources of income from new markets, new products and new customers; working with existing customers to expand relationships; lowering the direct cost of products; and reducing the working and fixed capital needed to support a given level of business (see Figure 8.6).

Customer Perspective

The objectives under this perspective include pushing the product into the realms of the unknown, the untried or the highly desirable; building bonds with customers; and delivering products that have good quality, low price and ease of purchase (see Figure 8.7).

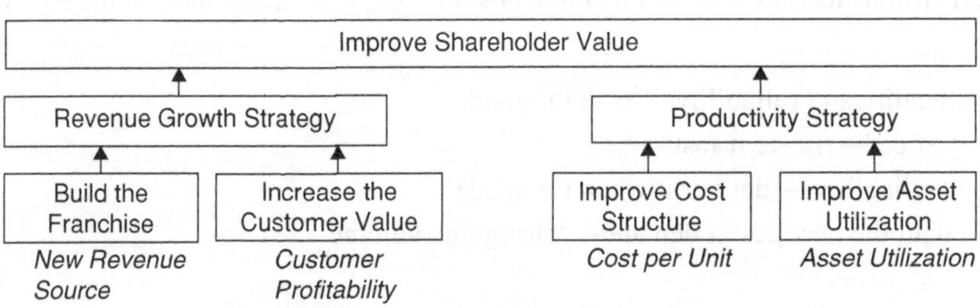

Figure 8.6 *The Financial Perspective*

Internal Perspective

The general objectives under this perspective are innovation process to create new products; customer management process for relationship management and solutions development; operational excellence emphasizing cost, quality, the quickness of operating process, excellent supplier relationship and speed of servicing the customers; and efficiency of supply and distribution process (see Figure 8.8).

Learning and Growth Perspective

The general objectives under this perspective are the strategic skills and knowledge required by the workforce to support strategy, materials, process technologies, information systems, databases, and tools and network; and the cultural shift required to motivate, empower and align the workforce behind the strategy (see Figure 8.9).

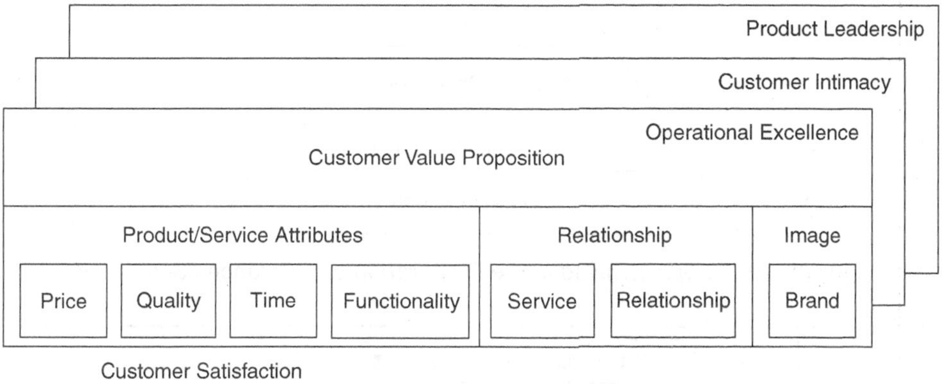

Figure 8.7 *The Customer Perspective*

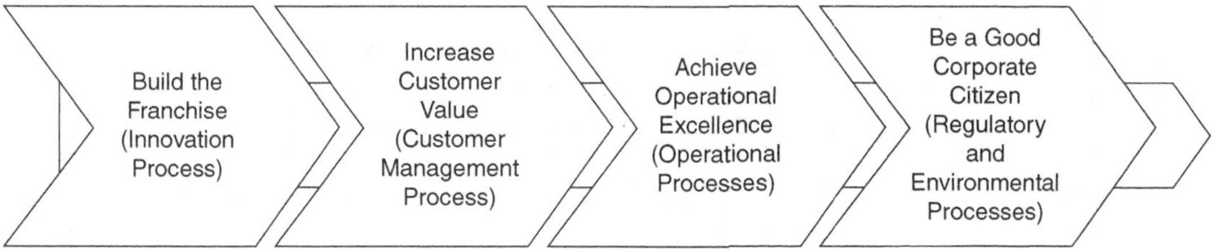

Figure 8.8 *The Internal Perspective*

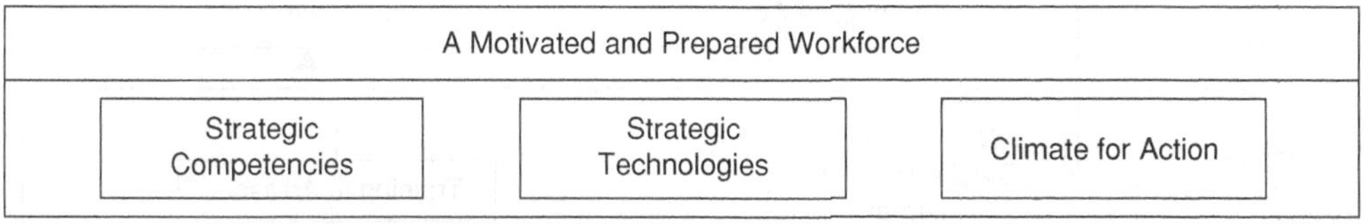

Figure 8.9 *The Learning and Growth Strategy*

STEPS INVOLVED IN THE PREPARATION OF A BALANCED SCORECARD

Figure 8.10 gives the steps involved in the preparation of a balanced scorecard:

1. The senior management decides the operations strategy based on the vision, mission and corporate goals of the organization.
2. The strategic objectives are then formulated and categorized into one of the four perspectives of the balanced scorecard.

Figure 8.10 ***Steps Involved in the Preparation of a Balanced Scorecard***

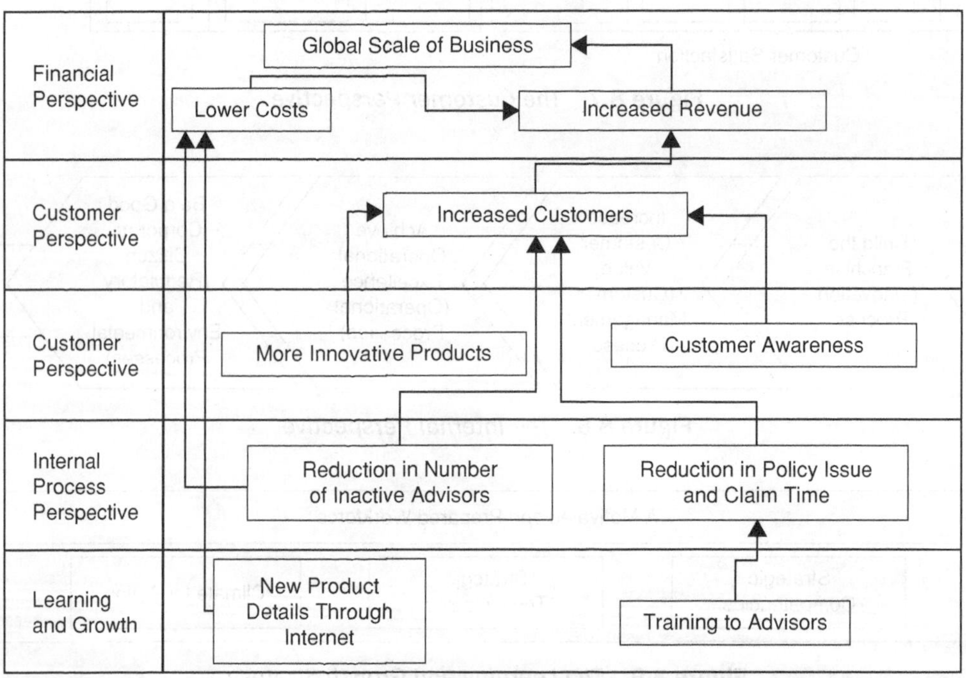

Figure 8.11 ***Strategic Map***

3. The metrics that measure the performance of the strategy are devised.
4. The strategic initiatives that are required to convert the aforementioned strategic objectives into action are formulated and then communicated to all in the organization.

Based on the company's vision and strategy, the strategy map shown in Figure 8.11 has been formulated.

USE OF INFORMATION SYSTEM IN INSURANCE INDUSTRY

The use of an information system in the insurance industry helps the industry in the following ways:

1. Manage customer relationship
2. Manage sales force effectively
3. Help customers to instantly access information, and provide solutions instantly
4. Remind customers of service requirements, and provide periodic follow-up and alerts
5. Online enquiry and transactions providing customer satisfaction
6. Automatic reporting and metrics to monitor performance and productivity

Now, let us look at the information flow in some of the processes.

FUNCTIONAL AREAS

Most businesses consist of a number of different departments, each of which has a specific job or task to do; these are called *functions*. Different functional areas that a company can have are as follows:

1. Human resources
2. Customer services
3. Marketing/sales
4. Administration/IT services
5. Operations
6. Finance/accounts
7. Sales and distribution process
8. IT services process
9. Customer relationship management

Human Resources

The human resources department is responsible for all aspects of managing the people who work in a business. The department does the following:

- Organize the hiring of employees (recruitment)
- Set up policies for making sure employees know the rules of the business and what is expected of them
- Deal with employees who may not stick to the rules
- Help with the training needs of staff
- Monitor the working conditions of employees

- Discuss important issues with representatives of the workforce
- Ensure that health and safety considerations are enforced

Customer Services

The customer services function in an organization is responsible for dealing with customer queries and complaints, for solving problems and for offering advice and support. This function is important because without customers a business cannot survive.

Marketing/Sales

The marketing department tries to find out what customers want from a business in terms of the goods and services it provides. The department uses this information to develop strategies to ensure that the business can meet the needs of customers and at the same time make a profit or at least cover its costs if it is a public sector organization.

Administration/IT Services

The administration/IT department is an extremely important part of any business. It can be seen as the glue that binds together all the departments of the business. It gives essential support to the whole business. Some of the tasks that the administration department might carry out are fairly routine, like answering telephone calls, filing information, photocopying documents, preparing letters and dealing with the mail. However, its work ensures the whole business runs smoothly. For example, if you need a new piece of software for your computer someone has to order it, make sure there is a license for its use, install it and make sure it runs properly. If you need a new pen, someone has to make sure there are supplies available. That is the job of the administration staff.

Operations

The functions of this department depend on whether the business produces a good or a service. If it is a good, then someone has to make it. To do that, the business needs equipment, materials and good planning to ensure everything gets done properly. The business also needs to make sure that the good produced meets the quality standards expected by customers. If the business produces a service then, again, it has to be planned, the production monitored and organized and the product delivered. The production/operations department carries out these tasks.

Finance/Accounts

The finance and accounts department looks after all the money in the business. Money comes *in* from

- Sales to customers (revenue) for private sector businesses
- Government for public sector organizations

Money goes *out* to

- Equipment
- Claims
- Wages
- Expenses
- Taxes

All these *ins* and *outs* must be recorded. This is what the accounts department does. Accounts are a record of all the money going in and out of a business. These records give information to managers. With this information, managers can make plans for the future.

Sales and Distribution Process

The sales concept proposes that customers, whether individuals or organizations, do not buy enough of an organization's products unless they are persuaded to do so through selling efforts. Therefore, organizations should undertake selling and promotion of their products for marketing success. Consumers are typically inert, and they need to be goaded for buying products by converting their inert need into a buying motive through persuasion and selling action.

This approach is applicable for unsought goods like life insurance; vacuum cleaners; and fire fighting equipment, such as fire extinguishers. These industries are, therefore, seen to have strong sales networks. The complete, integrated approach is shown in Figures 8.12 and 8.13.

Let us see how a life insurance is sold in RLI. The customer is approached through the distribution channel. The distribution channel is discussed in detail in the latter part of this section. The customer is given details about the policy and is persuaded to buy it. If the customer is willing to buy the policy, he or she provides the necessary documents for approval. The documents are submitted to the sales manager for approval. They are sent to the branch office and then to the regional office after their approval. In the regional office, the documents are verified and then scanned and sent to the zonal office. New policy requests from all the regions under the zonal office are then sent to the head office for

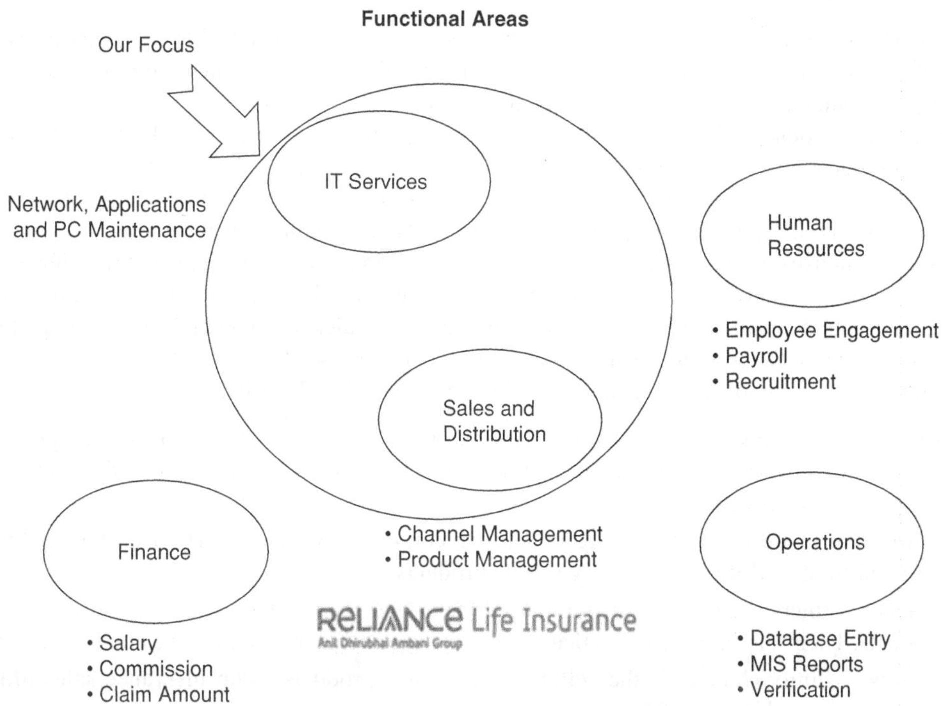

Figure 8.12 *Integrated Functional Views*

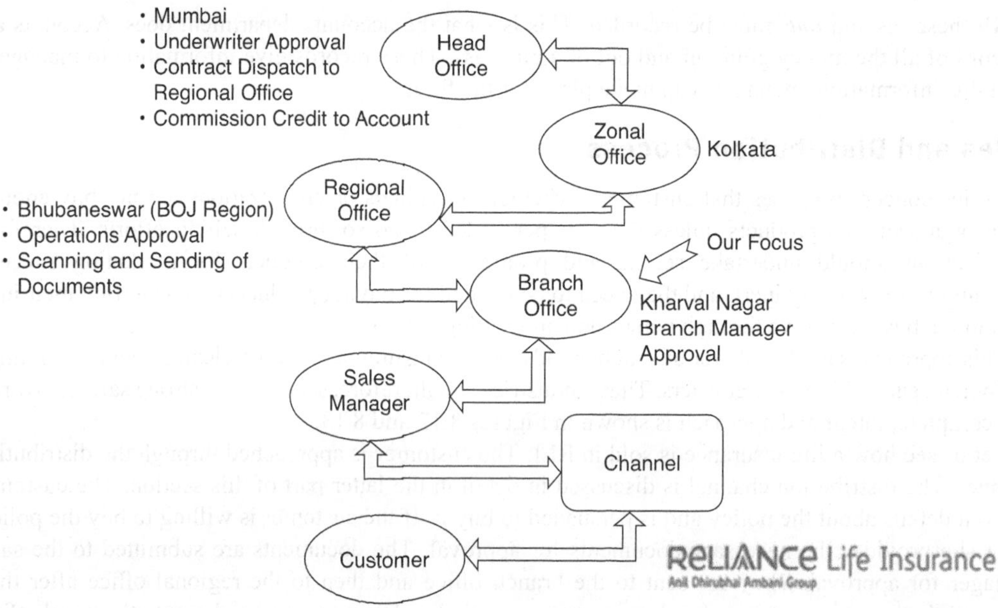

Figure 8.13 *The Sales Process*

underwriter's approval. After approval, the contract is printed and dispatched to the zonal office. It is then finally sent to the customer from the regional office. After the underwriter's approval is received, the stipulated commission is credited to the agent's account.

To make any product visible in the market, the distributor plays a key role. Particularly in areas where the products are intangible, the prospect may need to be educated about its merits before the actual sales results. In the insurance sector, the marketing of insurance products is not directly involved with the customers. Insurance companies sell their products through their agents at the grassroots level. The insurance industry in India is undergoing major transformation after the entry of new players into the market. The new players bring new technology and new products and at the same time usher in multiple distribution channels in order to have economies of scale. New channels have emerged in the form of Bancassurance, corporate agents and authorized brokers (see Figure 8.14).

The different distribution channels through which insurance is sold in RLI are

1. Agents: Sales of insurance products is done through individuals who are off roll by providing incentives. They are the points of contact for customers, and it is essential that they are trained properly to address customers' needs.
2. Third-party distribution: Insurance is sold by corporate agents. In the case of RLI, Punjab National Bank and Reliance Money sell its products.
3. Channel partners: Sales is done through partners who recruit the agents themselves and sell products. Their roles are similar to that of sales managers, but they are not the employees of RLI.
4. Affinity: Affinity channel is the selling of insurance products using insurance sales officers who are the employees of RLI.

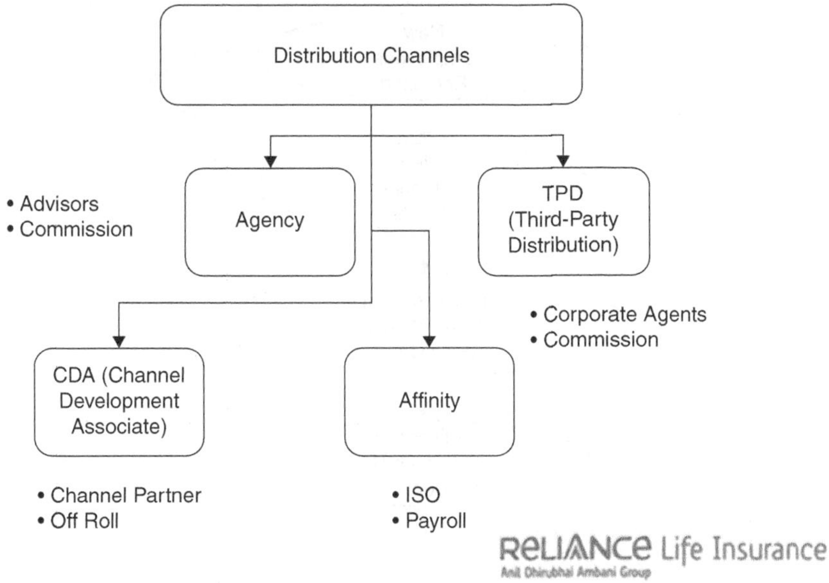

Figure 8.14 *Distribution Channels*

IT Services Process

IT support processes form the backbone of all functional areas. Because of the use of new technology, it is important that computer applications that support the business processes run without any issues. Most of the operations depend on the use of a computer and it is very essential that downtime is maintained very low. Let us see in detail how the IT needs of employees are taken care of when they join RLI and also how an IT-related issue is resolved in RLI (see Figure 8.15).

When employees join RLI, they fill their personal details, which are sent to the head office. When employee details are entered in the database, a SAP ID is generated and sent to the branch's IT department. The IT department allocates a desktop computer if the designation of the employee is below that of branch sales manager and a laptop if the designation is above that of branch sales manager.

When an employee faces a problem either in network access, computer hardware or access to applications, the employee raises a call using the Web-based application ITIS centre. A call is something like a work request to the IT department in the head office. The IT department in the head office tries to resolve the issue using its NetMeeting facility. If the problem requires physical presence at the problem site, then the call is transferred to regional IT operations, which solves the issue and closes the call.

Customer Relationship Management (CRM)

CRM is a process or methodology used to learn more about customers' needs and behaviours in order to develop stronger relationships with them. Since today the focus of insurance industry is selling more products to existing customers and acquiring more customers, CRM with business intelligence can help insurers in monitoring customer behaviour and giving a holistic 360° view of the customer. CRM helps to obtain granular details about a firm's customers, helping the firm to design better products, improve service levels and reduce operational costs.

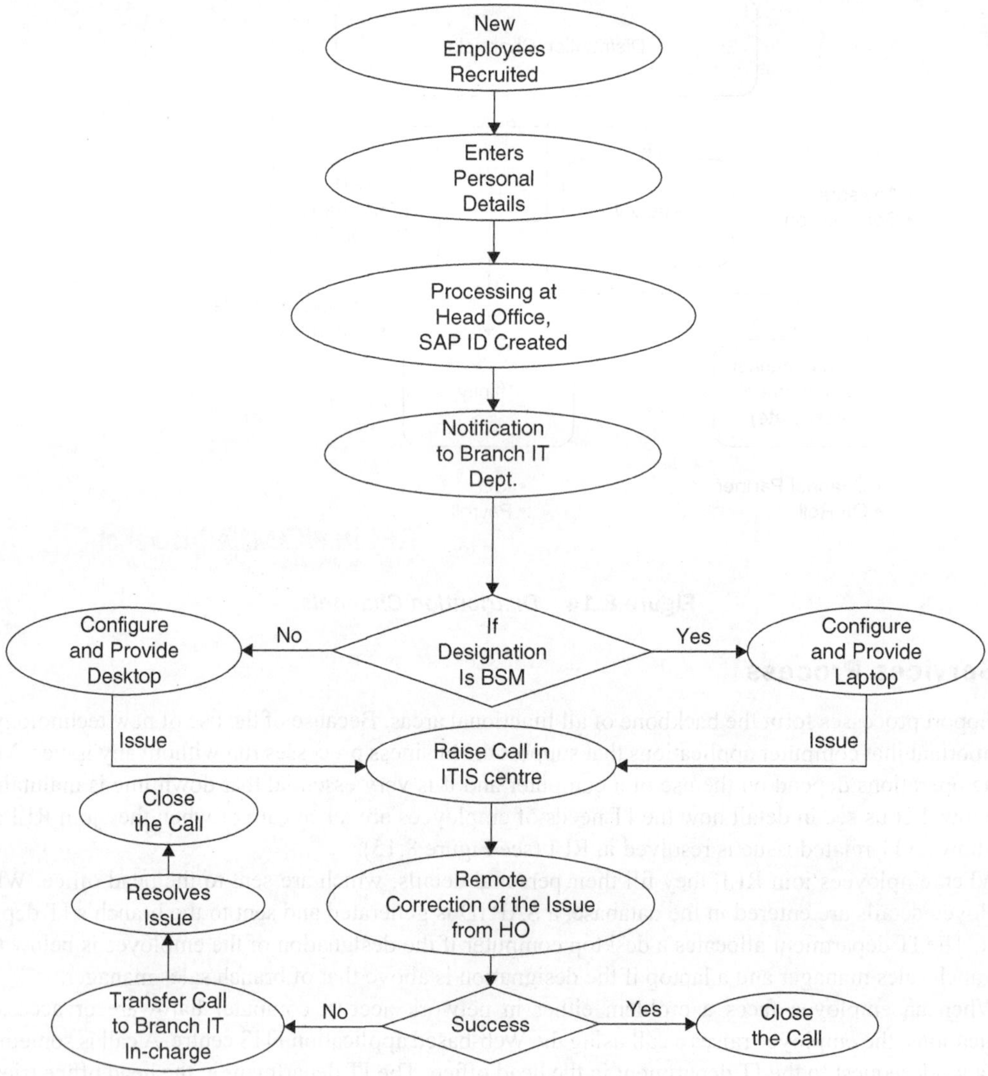

Figure 8.15 *IT Services Process*

From using CRM, insurance companies can have the following benefits:

1. It helps the company to interact with the customer in a more informal way.
2. It helps the manager, agent and other officials to understand the status of the client; his or her past transactions; last meeting with the agents; comments of the agent, managers and employees; etc.
3. CRM helps in maximizing revenue by carefully targeting the customers and offering more products and services. One can cross-sell and up-sell. It also helps the firm to identify the most profitable customers. By paying special attention to those customers, the firm can earn their loyalty.

Figure 8.15 is the general structure of a CRM system. It shows how data flows from a customer touch point like the Internet to the marketing automation process that processes the data to help drive a more effective and efficient marketing campaign. The data is further analyzed, and it provides information about customer segmentation.

Collaborative CRM: Collaborative CRM deals with applying collaborative interfaces (such as email, conferencing, chat and real-time services) to facilitate interactions between customers and organizations, as well as among organizational entities dealing with customer information (customers to sales representatives, sales to marketing, agent to provider).

Operational CRM: Operational CRM is the automating of horizontal integrated business processes involving front-office customer touch points, such as sales, marketing and customer service, via multiple, interconnected delivery channels and integration between front office and back office.

Analytical CRM: Analytical CRM involves analyzing the data created on the operational side of the CRM equation for the purpose of business performance management. Analytical CRM is tied to data warehouse architecture; it is most often evident in analytical applications that leverage data marts.

SOFTWARE TOOLS USED IN RLI

IBM Lotus Notes: The Notes client is mainly used as an email client, but it can also be used as a browser, notebook and calendar/resource reservation client, as well as a platform for interacting with collaborative applications.

SAP R/3: The enterprise software helps to store and retrieve all details about transactions related to different departments. These are Web-based transactions that help RLI to carry out its business in an efficient manner.

PTS: PTS is used to retrieve the information of all policy holders and policies, collection remainder, overdues and penalties.

SafeBoot: This is used for data security by encrypting customer data so that unauthorized accesses can be reduced.

REDRESS PERCENTAGE

With the increase in competition in the insurance sector in India, there is a dire need for each and every insurance company to not only attract customers but also retain the customer base. For a new company like RLI, it is important to strive in a highly competitive market. For this, customers should be given prime importance and their problems must be addressed without any delay so as to retain them.

Redress percentage is measured to achieve the strategic objective in customer perspective. This is a part of grievance management. This is done in order to know how far the company has been successful in solving the problems of its customers. This is calculated using the following formula:

$$\text{Redress percentage} = \frac{\text{Number of grievances addressed}}{\text{Number of grievances intimated}} \times 100$$

Customers lodges their complaints or grievances, and the branch manager uses this metric every month to assess how far a branch has been successful in addressing the complaints lodged by customers. According to this information, the manager makes the decisions regarding the upgrade of the CRM of the branch.

PERCENTAGE CONTRIBUTION OF NEW OFFERINGS

This metric helps in knowing the success of new products. By assessing the success rate, decisions related to the promotion of a particular product will be made by the marketing department. This metric is calculated using the following formula:

$$\text{Percentage contribution of new offerings} = \frac{\text{Number of new policies sold}}{\text{Total Number of policies sold}} \times 100$$

This metric is used for attaining the strategic objective in both customer perspective and learning and growth perspective. This is used by the marketing manager to assess how far the new product has succeeded in reaching the customers.

PERCENTAGE OF ACTIVE ADVISORS

In a field like Insurance, an advisor, who interacts with the customers and sells a company's plan, plays a key role in the company's development. For a company to be successful, its advisors should be very active in selling the plans. This metric is used to assess the potentiality of a company's advisors. By using this metric, a company can know about its inactive advisors and thereby plan for improving the efficiency of inactive advisors by providing training. It is also useful to improve the efficiency of active advisors. By doing so, the sales and the income of the company increases.

This metric is calculated using the following formula:

$$\text{Percentage of active advisors} = \frac{\text{Number of advisors who sell products}}{\text{Total Number of advisors}} \times 100$$

A branch manager uses this metric to find who the inactive advisors are and plan for improving their performance. The data will be provided by the operations department, whereas policies are logged and are assessed monthly.

AVERAGE NUMBER OF PRODUCTS SOLD PER ADVISOR

As mentioned in the section titled 'PERCENTAGE OF ACTIVE ADVISORS', the success of an insurance company depends upon the potentiality of its advisors. So, it is very necessary to assess the potentiality of a firm's advisors.

This metric is calculated and assessed to achieve the strategic objective in the learning and growth perspective. This gives a clear picture about how far advisors benefit from training programmes. By assessing this, a company can plan efficient training programmes and thereby increase the productivity of its advisors and thereby improve the business.

This metric is calculated using the following formula:

$$\text{Average number of products sold per advisor} = \frac{\text{Total number of policies sold}}{\text{Total number of advisors}}$$

The branch manager uses the metric and accordingly plans the training programmes to improve the productivity of advisors. The operations department enters the data required for the calculation of the metric. This is to be assessed very frequently for the company to grow, and this is measured once a week.

FREQUENCY OF NUMBER OF CALLS LOGGED

This is an indirect metric. This measures the number of IT-related problems faced by the employees in a given period of time. This is used to attain the strategic objective in the employee perspective. This is used to assess the technological problems faced by employees and how far the company has succeeded in addressing such problems. This metric is calculated using the following formula:

$$\text{Frequency of number of calls logged} = \frac{\text{Total number of calls logged}}{\text{Time period}}$$

This metric is used by the IT service manager to assess the problems faced by employees and to rectify them in order to improve the efficiency of employees.

AVERAGE TURNAROUND TIME (TAT)

This is the time in which customers' applications have to reach the head office from the branch office. Usually, the TAT for most of the policies in RLI is one day.

SAMPLE MANAGEMENT INFORMATION SYSTEM (MIS) REPORT

Before selling a particular policy to a customer, the advisor gives the customer a policy brochure, which contains all the details about the policy. Then, if the customer is satisfied with the plan, the transaction process starts. The policy purchased by a customer is mentioned in the MIS template.

Every customer is given a separate application form with a unique number. This application is forwarded by the advisor to the branch office from where, after verification, it is sent to the head office. The time taken for the process is called TAT. This is mentioned in the sample MIS template.

Each and every advisor has a unique code. This also is mentioned in the MIS template, and whenever the advisor sells a policy the transaction gets updated in the corresponding code. This helps in identifying a particular advisor and assessing his performance. The area manager name, under which a particular advisor comes, is also mentioned in the MIS template. In the MIS template, one can observe the following information:

1. Date on which a customer applied for a particular policy
2. Application number
3. Applicant name
4. Name of the policy
5. Sum assured
6. Weighted first-year premium
7. Advisor code
8. Advisor name

9. Name of the area manager under which the advisor comes
10. Status of the application
11. Contract number
12. Standard Terms and Conditions (STC) date
13. Issued date
14. Issuance TAT
15. Dispatch date
16. Date on which the customer received the policy
17. Remarks

(Please refer to ANNEXURE, Table A1 for a sample MIS report.)

COST–BENEFIT ANALYSIS

Cost Involved

There are three types of costs involved in implementing a MIS. They are as follows:

- Acquisition cost—These are the costs related to the initial purchase of software and hardware. Hardware includes server, router, switch, hub and magnetic storage, whereas software includes SAP R/3, Lotus Notes and link charges.
- Directly related costs—These are the costs involved in deploying and maintaining the technology platform, along with the cost of developing, supporting and integrating applications. Commissioning of SAP, application development and system maintenance come under directly related cost.
- Consequential cost—These costs include the costs of both planned and unplanned downtime, which are often hefty and difficult to quantify, and can include loss of revenue opportunities, the cost of capital wasted in idle productivity or the cost of damaged business relationships with partners and customers.

Benefits of Using MIS

- By using MIS, RLI can respond effectively to the needs of its customers; more customers are willing to buy the insurance products, resulting in an increase in the number of RLI's customers.
- Efficiency of the sales team goes up as their systems and processes are computerized and as they have discarded paper systems. The time gained in this manner can be spent for customer engagements, thereby increasing the company's productivity, which in turn results in increased sales.
- Ease in the collection of data regarding claims and also in the collection of feedback.
- Ease in paying premium for customers.
- Increased marketing efficiency and effectiveness.

CONCLUSION

Insurance industry must tap new geographical areas. They must introduce innovative products to reach wider segments of the population. They must ensure that customers get the right kind of information and solution so that customers can meet their real needs. The life insurance industry is in its infancy in India, and the focus of all the current players is geared towards growth in an underinsured market. But ultimately, the survivors will be the ones who are able to build a sustainable business. As has been discussed throughout the chapter, information systems help the companies to sustain their business through increased customer focus, efficient sales force management and lower cost of operation.

DISCUSSION QUESTIONS

1. How is the MIS of ICICI Lombard different from that of RLI?
2. Prepare a table indicating corporate strategy, metrics for measuring the success of corporate strategy and the corresponding MIS report.
3. Prepare a consolidated MIS report for one month for RLI, which indicates the status of business development activities in a zone.

BIBLIOGRAPHY

1. http://www.reliancelife.co.in, 2008.
2. *Insurance Today* Monthly magazine
3. http://en.wikipedia.org, 2008.
4. http://www.ibef.org, 2008.
5. http://www.indianmba.com, 2008.
6. http://www.nriol.com, 2008.

ANNEXURE

Table A1 *Sample MIS report*

Serial Number	Date	Application Number	Life Assured Name	Products	Sum Assured	WFP	Advisor Code
1	4 November 2009	PP16121875	Velmurugan. S	Reliance Whole Life Plan	1,00,000	12,000	00758583
2	5 November 2009	PP13540915	Selvan. N	Reliance Connect 2 Life	1,00,000	25,000	00534555
3	6 November 2009	CR20471576	Saravanakumar. S	Crisis cover	7,00,000	3,319	00502124
4	7 November 2009	CR20471578	Veerasikkammal. K	Crisis cover	3,00,000	2,834	00496063
5	8 November 2009	LL20288787	Sundar. M	Reliance Whole Life Plan	1,10,000	12,000	00409533
6	9 November 2009	HC20480887	Chitra. K	Hospital care	Plan A	5,353	00494324

Advisor Name	UM/AM Name	Status	Contract Number	Decision	STC Date	Issued Date	Issuance TAT	Despatched On	Received On
Kasthuribai. A	Premkumar	Reject							
Balajikadiravan. K	Saravanan	In force	9333035	Jet	5 July 2008	6 July 2008	1		
Jalajarani. S	Saravanan	Accept							
Subha. S	Vijaya	In force	9350255	Jet	8 July 2008	9 July 2008	1		
Karthikeyan. K	Premkumar	Accept							
Jothilakshmi. R	Vijaya	In force	9345552	Jet	7 July 2008	8 July 2008	1		

9

Case Study on Pantaloons: Value for Money

VISION OF A FIRM

Vision of a firm is a statement that describes what the firm intends to achieve in the long run. It explains what the firm's position would be after a period of time. Vision refers to a firm's final, all-inclusive and forward-thinking intentions, which can be at the macro level.

VISION OF PANTALOONS

Pantaloons has a broad vision of delivering everything, everywhere, every time for every Indian consumer in the most profitable manner.

MISSION STATEMENT OF A FIRM

Mission statement explains why a firm exists; it further defines the means for achieving its vision. In the mission statement, we find a concrete form of actions that will lead to the realization of vision. In short, mission is an organization's vision translated into the written form. Mission helps the organization to decide its priorities.

MISSION STATEMENT OF PANTALOONS

- Pantaloons share the vision and belief that its customers and stakeholders can be served only by creating and executing future scenarios in the consumption space leading to economic development.
- It will be the trendsetter in evolving delivery formats, creating retail reality and making consumption affordable for all customer segments—for classes and for masses.
- It will infuse Indian brands with confidence and renewed ambition.

- It will be efficient, cost conscious and committed to quality in whatever it does.
- It will ensure that its positive attitude, sincerity, humility and united determination are the driving forces that make it successful.

CORE VALUES AND BELIEFS OF PANTALOONS

- Indianness: confidence of the firm in itself
- Leadership: to be a leader, both in thought and business
- Respect and humility: to respect every individual and be humble in conduct
- Introspection: leading to purposeful thinking
- Openness: to be open and receptive to new ideas, knowledge and information
- Valuing and nurturing relationships: to build long-term relationships
- Simplicity and positivity: simplicity and positivity in thought, business and action
- Adaptability: to be flexible and adaptable, to meet challenges
- Flow: to respect and understand the universal laws of nature.

STAKEHOLDERS OF PANTALOONS AND THEIR OBJECTIVES

There are three major stakeholders for Pantaloons. They are

1. *The Future Group*: The company would always try to offer the best products at the best prices and make maximum profit in the process.
2. *Customers*: With the business scenario and dynamics evolving every day, it is very important to retain existing customers and at the same time create new customers to move the business forward.
3. *Suppliers*: Since the word retail means 'to break bulk', it is very important to have a very good vendor management system in place so that supply of products to the shop floor is done effectively.

BUSINESS MODEL FOR PANTALOONS

The process flow for Pantaloons involves the following steps:

1. *Supplier*: Suppliers are involved in carrying out the following functions:
   a. Vendor management
   b. Cost and deal management
   c. Purchase order management
   d. Collaborative management
2. *Purchase process*:
   a. Supply chain visibility
   b. Warehouse management
   c. Transportation management
3. *Store/shelf management*:
   a. Store planning
   b. Inventory management
   c. Replenishment management

   d. Fresh item management
   e. Item publishing
   f. Order management
4. *Sales/point of sales*:
   a. Point-of-sales management
   b. E-payment
   c. Content management
   d. Online retailing
   e. Kiosks
   f. Self checkout
5. *Customer*:
   a. Customer loyalty management
   b. Voucher gift management
   c. Customer ordering management
6. *Track and analyse*:
   a. General ledger and account management
   b. Sales audit and invoice matching
   c. Workforce management
   d. Payroll processing
   e. Sales analysis and loss prevention
7. *Planning*:
   a. Sales planning
   b. Pricing management
   c. Promotion management
   d. Customer profiling
   e. Assortment management
   f. Category management
8. *Central hub*:
   a. Process improvement
   b. Six sigma implementation
   c. Radio Frequency Identification (RFID) implementation
   d. Enterprise security

BUSINESS OBJECTIVES OF PANTALOONS

- To grab the full wallet of the consumer by capturing the whole consumer space: It is a concept given by Kishore Biyani, Chief Executive Officer (CEO) of Future Group; he believes that everything (petroleum, telecommunication, banking, etc.) comes under retail and thus the firm can grab the full wallet of the consumer.
- To realize the annual business plan (ABP; see Figure 9.1) by simultaneously achieving both the top line and the bottom line.

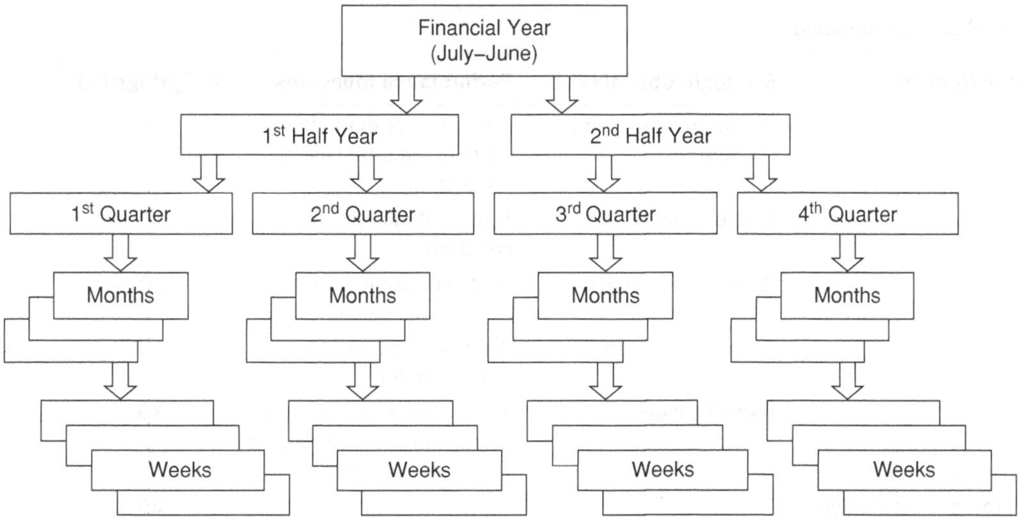

Figure 9.1 *Annual Business Plan (ABP)*

STEPS TO IMPLEMENT THE BALANCED SCORECARD TO DRIVE PERFORMANCE

1. Build consensus around strategies
2. Synthesize strategic objectives
3. Prepare a strategic map
4. Select performance measures
5. Select strategic initiatives
6. Prepare an implementation plan
7. Cascade the balance scorecard
8. Align the human resource with the balance scorecard
9. Set up a strategic feedback and review system

DERIVATION OF OBJECTIVES USING BALANCED SCORECARD FOR PANTALOONS

While deriving metrics for monitoring and control, it is essential that these metrics are aligned with business goals. In order to arrive at effective business alignment, we use the Balanced Scorecard technique (please refer Table 9.1), where we use four perspectives to derive strategy as well as metrics for Pantaloons.

Table 9.1 *Balanced scorecard for Pantaloons*

Serial Number	Strategic Objectives	Performance Measures	Weightage (%)
Financial perspective			**40**
F.1	Return on investment	Profitability status	20

(Continued...)

Table 9.1 (*...Continued*)

Serial Number	Strategic Objectives	Performance Measures	Weightage (%)
F.2	Return on marketing investment	Proportion of marketing costs in the total cost of production	15
F.3	Cost of sales	Total cost incurred by the company	20
F.4	Sales per employee	Employee contribution towards net sales	20
F.5	Claims percentage	Pilferage incurred during transportation	10
F.6	**Sales by demand**	Allows the comparison of sales of product categories within retail outlet	**15**
Customer perspective			**20**
C.1	Number of new customers	Customers acquired during a time period	25
C.2	Customer loyalty	Brand awareness and loyalty of customers towards Pantaloons	30
C.3	Dissatisfaction management	Effectiveness in operations	25
C.4	Conversion rate	Visitors turning into prospective customers	20
Internal process/ operational perspective			**30**
O.1	Inventory turnover rate	Assessment of how fast inventories are replenished	30
O.2	Effectiveness of distribution channels	Defects in distribution channels	20
O.3	Stock position	Material consumed during the period	20
O.4	Transit time	Time taken for the material to reach the end users	10
O.5	Resource utilization	Optimum utilization of the allocated budget	20
Learning and growth perspective			**10**
G.1	Percentage increase in market share	Measures market penetration and market coverage	40
G.2	Percentage growth	Intracompany growth and intercompany growth	**30**
G.3	Success rate	Measures operational and business excellence	30

DESIGN OF MANAGEMENT INFORMATION SYSTEM (MIS)

It is said that the recipe for making a good decision is 90 per cent information and 10 per cent inspiration. *MIS* can be defined as a set of capital and human resources that enable the collection, storage and processing of data to produce and communicate relevant information to all levels of management to provide support in performing management-related activities. It is viewed that the following areas in Pantaloons are the most important areas through which business efficiency can be promoted:

- Stockholding report
- Sales report
- Age analysis
- Operating parameters

Stockholding Report: First-hand information about stock availability is considered to be the most important information for use by department and store managers. A format marked 'A' has been evolved to provide information regarding the availability of each item every day. This format gives information about the opening and closing stocks of the day in terms of quantity and amount. This information is specific to one unit only because its storage capacity is limited and predetermined and may not compare with other sister units. Hence, this information is used for the appraisal by the department manager and store manager of respective units only.

Sales Report: Format 'B' is the proposed MIS for sales reports to provide data related to daily sales. The format includes cost price, maximum retail price, discount, margin (gross and net) and achievement for a particular item in the showcase. At the right end of the format, achievement is shown in terms of target sales and actual sales. The targets for different units will be different. Hence, comparison of this information may not be meaningful. The most important parameter is sales. Here, the column is widened to include the data in terms of amounts achieved by other sister units also. A comparison and view of this information on sales head will give rise to an expectation for the gradual increase in sales turnout. This will ultimately help in creating a sense of competition among the units and thereby the growth of the organization.

Age Analysis Report: It is important to keep track of stock movement for any item placed in the showcase. Format 'C' is proposed to be raised on a weekly basis. This gives specific information regarding the number of days for which any incoming consignment is held in the floor. This will be helpful in tailoring the frequency of accepting incoming consignment for a particular store. A detailed analysis of the information in this format will also provide knowledge about the fluctuation in demand with the change of seasons, that is, seasonal demands. This format, however, cannot be used for the comparison of performance of other units.

Operating Parameters: Format 'D' is planned to include information regarding the quantum of conversion of visiting/intending customers to real customers. This information is important to a very high degree for any unit. This speaks more of the efficiency of sales executives in converting individuals intending to buy a product to real customers. This indicates the positive and caring attitude of sales executives towards the visiting customers. In other words, increase in efficiency focuses on the ability to improve selling skills. The format includes information on the customer conversion head achieved by different units. This makes a unit aware of its efficiency compared with other units.

METRICS

Based on the business objectives discussed in the section 'BUSINESS OBJECTIVES OF PANTALOONS', operational strategies are derived using balance scorecard techniques under four perspectives, as discussed in the section 'DERIVATION OF OBJECTIVES USING BALANCED SCORECARD FOR PANTALOONS'. The various perspectives of balance scorecard are measured using different metrics, which are shown in Table 9.2.

Table 9.2 *Measurements for strategic objectives*

Serial Number	Strategic Objectives	Formulae
Financial perspective		
F.1	Return on investment	Net income/Capital employed
F.2	Return on marketing investment	Increase in sales – Marketing costs
F.3	Cost of sales	Factory cost + Administrative overheads + Selling and distribution overheads
F.4	Sales per employee	Net sales/Total number of employees
F.5	**Claims percentage**	**(Total loss and damage claims/Total transportation costs) × 100**
F.6	Sales by demand	Category-wise net sales/Stores total sales
Customer perspective		
C.1	Number of new customers	Customers in the current period – Customers during the last period
C.2	Customer loyalty	Tendency of customers to choose Pantaloons product/Total products in the market
C.3	Dissatisfaction management	Number of complaints after execution/ Previous number of complaints
C.4	Conversion rate	Visitors who take desired actions (purchase)/Total number of customers
Internal process/operational perspective		
O.1	Inventory turnover rate	Cost of materials consumed during the period/Average stock held during the period
O.2	Effectiveness of distribution channels	Defects in distribution channels (checkpoints)/Total number of checkpoints
O.3	Stock position	Inventory in the beginning + Purchases during the year – Sales during the year
O.4	Transit time	Number of days (hours) from the time a shipment leaves the organization to the time it arrives at the desired location versus transit time quoted by the carrier
O.5	Resource utilization	Budget spent/Total budget allocated

(*Continued*...)

Table 9.2 (*...Continued*)

Serial Number	Strategic Objectives	Formulae
Learning and growth perspective		
G.1	Percentage increase in market share	Comparison of business rate in a specific market/Trend of the market
G.2	Percentage growth	*Intra*: (Current year's share – Previous year's share/Previous year's share) × 100 *Inter*: Share of Pantaloons/Total market share of all the competitors taken together
G.3	Success rate	Number of successful projects/Number of projects held by the company

Table 9.3 *Periodicity, roles and tools used in MIS reports*

Activity	Role	Periodicity
Stockholding report	Operations department	Daily
Sales report	Marketing department	Daily
Age analysis report	Marketing and operations department	Weekly
Operating parameters	Human resources and operations department	Weekly

There is lot of information that Pantaloons gets from its MIS reports, like daily sales report (DSR), stock analysis, margin analysis, markdown analysis, plan versus actual sales analysis, operational reports, weekly stock covers and operational parameters (see Table 9.3). Through MIS, the store gets the Line of Business (LOB)–wise sales comparative reports and DSR of all eastern zone Pantaloons. All the Pantaloons stores require DSR; they also need weekly sales reports on the Monday of every week. The store manager also wants the age analysis and stock cover report at the store level and weekly sales comparative reports of the store's sister units. But data collection takes place every day as reports are updated each day to give a more accurate report at the end of the week.

While using the MIS none of the stores face any problems because before using it the MIS team undergoes training in using and handling MIS reports.

MIS TOOLS USED IN PANTALOONS

The MIS tools used in Pantaloons are as follows:

- SAP
- REM

All the Pantaloons store units are presently using SAP (BIW) and REM for generating reports from the system. Initially, they were using the REM system for generating reports. In 2006, Pantaloons first implemented SAP in its operation process. SAP is the upgraded version of REM, in which all the stores get all the reports required for their operations as well as the comparisons of their performance with other sister units.

DISCUSSIONS AND FINDINGS

- MIS of Pantaloons and MIS of other stores like Shoppers Stop, etc., differ on the basis of merchandise selection.
- MIS across the Future Group retail stores, viz, Pantaloons, Central and Big Bazaar, are similar with product diversification, that is, category of products across different retail outlets, as the major differentiator.
- Analysis of reports is done at one place using SAP (BIW), and it is found that SAP is more effective than REM, which was used earlier.
- It was found that REM is not able to give accurate data; so it was changed to SAP (BIW).
- In the transition period there were many difficulties: For example, eight to 10 people who were trained across the globe for implementing SAP left their jobs.
- In Pantaloons, the major thrust is on effective utilization of shop floor and of unused retail space.
- Any sister concern of the Future Group gives profit to the concerned store if the store utilizes its shop floor.
- Trend analysis for the demand is predicted, which helps to increase the sales for the season.

DISCUSSION QUESTIONS

1. Who are the stakeholders in Pantaloons?
2. How can you arrive at the corporate objectives of a stakeholder?
3. Discuss how MIS can be designed for each stakeholder so as to monitor his or her progress.

BIBLIOGRAPHY

1. Biyani Kishore (2007). *It happened in India.* New Delhi: Rupa & Co.
2. http://www.pantaloon.com, 2009.
3. http://www.scribd.com/doc/23575395/Pantaloon-Annual-Report-Analysis-FY09, 2009.
4. http://www.sebi.gov.in/dp/pantaloon.pdf, 2009.
5. http://www.moneycontrol.com/annual-report/pantaloonretail/directors-report/PR03, 2009.

10

Case Study on RPG: From Regional to International Music

RPG: BACKGROUND

RPG has several interests in the sub-continent market. One of the major business lines for which RPG is well known for its presence is the audio business. Its presence in the audio industry for the last 30 years has helped it to build a strong relationship with the music industry. For a long time, its name was synonymous with high audio quality of music. The organization has retail outlets in all the states of India, and it has also been successful in expanding its business to the overseas market. It sells cassettes and compact discs (CDs) in different packages and these packages are grouped into different categories, such as movie-, artist- and situation-based collections.

With so many different product lines, the company wants to simplify its manufacturing operations. It is also looking into improving and upgrading its supply chain management (SCM) systems. At present, it uses its homemade warehouse management system in different parts of the company. But the system is less than effective as is evident from the delay faced in the decision-making process. The delay is faced primarily when forecasting the sales figures for the next month. The company's system is an integration of systems comprising manufacturing, warehousing, inventory control, planning, shipping and logistics. Apart from these internal systems, the company has to interact with suppliers, musicians and other partners while taking care of both retail and wholesale customers.

Increasingly, Goenka, the Managing Director (MD), is finding it difficult to find the numbers related to monthly and annual sales. He wants to build a strong customer base with quality products while keeping his partners happy. He wants to use feedback mechanism to get information on the quality of cassettes being sold while improving research activities to keep the company abreast with modern manufacturing technology. Most of the time the partners provide much information on technology and the MD needs to make judicious and timely investments to get that competitive edge. His vision is for RPG to be the leading music-selling company in India at the national and regional levels and a recognized player in international market in due course of time.

CURRENT SITUATION

When Goenka passed out from his MBA school, he was full of ideas and he wanted to introduce these ideas in the form of initiatives in his father's company. He felt that these initiatives would facilitate the entry of the company into the international market. However, he had no clue as to what the condition of the company was at that time.

He divided the company into four regional areas, and in each region sub-divisions were made based on projected sales volume. But he was not able to give a correct projection of sales figures for each of these divisions and every month there was a wide fluctuation in the sales forecast versus actual sales. He used the models that he had learnt in the MBA school for forecasting; each forecasting model used past data to arrive at the forecasting and he had used the past data to derive sales forecasting! He went back to the actual sales figures again and found that the actual sales figures as recorded in the books are different from the ones he had used for forecasting. When contacted, the accounts department said: "This is the latest figure available from sales and these data are based on actual realization of money." His problem was compounded when within 2 hours a stockout situation in Coimbatore was reported whereas office in Cuttack refused to take any more inventories saying that the Cuttack warehouse was overstocked. One of the suppliers also informed that because of cold season, the supplier will not be able to supply the magnetic tapes in November and December and, hence, wanted to supply the excess quantity now to tide over any manufacturing problems that might occur later on.

The sales department reported a reduction in sales to the tune of 5 per cent in the quarter and net margin also showed erosion. A competitor T-series, on the other hand, had a good quarter and was able to increase its volume of sales by 17 per cent, most of the increase coming in at the cost of RPG.

Goenka called a meeting with the regional managers (RMs) of the company and asked them to present their issues, sales figures and projections. Most of them were not prepared to share any information as they noticed that some suppliers too were present in the meeting. They sulked and said they would send the information by courier as that was the preferred means of sending all information related to sales and inventory. "That takes hardly three days and we can definitely wait for that period." The sales figures usually arrive from different stockists within seven–eight days after sales and then the RMs compile them for two days and courier them to the head office.

CHALLENGES

Goenka wanted RPG to follow the model of Wal-Mart and become a true value supplier to customers. He wanted RPG products to be affordable and of high quality. He also wanted to increase sales figures with a reduction in cost while maintaining a healthy relationship with the partners of the firm. In fact, he wanted to improve the relationship between suppliers and the company to achieve the same end, "to sell as many products as possible without both of us having to maintain too much inventory. I also want to be linked to each and every customer so that we can react to their needs at the earliest".

Goenka decided to implement enterprise resource planning (ERP) and also customer relationship management (CRM) so that he could achieve his vision. He asked all the leading players in ERP and CRM to make presentations to the management team. During the presentation, he found that the management team could not answer many of the questions raised by the ERP and CRM vendors. The questions were related to the requirements of the company and the process flow of information. However, Goenka answered each and every question, and a detailed comparative statement was prepared and sent to the board for approval. He was sure that if implemented this Rs 1.5-crore-worth (including Annual Maintenance Contract [AMC] and hardware cost) implementation will change the way the company works and increase the operational efficiency manifold.

In the next board meeting, his proposal was rejected and he was back to square one. This case represents a scenario at RPG at the time when it was being converted from a family-owned business to a professionally driven firm. The firm at this point of time was losing market share to its major competitor T-Series due to internal inefficiencies and lack of proper planning. Hence, the firm needs to assess its current business objectives and determine how IT as an enabler can become a process differentiator for the company.

To correctly arrive at the current objectives of the company, the vision and mission of the company are considered first and company objectives are drawn based on them.

INDUSTRY OVERVIEW

The RPG case study presents a situation that is both interesting and challenging. In order to understand the case study and the company's situation, it is important to understand the larger picture regarding the position of the audio industry and then see the company in that context. The introduction of the CD in the 1980s marked the dawn of digital audio revolution. Before the turn of the new millennium, analogue-based audio systems were fast becoming a rare entity, whether at home or anywhere in the professional audio industry. Digital audio was fast emerging as the dominant technology. The then research trends in the industry, such as audio encoding and high-resolution audio; high-tech speakers and microphones; and high-quality audio recording, storage and processing equipment, were quickly changing the picture. Moreover, improved methods of transmission and broadcasting were emerging, which had given a concrete platform for the industry to grow at an accelerated pace. The broadcasting industry also benefitted from the technological improvements happening in all these spheres.

The introduction of digital audio created a quantum leap in the audio industry over the past three decades with enhanced sound quality, added flexibility and signal processing. With the advent of the new technology, the editing of sounds was fast becoming cheaper, with a regular personal computer loaded with high-tech software becoming the tool to create and edit music.

Although some segments of the industry have grown substantially over the past three decades, the audio segment still needs to reach its full potential. Out of the Rs 14,000-crore Indian consumer electronics market, audio products account for less than 10 per cent of consumer spending. Last year, the main growth in the audio industry came from three segments, namely, mini systems with VCD/MP3 players, CD radio cassette recorders and personal stereo. Devices like audio receivers and sound distribution devices like amplifiers still have a very small market.

COMPANY OVERVIEW

RPG enterprises, established in 1979, is one of India's fastest-growing business groups with a turnover touching $3.25 billion in the year 2007. RPG is a leading player in the Indian audio industry. Over a period of 30 years, it has developed a strong partnership with the music industry and has become a force to be reckoned with in India. The $25-million organization has its presence felt in almost all the states in India.

The group has more than 20 companies in diverse business areas like power, transmission, IT specialty, carbon black, tyre, retail and entertainment. RPG is one among the leading players in the Indian audio industry. Over a period of 30 years, it has developed a strong partnership with the music industry and has become a force to be reckoned with.

Company's Management

RPG's management board is the backbone of the conglomerate. Its members are highly qualified professionals, coming from diverse fields with much experience in their respective fields of work.

Quality

For RPG and for all the other companies in the audio industry, quality determines success. Continuous process improvements are carried out to ensure complete satisfaction of customers and meeting of market requirements.

Now, let us look at some of the characteristics of the music industry. Some of these are extremely typical of this industry and are not seen elsewhere:

- Seasonal demand is varying.
- Demand is geographically spread.
- Technology innovation is fast.
- Technology obsolescence, hence, is quick too.
- There is partner dependency.
- Advertising is important.
- There is adherence to product life cycle.

VISION OF THE COMPANY

The company believes in the following vision statement: "We shall be the leading Indian group with a focus on market capitalization."

MISSION OF THE COMPANY

The vision of RPG translates to the following missions:

1. Leadership in profitability and revenue growth in the chosen business.
2. Be a customer-centric organization.
3. Be the most exciting workplace.

VALUES OF THE COMPANY

- Customer sovereignty
- People orientation
- Innovation and entrepreneurship
- Transparency and integrity
- Passion for superior performance
- Anticipation
- Speed and flexibility

OBJECTIVES OF RPG

Based on the mission, vision and values of RPG, the objectives of the company can be outlined as follows:

- Obtain maximum returns
- Minimize the cost of operations
- Resolve partner issues
- Resolve data integrity issues
    - Provide one-time entry of data
    - Ensure correctness of data
    - Availability of right information to everyone, across all functions

BALANCED SCORECARD

The balanced scorecard approach (see Table 10.1) can give a much clearer understanding of the firm's current situation and how the firm should proceed in the current situation.

Table 10.1 *Four perspectives of balanced scorecard technique*

Serial Number	Weight	Objective	Metrics	Data Required
A. Financial perspective (weight = 0.3)				
1	0.4	Revenue growth	Percentage increase in annual sales.	(Change in sales)/Total sales in year T-1.
2	0.25	Cost efficiency improvement (reduction in operational costs)	Return on investment (ROI). Return on capital employed (ROCE). Quality.	Cost savings/Total cost of ownership. Percentage of defective products for each product line.
3	0.25	Asset utilization	Increase in productivity. Regularization of cash flows.	Production rates for each product line. Percentage of orders met, percentage of change in the size of orders.
4	0.10	Increase in market share	Percentage share in the market.	RPG's sales/Total estimated size of the market.
B. Customer perspective (weight = 0.2)				
1	0.3	Product availability at all times	Percentage of sales lost due to stockout.	Number of stockouts/ Number of times the inventory is replenished.
2	0.3	High quality	Percentage of defective products (as complained by customers). Percentage of customers returned by channel partners.	Customer complaints. Stocks returned to the factory.

(*Continued...*)

Table 10.1 (...*Continued*)

Serial Number	Weight	Objective	Metrics	Data Required
3	0.2	Better inventory management	Lead time.	Decrease in time taken to deliver/Total lead time.
4	0.2	SCM	Amount of inventory held.	Cost of capital invested in the inventory, in relation to percentage of lost sales.
C. Internal process perspective (weight = 0.3)				
1	0.2	Integration with suppliers	Percentage improvement in lead time and orders delivered.	Change in order delivery time. Fill rate.
2	0.2	Integration of data	Number of instances of inconsistent data across different processes/applications. Number of duplicate entries. Correctness of data. Number of times data was not available to a certain person.	Number of data mismatches, counts of erroneous data.
3	0.2	Forecasting accuracy	Percentage of forecast error.	Forecasted data by product line, actual sales data by product line.
4	0.2	Innovation	Number of new product developments. Number of new performers. Number of new partnerships.	Increase in the number of patents held by the company. Increase in new service offerings by total offerings.
5	0.2	Information transparency	Time spent in collecting data.	Percentage of time spent by individuals in looking for information.
D. Learning and growth perspective (weight = 0.2)				
1	0.5	Improve employee efficiency	Number of training hours. Training budget. Percentage of budget utilization. Revenue/employee. Cost/employee.	Training hours. Training budget. Training budget overspend/not spent. Revenue. Costs.

Serial Number	Weight	Objective	Metrics	Data Required
2	0.5	Improve employee retention	Employee satisfaction index. Number of new recruits. Employee turnover.	Employee satisfaction index by means of a survey. Number of new positions created/Total head count. Attrition ratio.

CORPORATE STRATEGY

1. Be a customer-centric company/group with strong emphasis on high-quality product and service, accurate forecasting and faster response to changing demands.
2. Become a true value supplier to customers, increase sales figures with reduction in costs and maintain healthy relationship with partners.
3. Sell as many products as possible, without having to maintain very high levels of inventory.
4. Maintain and improve market share though better CRM.
5. Improve product quality as well as continuously evolve new products and avenues for revenue growth.
6. Reduce costs through better sharing of resources and information and enhanced employee involvement.

IT STRATEGY

The corporate strategy of RPG, along with its vision, mission and values, create a very clear picture of the company's IT strategy. The IT strategy can be primarily created from the corporate strategy, although not all points from corporate strategy have a corresponding element of IT strategy (see Table 10.2).

Table 10.2 *Mapping business need with IT strategy*

Business Need	IT Strategy
1. Faster information transfer 2. Improved information availability throughout the company 3. Single data entry point (data is entered only once) 4. Avoid entry of incoherent data 5. Higher transparency across the company	Can be achieved through the implementation of an ERP.
1. Better CRM by meeting customer preferences and improving customer relationships 2. Ability to track market trends and changes in customer preferences and taste patterns	Can be achieved through the implementation of SCM and CRM (ideally they should be additional components of ERP and should 'fuse' with the ERP application).

(***Continued...***)

Table 10.2 (...*Continued*)

Business Need	IT Strategy
3. Better, improved partner relationship management through information sharing	
1. Better forecasting 2. Better data tracing 3. Improved productivity 4. Better capacity usage 5. Better resource utilization	Systems like data warehouses that allow data crunching to view aggregate data, and perform analysis. These improved processes can support the change management initiatives introduced by the management.

In the company situation discussed in the chapter, the organization has to ramp up all its information systems. It has to do a complete 'overhaul' of its IT systems to meet its IT objectives and, in turn, its corporate objectives. Considering the problems faced by the organization in terms of data transparency and information management, it is advisable for the company to go for enterprise-wide applications like ERP, which would integrate all the various elements of the company's operations. The company can also plan to implement SCM and CRM products that share the same technology as the ERP product, so that together they create a common platform for data creation and exchange.

Implementation of an ERP or any other enterprise-wide application is a mammoth task. The following issues must be taken into account before embarking on a task like an ERP implementation:

- There must be clear visualization of 'as-is' and 'to-be'.
- There must be proper formulation of strategy.
- Conduct planning of resources (financial, information, human) and proper business planning.
- Conduct proper structuring and prioritizing.
- Time of transition between the systems is the toughest time to handle, and transitions always create very difficult situations, which can sometimes severely affect a business.
- The correct method of deployment must be followed.

In the context of the company, it is important to consider the factors that would affect the implementation of the IT strategy:

1. Since RPG plans to establish itself as a global player, quicker and efficient methods of information and process handling are required.
2. Information flow must be handled in a centralized, integrated fashion. But this integration also creates a threat to data, as all the data is available at one place.
3. With an efficient IT strategy, supply chain responsiveness increases. Operating costs decrease due to less stockouts and better management of inventory. So, an efficient IT strategy will have a continuous and enlarging business impact.
4. With better information capturing, processing and analysis, challenges posed by seasonality and other demand trends can be determined.

CALCULATING THE ROI

More often than not, calculation of ROI is an extremely difficult task, and it is largely based on estimates rather than on actual data. The availability of actual data provides the ability to view the improvements in the company that take place after ERP and other associated applications are put to use.

By implementing ERP, the benefits can definitely be measured, but how can it be ensured that these benefits are originating from factors other than ERP? It is quite possible that ERP is acting only as an enabler, while the real improvements are coming from areas such as better planning and employing smarter people. In such cases, it is extremely difficult to measure a benefit and define what exactly resulted in the benefit and to what extent. ERP ROI analysis can usually be thought of as a four-step process (see Figure 10.1):

Step 1: Define the key performance indicators or key result areas that would be used to measure the success of ERP.

Step 2: Recording costs is quite a big task as the costs are often split into several different categories and are not always clearly attributable to a certain area.

Some of the common costs of a software project, especially an ERP, can be identified under the following categories:

Category: direct, one-time costs

1. Hardware and peripherals
2. Packaged and customized software costs
3. Network, peripherals, supplies and equipment
4. Initial data collection and conversion of archived data
5. Facilities upgrade, including site preparation and renovation

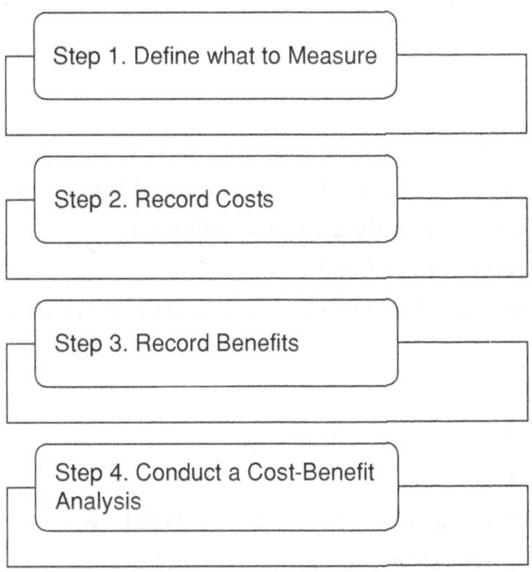

Figure 10.1 *ROI Analysis*

6. End-user project management
7. Project planning, contract negotiation, material procurement
8. Application development and deployment
9. Configuration management costs
10. Office accommodations, furniture and related items
11. Initial user training
12. Workforce adjustment for affected employees
13. Transition costs (parallel systems, converting legacy systems)
14. Quality assurance and post-implementation reviews
15. Consulting-fee expenses

Category: direct, on-going costs

1. Salaries for IT staff and the assigned user staff
2. Software maintenance, subscriptions and upgrades
3. Equipment leases
4. Facilities rental and equipment
5. Professional services
6. On-going training
7. Reviews and audits

Category: indirect, on-going costs

1. Data integrity
2. Security
3. Privacy
4. IT policy management
5. Help desk

Step 3: Record benefits

1. Cost savings due to less stock wastage
2. Reduced inventory and cost of capital invested in the inventory
3. Cost savings due to correct handling of raw materials
4. Cost savings due to reduction in head count
5. Cost savings due to proper planning of supply and hence reduction in the cost of logistics

Incremental revenues:

1. Increase in total sales
2. Increase in margins due to higher efficiency
3. Improved customer retention

Other benefits, which cannot always be quantified, are as follows:

1. Increased customer satisfaction and partner satisfaction
2. Increased customer satisfaction and stronger brand equity
3. Better feel of the market pulse
4. Higher employee satisfaction levels

Step 4:

$$\text{ROI} = \frac{\text{Net present value (NPV) of (benefits} - \text{cost)}}{\text{Total investment in the project.}}$$

MANAGEMENT INFORMATION SYSTEM (MIS) IMPLEMENTATION

An MIS for a company of this size can have thousands of data points, several hundred information creation processes and many hundred processes that are the consumers of that information. A complete listing of such processes would be very comprehensive. Some of the key information from some of the business functions, as a sample to the listing that can be generated, have been presented in Table 10.3.

Table 10.3 *Some sample metrics for MIS*

Serial Number	Metric	Publisher	Frequency
1	Inventory of finished product	Inventory manager	Weekly
2	Supply chain cycle time	Inventory manager	Monthly
3	Cost of inventory operations	Inventory manager	Annual
4	Inventory obsolescence	Inventory manager	Monthly
5	Safety stock	Inventory manager	Monthly
6	Inventory turnover ratio	Inventory manager	Quarterly
7	Gross margin return on inventory investment (GMROII)	Inventory manager	Annual
8	GMROII	Inventory manager	Annual
9	Inventory accuracy (inventory audits)	Inventory manager	Annual
10	Number of man-days required for month-end closing	Inventory manager	Quarterly
11	Number of purchase orders generated	Procurement department	Annual
12	Total volume (spending) of purchases	Procurement department	Monthly
13	Accuracy of delivery by suppliers	Procurement department	Monthly
14	Cost of purchasing as a percentage of gross sales	Procurement department	Quarterly
15	Total procured spent as a percentage of total business costs	Procurement department	Annual
16	Cost of purchasing as a percentage of gross sales	Procurement department	Annual
17	Cost of purchasing as a percentage of gross sales	Procurement department	Annual
18	Cost per quote	Sales manager	Annual
19	Create customer order costs	Sales manager	Annual
20	Closed sales year to date (YTD)	Sales manager	Annual
21	Closed sales quarter to date (QTD)	Sales manager	Quarterly
22	New business (in pipeline)	Sales manager	Monthly

(*Continued...*)

Table 10.3 (...*Continued*)

Serial Number	Metric	Publisher	Frequency
23	Key opportunities in pipeline (percentage) or dollar value	Sales manager	Monthly
24	Order conversion rate	Sales manager	Quarterly
25	Average order value	Sales manager	Annual
26	Buyer conversion rate	Sales manager	Annual
27	Revenue per customer	Sales manager	Annual
28	Lead conversion rate	Sales manager	Quarterly
29	Hit rate	Sales manager	Annual
30	Percentage of neglected opportunities	Sales manager	Annual
31	Perfect order fulfilment percentage	Sales manager	Annual
32	Sales order by FTE	Sales manager	Annual
33	Average number of new appointments generated per sales representative	Sales manager	Quarterly
34	Average customer conversion	Sales manager	Quarterly
35	Involuntary customer churn	Sales manager	Quarterly
36	Voluntary customer churn	Sales manager	Quarterly
37	Average customer lifetime value	Sales manager	Quarterly
38	Percentage of new customers	Sales manager	Quarterly
39	Percentage of repeat business turnover	Sales manager	Quarterly
40	Past due order	Sales manager	Monthly
41	Back order	Sales manager	Monthly
42	Days sales outstanding	Sales manager	Weekly
43	Order management costs	Sales manager	Monthly
44	Order receipt-to-order entry complete time	Sales manager	Monthly
45	Sales cycle time (orders)	Sales manager	Monthly
46	Category sales	Sales manager	Weekly
47	Percentage of defects	Production manager	Daily
48	Production rate	Production manager	Weekly
49	Orders received	Sales manager	weekly
50	Orders filled	Sales manager	Weekly
51	Inventory level at warehouse	Warehouse manager	Weekly
52	Number of customer complaints	Quality assurance manager	Weekly
53	Returns	Operations	Biweekly
54	Changes in revenue	Finance	Monthly
55	Changes in cost structure	Finance	Monthly
56	Profits earned	Finance	Quarterly

Similarly, there would be several data points from functions like finance, marketing, human resources, sales and distribution, etc. Table 10.3 is just a small sample of the list of metrics for MIS. The entire exhaustive list can contain several hundred objects.

CONCLUSION

A good corporate strategy is able to provide all the stakeholders of a firm with the results that they need. A strategy can be deemed successful when it can get "the right information to the right person at the right time". In real-life situations, satisfying this statement becomes quite a challenge, as meeting all the three criteria at the same time is very difficult. Companies tend to falter on one or more of the criteria, and the long-term implications of these failures are huge. Hence, it is very important that firms give adequate importance to planning and defining a proper road map for their corporate strategy. A well-defined strategy can drastically change the way the operations of a company are handled, and the benefits can be far reaching. Just like any other project, proper planning and forward thinking can save considerable effort and money, and many a time this becomes the differentiating factor between a successful project and a project that is termed a failure. As companies realize the importance of systematic and scientific approach for strategy in the success of the company, balanced scorecard as a tool is getting more importance in the overall planning in the company. And many a time balanced scorecard takes the centre stage in the entire planning exercise of a company. Although it is believed to be just an enabler, balanced scorecard can contribute far more in certain situations.

DISCUSSION QUESTIONS

1. How do the vision, mission and corporate objectives of a company help in the design of its MIS?
2. Why is it important to take care of the objectives of each and every stakeholder?
3. How should MIS be used for taking quick and correct decisions?

BIBLIOGRAPHY

1. http://www.rpggroup.com/, 2009.
2. www.rpgnet.com, 2009.
3. www.rpgplanet.com, 2009.

11

Case Study on Tata Sky: Strategic Advantage Through Technology

INTRODUCTION

Direct-to-home (DTH) service involves the transmission of programmes via satellite to individual homes where personal dish antenna is installed for the reception of signals. This technology does away with the cable operator as a medium between mass broadcaster and viewers of programmes. Due to the advantages of DTH such as doing away with middlemen, that is, the cable operator, and absence of the need for cables covering the last mile, DTH is able to reach even the remote corners of the world. It also allows more channels to be beamed. In India cable transmission is still analogue, so DTH offers better-quality pictures and stereophonic sound. DTH also allows interactive TV services like email, videoconferencing, Internet access and movie-on-demand. Broadcasters show preference for DTH as it reveals actual TV programme viewers, which is usually underreported by the cable operator.

The DTH network consists of a broadcasting station, satellite, encoders, multiplexers, modulators and the receiver. The service provider leases Ku-band transponders on the satellite. Video, audio and data signals are converted by an encoder to the digital format and mixed by a multiplexer. The viewer uses a small dish antenna, which can be as small as 45 cm in diameter, and a set-top box (STB) to decode the encrypted transmission and view a number of channels.

DTH services have been allowed in India since 2001. There is a licence fee, and there are restrictions like a foreign equity cap of 49 per cent. The first DTH service was Dish TV, which was launched in 2003 by the Essel Group, the owner of Zee telefilms. The government-owned DD+ Direct from Doordarshan was launched in 2004. In 2005, DTH licences were given to four companies: Tata Sky, an 80:20 joint venture between the Tata and Star groups, Sun Direct from Kalanidhi Maran's Sun TV and Reliance. One pattern that is seen the world over is that there is a huge first-mover advantage between technologies in this industry. India already has the cable system and hence DTH has an uphill task in finding acceptance initially. The reverse has happened in Europe where DTH had developed before cable and currently holds 80 per cent of the total satellite TV programme subscriptions. In the United States, though, as cable had come first it dominates over DTH. In India, DTH is making inroads into the rural and remote areas where cable has not yet reached, as well as among niche urban homes where interactive innovative content is in demand. Apart from the service providers mentioned earlier, there are other DTH service providers in the country today like Airtel and Videocon.

INDUSTRY ANALYSIS

A feature of the DTH service in India is that although all service providers are reporting losses, new players are regularly entering the fray. Dish TV reported a loss of Rs 413 crore in 2007–08 and a loss of Rs 200 crore one year before, in 2006–07. Tata Sky showed a loss of Rs 1,100 crore in 2007–08 and a loss of Rs 886 crore one year earlier, in 2006–07. Sun Direct expects to lose Rs 200 crore from 2005–10. Some observers have labelled the sector as 'direct to loss TV'!

The reason why new entrants find the sector attractive despite its propensity to create losses is the very high potential promised by the **sector**, even if it takes a minimum of five to six years to break even. The potential market for DTH is **high** and totals 71 million households. This is too big an opportunity to ignore. As there are many players in the market now, they are competing in offering innovative packages and interactive content. A challenge for the sector is the rapid development of technology. In the future, DTH will face string competition from Internet Protocol TV (IPTV) and mobile TV, although the current threat from these areas is not that high.

ENVIRONMENTAL ANALYSIS

Based on Figure 11.1, the environmental analysis of the DTH industry is discussed in the sub-sections of this section.

Bargaining Power of Supplier—Very High

DTH relies on three major suppliers: customer premise equipment (CPE)—satellite dish, STB and access card, and Ku-band transponder and content.

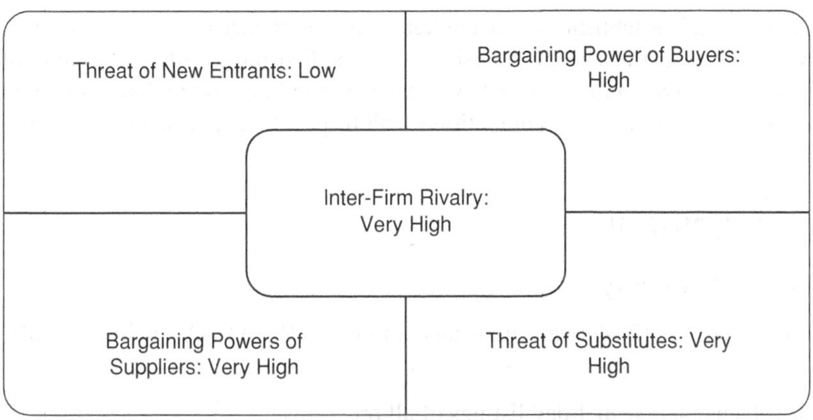

Figure 11.1 *Environment Analysis for the DTH Industry*

The bargaining power of DTH operators with CPE suppliers has increased due to supply. Transponder is provided by Astrix, Indian Space Research Organization (ISRO); hence dependency exists, and due to there being no regulations regarding channel pricing DTH operators are at the mercy of broadcasters.

Bargaining Power of Buyer—High

Consumer has the power to choose in this industry as different providers offer a variety of services. Unless players can differentiate themselves from the competition, the market will remain mostly homogeneous. Customers will have high bargaining power and be influenced by costs versus services.

Threat of Substitutes—Very High

DTH services face major competition from terrestrial TV, cable TV and IPTV. Doordarshan is the world's largest terrestrial broadcaster with over 1,400 transmitters, covering 88 per cent of India's geographical area. They offer digital services in collaboration with BBC resources. This wide reach and low-cost approach are offset by its lack of attractive content.

Cable TV operates in two modes: CAS<Metros> and IPTV, which requires a separate STB and non-addressable system. Its cost varies from Rs 100 to Rs 350 depending upon the location. Because local cable operators will lose out to DTH operators there is bound to be resistance from local cable operators.

IPTV is a service where television signals are digitally sent over telecommunications lines. Mahanagar Telecom Nigam Ltd. (MTNL) and Bharat Sanchar Nigam Ltd. (BSNL) plan to tap these lines. Even with strict regulations (not yet enforced), it is a considerable threat due to its new level of interactivity.

Threat of New Entrants—Low

With there being already seven players in the DTH space, threat posed by new entrants is relatively low due to the presence of enough competition. Getting a licence is relatively easier but issues related to pricing of CPE and getting required transponders are quite challenging. Also, first-mover advantage exists in this industry.

Competitive Rivalry—Very High

With seven players already established in the market, inter-firm rivalry is intense. DD offers free service but has a very small bouquet of channels. Dish TV has the first-mover advantage and holds the highest market share. New players in the sector have very big brand names and have started their business with extensive publicity. There is also competition with respect to acquiring content. Further, there are regional discrepancies.

COMPANY OVERVIEW

Offerings from Tata Sky

Tata Sky has leased all its 12 Ku-band transponders on the INSAT 4A satellite. Its offerings to the customer are

- More than 160 channels with 4-day listings of all programs.
- Interactive series, which includes Active Stories, Active Games and Active Darshan.

- Offers options like guide, parental control, search and scan banner and favourites.
- Tata Sky + is the newest offering from the stables of Tata Sky, which allows its viewers to pause, record and rewind live TV.
- Whereas Tata Sky basic starts at Rs 2,499 + channel packages, Tata Sky + starts at Rs 9,999 + channel packages.

Vision of Tata Sky

- Connecting every television home
- Empowering every television viewer and revolutionizing home entertainment

Mission of Tata Sky

- Tata Sky aims to revolutionize Indian home entertainment by offering superior digital versatile disc (DVD)-quality picture and compact disc (CD)-quality sound.

STRATEGY OF TATA SKY

Tata Sky's target customers include people from various strata of the society, with different service packages available to each person. To improve its performance in the competitive DTH market, the Tata Sky management should assess the company's brand positioning in its target segment by establishing a distinctive image for itself compared to its competitors. But these initiatives present challenges, which Tata Sky is facing currently, caused by rising costs, the sporadic nature of demand and the relentless downward pricing pressure due to competition. Adding to these challenges, slackening of demand and higher interest rates are not welcome signs. With these in mind, Tata Sky should try to become fast paced and highly competitive. To counter these challenges and still be profitable, various strategies have been suggested based on what will suit the demands of Indian market and its consumer behaviour to increase Tata Sky's market share.

CURRENT SITUATION

- Tata Sky crossed the two-million connections mark in a period of 20 months, achieving its position as the fastest-growing DTH service provider across the globe.
- The *marketing budget of Tata Sky in the beginning* was 15 per cent of sales. This included around 5 per cent for advertisements, 7 per cent for discounts and promotions, and 1 per cent for sponsorships.
- Recently, Tata Sky roped in Aamir Khan (Bollywood actor) as its brand ambassador. Aamir Khan would feature in all of Tata Sky's brand and product communications, including advertisements in TV, print and radio.
- Further, tie-ups with ITC's e-Choupal and Godrej Aadhar give Tata Sky a wider rural reach. Also, for its distribution Tata Sky has a tie-up with ITC's international business division.
- The Web site www.24X7 guru.com has joined hands with Tata Sky to provide content for active learning.
- Tata Sky has adopted a 360° marketing campaign approach that encapsulates television, print, outdoor and radio along with on-ground activities and marketing on the digital platform.

- Tata Sky plans to enter into tie-ups with Sony Pictures and Fox Entertainment for content, with pay-per-view service for exclusive events.

Company Target

Tata Sky hopes to have about eight million connections by 2012.

STRENGTHS, WEAKNESSES, OPPORTUNITIES AND THREATS (SWOT) ANALYSIS

- Strengths
  - Leveraging on the brand TATA and high brand recall
  - Technological expertise with Newscorp's DTH arm SKY
  - Superior picture quality
  - Customer service
  - Rural penetration through ITC's e-Choupal and Godrej Aadhar
  - Interactive channels and program guides
  - Innovative product offerings
- Weaknesses
  - Second mover after Dish TV, which has higher market share
  - Cannot match free service like that offered by DD
  - Currently does not offer free STBs like Dish TV
  - Litigation issues in the court of law
  - Dependency on broadcasters; previously had issues with Sun TV
- Opportunities
  - Larger disposable incomes with India
  - Tapping niche markets with better service and product offerings
  - Expansion of the distribution network through exclusive stores
  - Interactive advertising—tie-up with Samsung
  - Increase in the number of TVs sold
  - Increase in geographical boundaries and untapped rural market
  - Growing demand for quality of service in the form of DTH over cable
  - CAS being made compulsory would encourage switch from cable to DTH
  - *Value-added services* (VASs) gaining steam
  - Cap on foreign direct investment (FDI) increased from 49 to 74 per cent
  - Reduction in licence fee from 10 to 6 per cent
- Threats
  - IPTV will provide superior technology if implemented
  - Cable STBs provide easy switching due to negligible switching costs
  - Increasing internal competition
  - Dependency on CPE suppliers to some extent
  - High dependence for transponders on ISRO
  - Dependency on broadcasters for channel content, which results in increased cost

- Videocon may enter the DTH sector by building its own STBs
- No exclusivity in content and prevalence of the rule of 'must carry'
- Interoperability regulations

PARAMETERS FOR BENCHMARKING

As a DTH operator, Tata Sky can use the following parameters for the purpose of benchmarking:

- Service-level agreement (SLA)
- Customer service
- Technology
- Number of channels
- Hardware

A few pointers must be mentioned:

- In the technology front, Tata Sky should be looking at MPEG4 technology, which is currently provided only by Reliance Big TV in India. MPEG4 not only gives better picture and sound quality but also increases the number of channels an operator can offer.
- In addition, offering IPTV is a good option; in this way Tata Sky will not just offer television services over the Internet but will be in a position to offer Web services and voice over IP too. IPTV will enable Tata Sky to target corporate houses, because of its ability to provide television content over corporate LANs.
- Telecom Regulatory Authority of India (TRAI) regulations currently state that there would be no exclusivity as far as channels are concerned, that is, all the channels will be available to all the operators, but as the DTH market gets bigger and more mature the clause of exclusivity might come in. Tata Sky should look forward to getting exclusive rights to niche channels.
- Try and reduce the price of procuring STBs and pass on the benefits to the customer.
- Increasing the number of channels as compared to competition would give an edge to Tata Sky. Currently, it provides lesser number of channels than Dish TV.

DISTRIBUTION NETWORK

Regarding the distribution network of Tata Sky we can safely conclude that it has the highest penetration in India. Through its tie-up with ITC's e-Choupal, Tata Sky has been able to reach out to the rural parts of India and it can leverage this reach to a greater extent by introducing cheaper packages for the villages. Including the local cable operators as distributors would be an extremely useful way of reaching out to the target market:

- Staff of cable operators to be made the distributors for Tata Sky (due to their familiarity with people)
- All distributors to be given the status of Tata Sky employees (due to the stakeholders' involvement)

Another focus could be the rural market. A snapshot of the rural market is as follows:

- 199 million total households in India out of which 119 million are (60 per cent of total households) TV households

- 55 million TV sets in rural areas
- Rural TV households growing by—three to four million each year, but only 2 to 3 per cent of the rural households have access to cable
- Growing focus towards more satellite channels

Strategies for the rural sector can be as follows:

- Customizing offerings.
- Offering combinations of various national channels and regional channels.
- Offering educational packages.
- Appointing the village head as the distributor and promoter, as villagers tend to listen to their village head.
- This can be supplemented by giving the connection for free to the village head initially.

Another avenue that can be explored is setting up mini-theatres in class B towns:

- Setting up mini-theatres in the rural sector to promote products.
- Conducting events like cricket matches, movies, etc.
- These mini-theatres can be the points of sales for Tata Sky.

Figure 11.2 is explained as follows:

- The Tata Sky logistics/commercial department sends the CPEs to the distributors who, in turn, send them to the dealers.
- The dealer sells and installs the equipment at the consumer premises and collects the first subscription.
- At the same time, the dealer sends a request for the activation of services at the customer premises and remits the first subscription. Thereafter, the customer contact centre deals with and takes

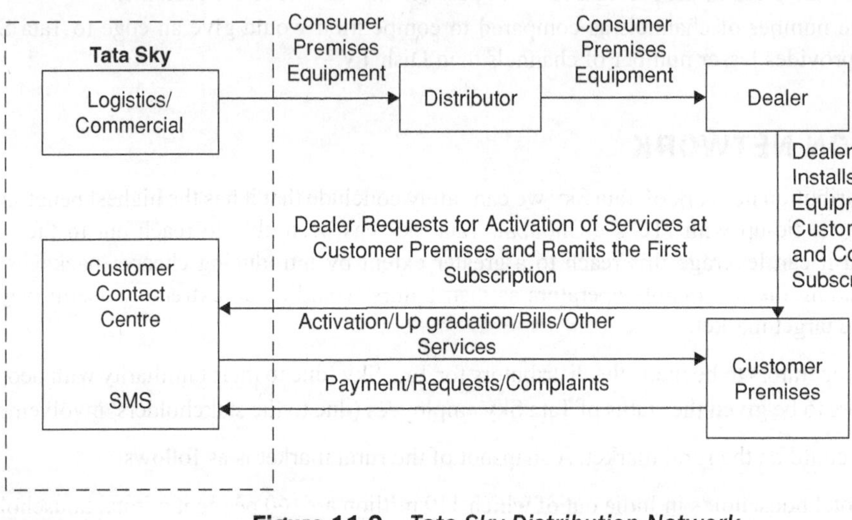

Figure 11.2 *Tata Sky Distribution Network*

care of the customer, right from providing VASs to the regulation of payments and handling of complaints.

CORPORATE STRATEGY

The corporate strategy is as follows: "To focus on best service delivery to customers by focusing on right technology implementation at the right time."

FACTORS AFFECTING THE IT STRATEGY OF TATA SKY

The following are the factors that affect the IT strategy of Tata Sky:

- *Business goals*—Goal setting will allow Tata Sky to be proactive, instead of being just reactive. Different units would need to be aligned for the achievement of the sub-goals. For Tata Sky, the two business goals that are important are
  - To reduce cost: The strategy will be to enhance efficiencies through cost reduction.
  - Automate all processes to enhance productivity: Technology will be used to enhance the productivity of people and processes.
- *Marketing*—The marketing of services provided is an important function of the organization, and technology can play a vital role in the enhancement of this feature.
  - To retain existing customers: Expansion always occurs when the base is retained. Efforts have to be made to ensure that growth is achieved not at the expense of existing customers.
  - To add new customers: The growth of the base of new customers is vital. The demand from existing customers coupled with increased demand from new customers will ensure the sustainability of the service.
  - Keep delivering the brand promise: Brand is an effervescent phenomena that will help in the sustenance and continuity of a business towards achievement of the goals of the business. The brand with it brings trust, respect and a bond that will be valued by both current and prospective customers. This is certainly an important fact to observe.
- *Service quality*—It being the service industry, the quality of service in this segment is one of the keys to charge premium and differentiate its service from that of its competitors.
  - Adherence to SLAs.
  - Minimizing customer complaints and grievances to retain customers and attract new customers.
- *Customer*—Enable and empower customers with innovative features that can be provided apart from the normal services provided by everyone in the market.
- *Partners*—Effective and long-term collaboration with partners in terms of technology is required.

IT STRATEGY FOR TATA SKY

- Automate all the processes according to a priority.
- Increase the number of best-quality interactive services provided to the consumer.
- Address complaints and grievances online, and adhere to SLA.

- Align all the IT services to ensure the right information flow from marketing, sales and operations through enterprise resource planning (ERP), customer relationship management (CRM) and Data Warehousing (DW) to enable business intelligence (BI).
- Train employees to make use of IT resources.
- Benchmark IT processes, and apply for international certifications.

Technology Partners

To get strategic advantage over competition, the organization has partnered with leading technology suppliers in the fields of digital technology and satellite television services. It uses the services of the INSAT 4A satellite, which was launched by India, and has taken lease for all 12 Ku-band transponders. This has given it an edge over its competitors as high quality of uninterrupted transmission can be provided for all its subscribers. All the channels beamed by Tata Sky have an edge over those beamed by others in terms of audio and picture quality.

Tata Sky has also implemented several decision support systems for taking faster and effective decisions. It has implemented a software developed by www.nds.com (NDS) for pay televisions. End-to-end architecture has been implemented, which helps nationwide customers to watch channels and pay for the movies they see (read purchase) through these channels. The conditional access system software developed by NDS has enabled Tata Sky to offer multiple programmes at multiple price packages. Similarly, software from Siebel has been able to support operations across the areas of call centres and field service, customer order management and product configuration. For residential and commercial customers, Comverse's Kenan FX billing software has been selected to support billing. Finally, all the software applications have been integrated with SAP, the leading ERP application suite. The modules that have been selected for implementation are materials management, sales and distribution, finance and control, and human resources (HR).

IT Infrastructure *Sun Microsystems*: Tata Sky has selected Sun Microsystems to provide world-class technology infrastructure, which helps the company to maintain a high level of service standards for its satellite television service.

Digicomp: Tata Sky has partnered with Thomson and Humax, world leaders in digital broadcasting technology, for building top-of-the line digicomps customized specifically for Indian markets. The technology's feature-rich design enables Tata Sky to deliver multiple programming and pricing packages and interactive services to its customers.

Systems Integration Partner for Tata Sky *Tata Consultancy Services* (TCS) is a systems integration partner for Tata Sky Ltd. It supports IT operations in the areas of billing, ERP, and other customer care and employee–related internal facing applications.

Service Support for Tata Sky *SerWizSol* provides Tata Sky with three high-end call centres, which offer round-the-clock support in 11 different languages at Pune (Maharashtra), Hyderabad (Andhra Pradesh) and Mohali (Punjab).

ROLES AND RESPONSIBILITIES OF CHIEF INFORMATION OFFICER (CIO)

The roles and responsibilities of a CIO can be stated as follows:

- CIOs must evaluate the overall operations of computing and IT functions and recommend enhancements.

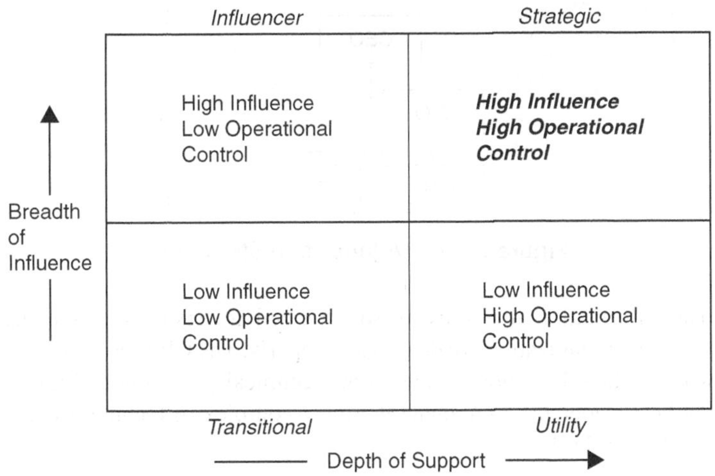

Figure 11.3 *CIO Roles and Responsibilities*

- CIOs must advise senior management on strategic systems conversions and integrations in support of business goals and objectives.
- They must prepare enterprise objectives and budgets to facilitate the orderly and efficient capture, storage, processing and dissemination of information.
- They must interact with company managers on internal and external operations that are impacted by the capture, storage, processing and dissemination of information.

The qualities expected in a CIO include the following:

- A CIO should be a business visionary.
- CIOs must help business executives to understand and appreciate the challenges of enabling IT for new business models.
- They should anticipate and implement the required changes (short term and long term), and not simply react to them.
- They should understand and effectively manage business risk.

The source of the analysis shown in Figure 11.3 is Gartner Inc. (2003, www.gartner.com). We see two axes (breadth of control and depth of support) and two quadrants (see Figure 11.3). Think of this rectangle as a national map; states that would be positioned along the top line of the rectangle have CIOs with very high influence. The states positioned along the extreme right of the rectangle are states where CIOs have high control over IT operations. The analysis has also created four quadrants—upper left (influencer), upper right (strategic), lower left (transitional) and lower right (utility) in Figure 11.3. In our opinion, the roles and responsibilities of CIOs should be placed in the extreme left corner with high influence and high operational control.

ORGANIZATION STRUCTURE

How the information hierarchy of Tata Sky should be organized so that the company gets the best out of it is a debatable topic. The proposal for a restructure in the company's information hierarchy can be thought about. The CEO being in the top should be assisted by a team of CIOs and two

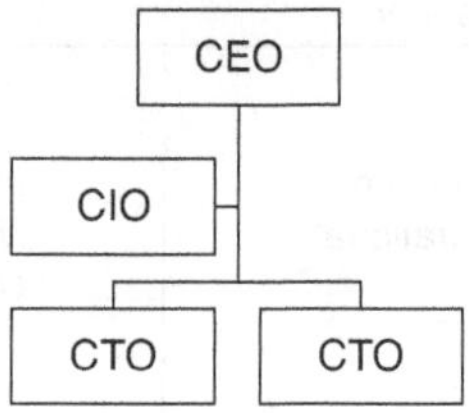

Figure 11.4 *Organization Structure*

reporting CTOs. The information hierarchy is so arranged to ensure that the various technology implementations across the organization are dealt with properly. The CIO should have vast experience in implementations, whereas the CTOs should come from a technical background. With such a combination, Tata Sky can get the best leadership to manage the most complex of technology implementations for business benefits (see Figure 11.4).

IMPLEMENTATION

Tata Sky's implementation strategy would include the consolidation of different implementations, such as ERP and CRM packages. Let us begin with business process inter-mapping. Implementing BI would be a major step for Tata Sky to undertake. The major agendas under this step would be

- Integration with ERP
- Integration with Seibel and other software
- ELT—data transformation tool

The implementation of a global data warehouse will be the focus on which the company plans to go ahead. Initially, there will be enterprise warehouses for each application. Then they can all be integrated into a global data warehouse.

ROADMAP

- Take a relook at the business processes: 6 months
- Implementation of enterprise data warehouse (EDH): 6–8 months
- Integration of other applications with BI: 1–1.5 years

IMPLEMENTATION APPROACH

The approach that has been followed for the case study can be divided into three components, as summarized in Figure 11.5:

Globalization: This component reflects the global opportunities that Tata Sky can make use of. The competition from different sources can be reflected here.

IT Evolution: With the evolution of IT, the organization needs to use technology to get maximum business benefits from the same. The company has planned to implement the BI suite to facilitate and integrate the different technology applications currently used by Tata Sky to render its services.

Figure 11.5 *Implementation Approach*

Tata Sky Services: Tata Sky services stand for quality, efficiency and compliance to customer satisfaction. The company proposes to implement Information Technology (IT) by understanding the business metrics powered by information systems.

BUSINESS INTELLIGENCE

Business intelligence (BI) refers to skills, knowledge, technologies, applications and practices used to help a business to acquire a better understanding of the market behaviour and business context. For this purpose it employs collection, integration, analysis, interpretation and presentation of business information. In simplified meaning it may refer to the collected information itself or the explicit knowledge developed from the information.

BI applications provide historical, current, and predictive views of business operations, most often using data that has been gathered into a data warehouse or a data mart and occasionally working from operational data. Software elements support the use of this information by assisting in the extraction, analysis, and reporting of information. Common functionality of Business Intelligence Applications includes Reporting, OLAP, Analytics, Dashboards, Scorecards, Data Mining, Corporate Performance Management (CPM) and Predictive Analysis (Figure 11.6).

Figure 11.6 presents the business analytics used in BI:

Top-line growth: Demand analysis is followed by external analysis, marketing analysis and customer analysis. All these belong to top-line growth.

Balancing act: Forecasts and plans refer to bottom-line cost.

Bottom-line costs: Supply analysis refers to the costs that comprise the bottom-line costs. Supplier analysis, service or product quality analysis and warranty analysis all belong to bottom-line costs.

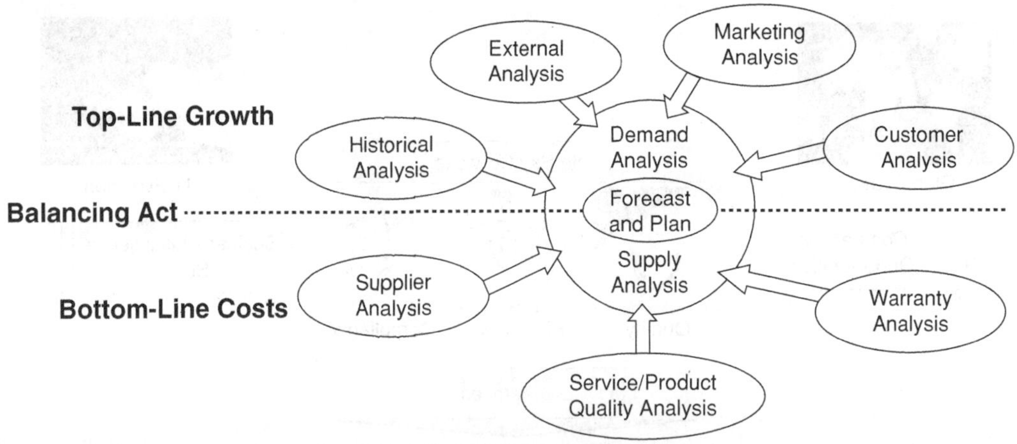

Figure 11.6 *Business Analytics in BI*

The ideal goal of planning and forecasting in any organization is to balance the demand side with the supply side:

- BI is an integral part of planning and forecasting.
- It is possible to gain sustainable competitive advantage with BI.
- The plan delivers this capability via its integrated BI stack.

ARCHITECHTURE

Let us take a look at the enterprise architecture of the warehouse model followed by the Tata Sky (see Figure 11.7). The flow of information is as follows:

Data → information → knowledge → decision

Data is derived from various external sources, which include legacy applications, spreadsheets, operations data or other external sources. The data is processed in the EDH, which is fine-tuned to derive information. The decision-making phase is when the business users interact with the EDH.

A COMPONENT-BASED ARCHITECHTURE

In terms of implementation, a 'big bang' approach is risky in general. SAP/BW as the Globally Distributed Work (GDW) focus does not make sense, whether big bang or not. ERP can be only a part of the picture. Estimates show that 25 to 30 per cent of all analytic data come from SAP/R3. The real-time analytics needs of the supply chain and some manufacturing plants present a particular challenge. It is needed to avoid over-architecting while still meeting the business mission.

The proposed architecture (see Figure 11.8) consists of several EDHs connected by a single global data warehouse. The different IT partners of Tata Sky can all connect to their respective warehouses (EDHs) from where the global warehouse can be linked. There will be data transformation tools in between, which will be responsible for the proper transformation of data.

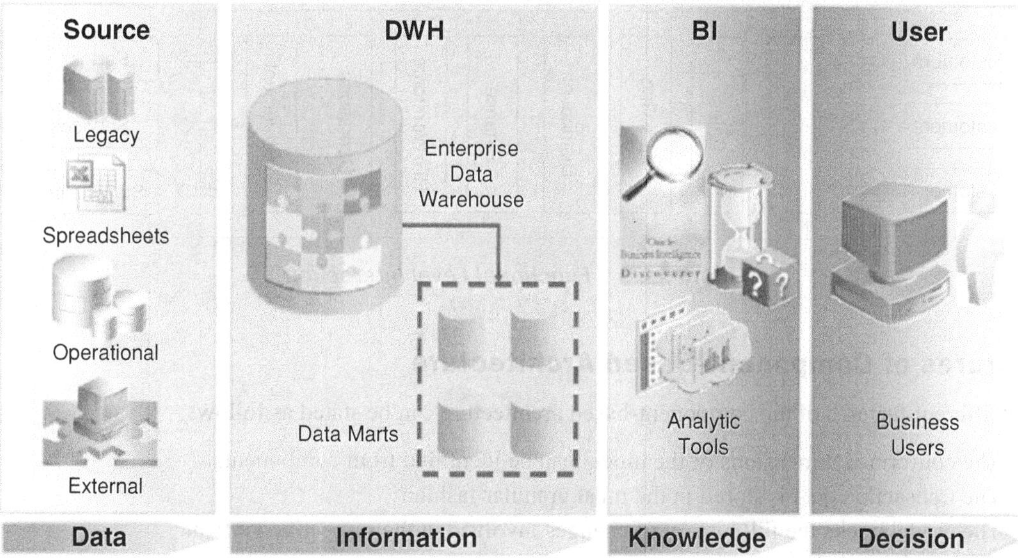

Figure 11.7 *Architecture for Warehouse Model*

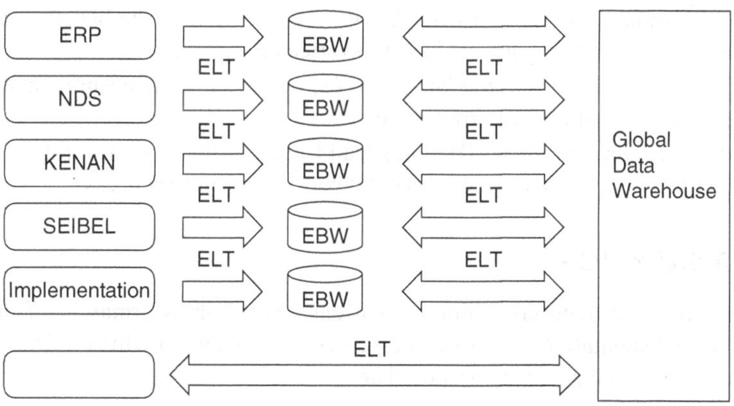

Figure 11.8 *Component-Based Architecture*

Let us understand the entire proposed structure in greater detail. We plan to align the entire structure along the lines of functional levels (Figure 11.9). The data will be imported from a management information system (MIS), which had been designed based on functional expertise. The inputs to the system will be given by partners, services and stakeholders, whereas the outputs will affect the customers. The business analytics will be evaluated based on different verticals like services, sales and marketing, distribution, finance, HR and so on.

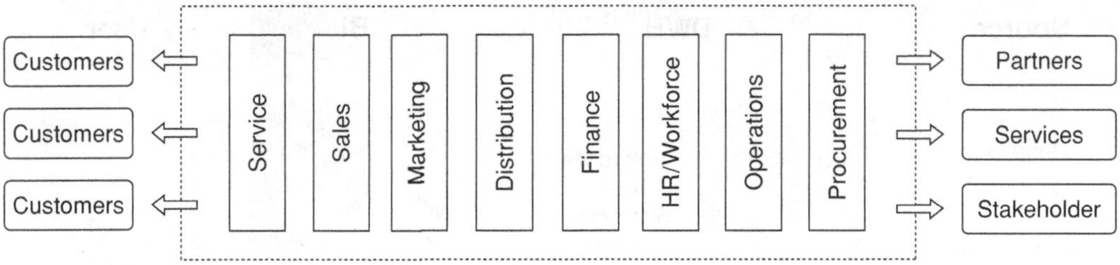

Figure 11.9 *Functional Level Interaction*

Features of Component-Based Architecture

The different features of the component-based architecture can be stated as follows:

- The conformed dimensions of the model can be identified from components.
- The transaction data is stored in the most granular fashion.
- The model tracks the full history of changes involved in the respective vertical.
- This model is prebuilt and is extensible in purpose.
- This model has been proposed keeping performance speed in mind.

Benefits of Component-Based Architecture

- *Enterprise-wide business analysis (across the entire value chain)*: The benefits can be felt across the entire business. The entire value chain will be affected.
- *Access summary metrics or drill to the lowest level of detail*: This will ensure that the firm manages to handle the issues even at the grassroots level.
- *Accurate historical representations*: BI suites lead to one of the most accurate representations of data. Proper maintenance of data warehouses is a part of the entire process.

BUSINESS ANALYTICS

Analytics basically refers to data crunching, which ensures the transformation of business insights into processes and implementations. There could be several streams in which a firm applies business analytics. The common ones that can be proposed are

- Financial analytics
- Marketing analytics
- Sales analytics
- Distribution analytics
- HR analytics
- Services analytics

Services Analytics—A Sample Case

Services analytics can be considered as a sample case to determine how a firm derives business benefit from a proposed structure.

The service metrics are as follows:

- Complaints 20 per cent
- SLA and adherences 20 per cent
- Technical problems 15 per cent
- Pricing vis-à-vis competition 20 per cent
- VAS 25 per cent

The different metrics assigned to each of the aforementioned parameters can be stated as follows:-
To determine the service-level efficiency:

$$x = 0.2 \times (\text{Complaints}) + 0.20 \times (\text{SLA}) + 0.15 \times (\text{Technical problems}) + 0.20 \times (\text{Pricing}) + 0.25\,(\text{VASs})$$

Now, this equation states that the variable x is dependent on a number of variables, namely, complaints, SLA, technical problems, pricing and VASs. We have already allocated weights based on which we get the final value. Based on the score, we can rate the service level in some particular zone:

If $3 < x < 4.5$, green
If $2 < x < 3$, yellow
If $0 < x < 2$, red

Based on the different points allocated to each of the parameters, we can get the values of customer service factors. If a value lies within 3 to 4.5, green mode is activated, which indicates high services ratings. Similarly, red region signifies a low in services ratings.

RISK MANAGEMENT

- Risk management
- Risk analysis
- Risk evaluation
- Development of mitigation plans

Risk management is the name given to a logical and systematic method of identifying, analysing, treating and monitoring the risks involved in any activity or process. Risk management is a methodology that helps managers makes best use of their available resources. Effective risk management is a recognized and valued skill. Risk management is now an integral part of business planning. The risk management process steps are a generic guide for any organization, regardless of the type of business, activity or function.

Establish the context, identify the risks, analyze the risks, evaluate the risks, treat the risks, monitoring and review, and communication and consultation.

Establish the context—The strategic and organizational context in which risk management will take place: for example, the nature of the business, the risks inherent in one's business and priorities.

It tries to match customers' needs with the resources available. (as shown in Figure 11.10).

Responsibilities must be allocated:

- Appoint a risk management champion with appropriate qualifications, including relevant experience and analytical skills.
- Form a risk management committee, comprising representatives of operational areas.
- Conduct risk management workshops.
- Determine operating procedures.

Sources of information for risk assessments are as follows:

1. Identify control risks: for example, high duty rates or quantity controls and the demand for certain services.
2. Research existing databases and records on customer histories.

- Evaluate current procedures to identify potential control weaknesses.
- Evaluate the risks.
- Evaluate the likelihood of occurrence of a risk event:
    - Almost certain
    - Likely
    - Moderate
    - Unlikely
    - Rare

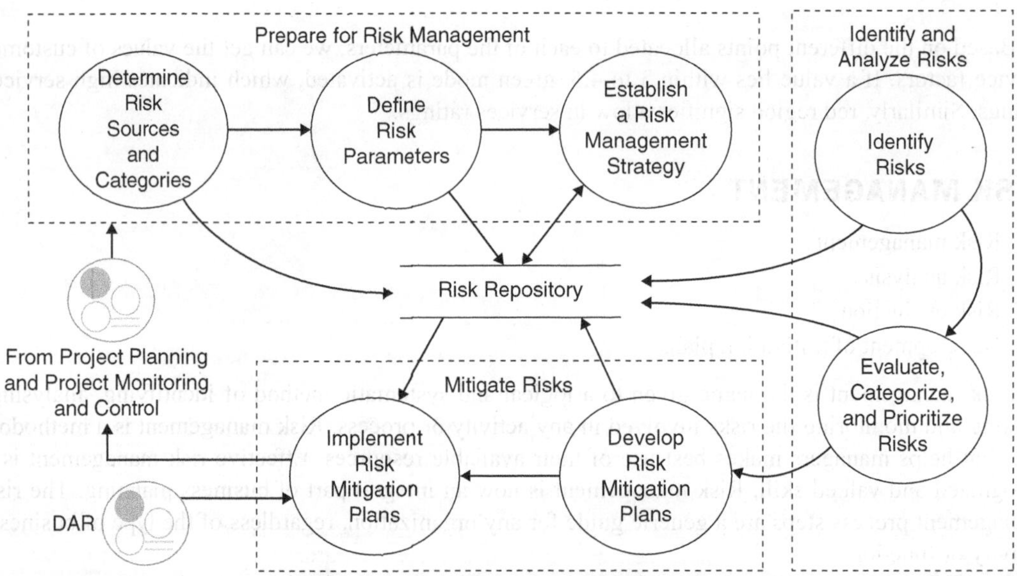

Figure 11.10 *Risk Management in Tata Sky*

Monitor and Review

The initial assessment made regarding the existence of risks and the level of risks must be evaluated on a regular basis. The effectiveness of risk profiles needs to be measured and updated as necessary. Reliable reporting of examination results is required. Compliance measurement activities must be done. Feedback from the business community is sought. Then, results analysis and data comparisons are conducted.

Using Risk Management

The starting point is the action plan:

1. Allocate responsibilities: for example, a risk management champion and a working party.
2. Evaluate how risk management processes can be best applied in your natural environment.
3. Survey existing skills and perform training needs assessment.
4. Catalogue existing sources of data or information that can help in identifying risks.
5. Flowchart existing processes.
6. Communicate and consult with custom's department, other agencies, the trading community and the transport industry.
7. Obtain IT tools, or set up processes for effectively operating a selectivity system.
8. Provide training in profiling/selectivity skills.
9. Test and gain confidence in the risk management process.

RECOMMENDATIONS

Presently, the local data warehouse handles most of the internal operations for the corresponding office. We strongly recommend that this be changed to a centralized architecture, as in establishing a central data warehouse having more control over regional warehouses. The benefits of having a centralized server architecture over the present system are as follows:

- *Ability to centralize information and security*: A centralized server infrastructure helps businesses to protect and access critical business information and stay connected to their customers. With the right server technology in place, owners can concentrate on taking their businesses to the next level.
- *Enhanced data security and reliability*: It prevents data loss by automatically backing up company information. With the right server, employees can easily retrieve accidentally deleted files and restore previous versions of files. It also protects the business and prevents any loss of productivity with a secure infrastructure, including built-in firewalls and password protection.
- *Ability to centralize information*: The company can take advantage of central data storage so that employees can easily share information and work together more efficiently and cost-effectively. Business information can be accessed away from the office, on a PC with an Internet connection or a Windows Mobile®-powered device.

CONCLUSION

This case study was tested in the classroom and was a great learning experience, especially regarding the practical application of the strategic management theories learnt in the classroom. We did not find any major flaws within the system in place to come up with any major recommendations. As a client, Tata Sky is very satisfied with its present system and does not have any major complaints with respect to the IT Strategy in place. The only flaw in the firm's approach is that it is not looking for ways in which it can better utilize its existing infrastructure as per the latest technology. Although financial considerations could be a reason, instead of satisfying only the needs, the firm should be concerned about how to make the present working strategy more efficient in terms of the effective use of prevalent technology, especially when the vendor has the capability to provide it. Integration is the need of the hour and it must respond to it.

DISCUSSION QUESTIONS

1. Explain the differences between SWOT analysis and benchmarking techniques.
2. What are the characteristics of the DTH industry?
3. How can an organization differentiate itself from its competition using technology-enabled strategy?

BIBLIOGRAPHY

1. http://www.tatasky.com, 2007.
2. http://broadbandforum.in/tata-sky-dth, 2007.
3. www.indiabroadband.net/tata-sky, 2007.

12

CASE STUDY ON ICICI BANK: LEADERSHIP IN RETAIL BANKING THROUGH TECHNOLOGY ADOPTION

INTRODUCTION

In the 1990s, Indian industry was liberated from 'licence raj' with the introduction of new measures and policies. The financial reforms introduced at the time ushered in globalization, and a completely new environment was seen in the banking sector. Whereas earlier the banks had been operating in a protected environment, they were now competing against each other with private players jumping into the fight. Foreign investment in the banking sector was now allowed and, as a result, Indian market saw the sudden entry of a number of foreign players in the banking and financial institutions segment. This required the banks to scale up their operations without diluting their quality of service. Consistency and predictability became the keys to success in the banking industry. Unless state-of-the-art IT was introduced as early as possible, winning new businesses and even holding on to the old ones was becoming increasingly difficult. With concepts such as 'anywhere banking' and 'telebanking' being introduced along with Internet banking, automation in banking operations was becoming a must. A combination of regulatory and competitive reasons led to an increase in the importance of total banking automation in the Indian banking industry.

INDUSTRY OVERVIEW

In the last one decade, banks all around the world have operated in an environment of major and minor changes and have to a large extent shown an ability to transform themselves to keep up with the evolving and growing environment. Consolidation is also moving ahead where cross-border mergers and acquisitions are creating ever larger financial institutions. Globalization remains a basic concern, with the growing importance of offshoring and the continuous need to expand into new markets. This is necessary not only to keep one jump ahead of competition but also to take advantage of the new opportunities of these emerging markets. In India alone, the growing middle-class population adds 22 million new customers every year, and in 2010 the number of middle-class customers reached 250 million. China's growing market is expected to create a credit card market of some 75 million population by 2010. It is a world where banks are reshaping themselves to succeed and where they need to keep on doing so to create a profitable future. To succeed, banks need to understand the fundamental industry trends and to have the management stability to execute their chosen course of action. The global banking industry has been continuously focusing on the following issues:

- Consolidation
- Implementation of Basel II norms
- Risk management
- Credit quality and management of distressed assets
- Corporate governance
- Technology
- Funding the economic growth with inclusion
- Creating global brands
- KYC norms and anti–money laundering

Banks in the current scenario not only need to cater to their existing clients but also make sure that their services are ready to meet the challenges posed by new clients and at the same time improve their profitability in the market. In the present day, the banking industry is going through a major downturn. The crisis occurred when Indian banks were in the consolidation stage; so the threat of acquisition or dilution of market value is very high. Due to this reason, there has been a change in the focus of the Indian banking industry.

TECHNOLOGY IN THE INDIAN BANKING INDUSTRY

The trend in technology adoption in the banking industry has seen a sea change. It has had a tremendous impact in India. Earlier, in the 1990s banks used to market Internet banking as a unique selling proposition; now, without Internet banking no banking operation is considered sustainable. Anywhere banking and 'anytime banking' have become a reality. The financial sector now operates in a more competitive environment than before and intermediates relatively large volumes of international financial flows. In the event of sub-prime lending crisis and tighter monetary control and regulations imposed by federal governments, the biggest challenge for the banks has been to adopt processes and systems as per the changing market dynamics. Here, technology has become the tool for survival.

With the introduction of technology at all levels of banking operations, automation has moved beyond the computerization of a bank's branches to laying a common platform by implementing core banking solution in all the branches. Internet banking has become a norm and an important tool in the retail space. Many banks have also adopted enterprise-wide applications that integrate customer databases as well as different applications so that duplicity can be avoided. This has led to an increase in productivity as well as credibility in banking operations, which is crucial to a country's economy as well. However, there still exists a lot of scope for future improvement. Business intelligence (BI) systems of banks can track the movements of customers so as to service existing customers better, while concentrating on increasing their customer base through new customer acquisitions. Using technology, it is possible to expand service delivery to a growing customer base without creating a large branch network. It will also help in reaching out to newer segments, for example, the customers of rural India.

IT can be used in banking mainly for the following processes:

1. Communication and connectivity
2. Business process reengineering
3. Access to liquidity
4. Transformation of assets
5. Monitoring of risks

Short-term industry focus is on the following points:

- Risk management—Basel II norms
- Credit quality and management of distressed assets
- Corporate governance

Long-term industry focus is on the following factors:

- Funding economic growth with inclusion
- Creating global brands
- Know your customer (KYC) norms and anti–money laundering

Technology has become the tool for survival for the banks. Technology today comprises not just the computerization of a bank's branches but has moved beyond that to laying a common platform by having core banking solution in all the branches. Internet banking has become a norm and an important tool in the retail space. Although bank automations have already been implemented in most of the major banks, there is still a lot to be done in terms of intelligent systems that can track the movements of customers and offer customized solutions to them. It is the new age of innovative products where the customer is the king and a bank's survival depends on offering the right mix of services to the right customer. Technology is both the enabler as well as the differentiator in the case of banks. It can help to expand the service delivery of banks to a growing customer base without creating a large branch network. It will also help in reaching out to newer segments, for example, the customers of rural India. IT enables them to cross-sell, as well as improving their internal processes; most importantly, it helps them to compete against global competitors and in building a global delivery platform.

ICICI BANK COMPANY OVERVIEW

ICICI was formed in 1955 as an initiative of the Government of India, World Bank and the representatives from Indian industry. The following is the brief chronology of events:

- 1955 to 1964: *Industrialization*
  - Era of rapid industrialization
  - ICICI emerged as an important source of foreign currency loans in the country
- 1965 to 1974: *Reorganization*
  - Focus shifted to other sectors
  - ICICI started export finance, concessional funding in industrially backward areas and loans for small enterprises

- 1975 to 1984: Consolidation
  - Set up state-level financial and technical institutions and the country's first specialized housing finance institution
  - First financial institutions to harness the power of IT
- 1985 to 1994: Liberalization
  - ICICI set up the country's first rating agency and the first venture capital company, and entered into asset management

ICICI Bank

ICICI Bank is the biggest private player in India. It has the largest customer base among private banks and the largest market capitalization. As of March 2008, it has total assets worth $100 million, a network of over 1,399 branches, 22 regional offices and 49 regional processing centres, about 4,485 automatic teller machines (ATMs; September 2008) and 24 million customers. The bank has retail and corporate customers and uses a variety of channels in the areas of investment banking, life and non-life insurance, venture capital and asset management. ICICI Bank is also the largest issuer of credit cards in India. ICICI reported a 1.15 per cent rise in its net profit to Rs 1,014.21 crore on a 1.29 per cent increase in total income to Rs 9,712.31 crore in the second quarter of 2008 (September 2008).

VISION

The vision of ICICI Bank is 'to be the leading provider of financial services in India and a major global bank'.

MISSION

"We will leverage our people, technology, speed and financial capital to

- Be the banker of first choice for our customers by delivering high-quality, world-class products and services.
- Expand the frontiers of our business globally.
- Maintain a healthy financial profile and diversify our earnings across businesses and geographies.
- Maintain high standards of governance and ethics.
- Contribute positively to the various countries and markets in which we operate.
- Create value for our stakeholders."

ORGANOGRAM

The basic organogram of ICICI Bank is shown in Figure 12.1.

BALANCED SCORECARD

Table 12.1 shows the balanced scorecard for ICICI Bank.

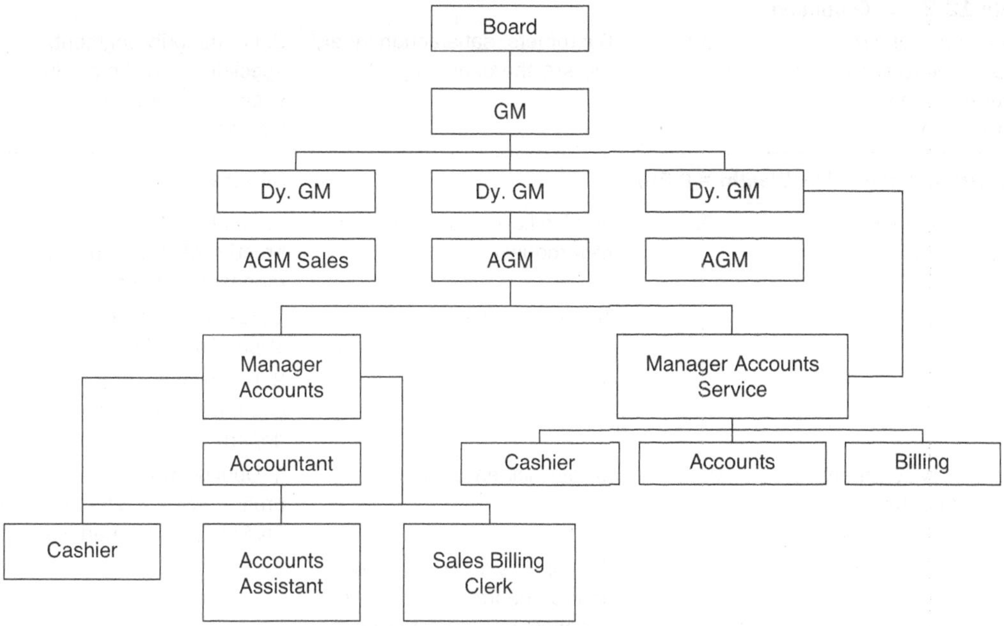

Figure 12.1 *Basic Organogram of ICICI Bank*

Table 12.1 *Balanced scorecard for ICICI Bank*

1. Financial Perspective (Weight = 0.3)		**Objectives**	**Initiatives**
Return on capital	0.3	Return on capital employed at periodic intervals with segment-wise details	1. Regular checks and balances—ensuring that borrowing short and lending long do not happen
Projected cash flow	0.35	Actual cash flow at periodic intervals and reporting of variance	2. Improve service quality and introduce better innovative products with risks neutralized
Project profitability	0.2	Periodic profitability report on each project with analysis of causes of variances and suggested areas of improvement in case of adverse variance in particular	3. Increase process efficiency and remove bottlenecks—take care of the underutilized human resource
Reliability of performance	0.15	Report on (a) project forecast reliability (b) sales backlog	
2. Customer Perspective (Weight = 0.25)			**Initiatives**
Value for money	0.6	Customers' ranking survey	1. Satisfy the major customer segment requirements by making affordable and safe product schemes

(***Continued...***)

Table 12.2 (*...Continued*)

Competitive price/ hassle-free relationship/ innovation and satisfaction	0.4	Customers' satisfaction index/ market share/pricing index	2. For minority segment, specialize in niche product segment, reducing waiting time
3. Internal Perspective (Weight = 0.35)			**Initiatives**
Shape customer requirements	0.3	Service Level Agreement for new request	1. Ensure adoption and practice of standard risk management norms
		Tender success rate	2. Faster processing time by streamlining the work flow
		Rework	3. Better and faster communication between departments and branches
Quality service/safety and cost control	0.45	Safety incidence index	4. Quality improvement programmes and try to achieve Six Sigma benchmarking
		Cost sheets and budgetary control reports, reporting of variance; revised estimates, revised project reports with requisite updates for cost and time overruns	
Superior project management	0.25	Project performance index	
		Project closedown cycle	
		Tender effectiveness	
4. Innovation and Learning Perspective (Weight = 0.1)			**Initiatives**
Product and service innovation	0.5	Revenue per employee; % of revenue from new product/ service	1. IT training programme for staff
Empowered workforce	0.2	Staff attitude survey	2. Bridging the gap between present employee capability and required capability
		Number of employee suggestions	3. Train staff to have better interpersonal skills
Continuous improvement	0.3	Rate of improvement Index	
		Speed to market (new standards)	
		Speed of imitation (robustness)	
		IT system development	
		(a) Features	
		(b) Cost	

STRENGTHS, WEAKNESSES, OPPORTUNITIES AND THREATS (SWOT) ANALYSIS

SWOT analysis is done for a company to find out its overall strengths, weaknesses, threats and opportunities to gauge the competitive potential of the company. SWOT analysis enables a company to recognize its market standing and adopt strategies accordingly. In this section, SWOT analysis of ICICI bank is done to understand better the positioning of the bank:

Strengths

1. *Brand name*: ICICI Bank has earned a reputation in the market for extending quality services to the market vis-à-vis its competitors. It has earned a strong brand name in banking in a very short span of time.
2. *Huge network*: ICICI Bank has the highest number of linked branches in the country. The bank operates through a network of 450 branches and over 1,800 ATMs across India, which enables them to serve customers in better way.
3. *Diversified portfolio*: ICICI Bank has all the products under its belt that help it to extend its relationship with existing customers. ICICI Bank offers an umbrella of products to a customer once the customer establishes a relationship with the bank. Some of the products offered by ICICI Bank are
   - Retail banking
   - Business banking
   - Merchant establishment services (EDC machine)
   - Personal loans and car loans
   - Demat services with e-broking
   - Mutual fund (ICICI Bank is the distributor of all mutual funds)
   - Insurance
   - Housing loans
4. *Salary account*: ICICI has an edge over other banks in the case of salary accounts. Most of the major private sector companies in India are having their salary accounts with ICICI even when their current account is with some other bank. This is mainly because of the huge network of ATMs and branches of ICICI extending throughout the country.
5. *Working hours*: ICICI is the only bank having its working hours from 8 a.m. to 8 p.m., which is one of the major strengths of ICICI Bank with respect to the IT and ITES industry. As most of the IT and ITES companies are global players and most of them have their parent companies in the United States, they have to work according to the US office time. Thus, some have their office time in the morning and some have it in the evening; so if the working hours of a bank are from 8 a.m. to 8 p.m., it is very convenient for such companies.
6. *Aggressive marketing*: ICICI Bank is known for the aggressive marketing of its products. Recent endorsement of one of its products by Amitabh Bachchan (popular Bollywood actor) proves the same. This gives ICICI an edge over other banks.
7. *Technology*: From its inception, ICICI Bank has adopted a policy of selecting internationally proved and specialized packaged systems for its technology. ICICI bank's technology platform

has been acknowledged globally as one of the best in terms of robustness, flexibility and cost efficiency. The bank is now in a position to leverage this platform to further its cost and service advantage.

Weaknesses

1. *Transaction cost*: ICICI Bank charges high transaction costs for its services. Most of the smaller companies in India prefer nationalized banks because of this cost factor. There are companies that go for the multi-bank system, that is, they use only those facilities of ICICI Bank that are provided at cheap rates (see the section titled 'Strengths' for a description of ICICI Bank's salary account) and go to nationalized banks and multinational companies (MNCs; read forex) for other services. So there exists a huge potential for ICICI Bank if it is ready to make its transaction costs flexible.
2. *Focus only on high-end customers*: The bank targets only the top bracket of clients and does not cater to the needs of small customers. Due to this reason the bank sometimes loses good clients.
3. *Little presence outside India*: ICICI Bank has only little presence outside India because of which companies prefer MNC banks, mainly Citibank. So, if ICICI Bank extends its services outside India then it can tap a huge customer potential.
4. *Poor customer care/service*: With its aggressive marketing, ICICI Bank is rapidly increasing its customer base. It is not, however, increasing the number of employees accordingly. This is leading to the deterioration of the company's standard of customer service.

Opportunities

1. *New IT and ITES companies*: The IT and ITES sector is on a boom in the Indian market context, with new companies mushrooming; it opens the door for ICICI Bank to capture the huge untapped market.
2. *Remittances*: ICICI Bank has a very limited presence as far as exchange earner's foreign currency (EEFC) account is concerned. Companies prefer to bank with MNCs (which have greater presence in foreign countries) and nationalized banks (which, according to the companies, provide lower transaction rates) to get their inward remittances, although ICICI is the provider of one of the most competitive rates. So the bank must promote its EEFC account better and get access to the door of huge potential markets.
3. *Business advising for smaller players*: The concept of business advising, which is very popular with the higher end players, is virtually nonexistent in the lower end of the market. ICICI should take this opportunity to provide business advising to smaller companies at competitive rates and try to avail itself of the first-mover advantage.

Threats

1. *Advent of MNC banks*: Large numbers of MNC banks are mushrooming in the Indian market due to the friendly policies adopted by the Indian government. This can increase the level of competition and prove to be a potential threat to the market share of ICICI Bank.

2. *Dissatisfied customers*: Although most of the customers are satisfied with the products offered by ICICI Bank, the bank's poor customer support/service is creating a lot of dissatisfaction among its customers. This can prove to be a serious problem as far as the market reputation of the bank is concerned, and it can be a major threat to future business acquisitions.

CORPORATE STRATEGY OF ICICI BANK DERIVED FROM SWOT ANALYSIS

The corporate strategy of the bank is derived from SWOT analysis, as ICICI is in a matured stage:

- The bank should have an integrated franchisee system across all markets, be it retail, corporate or small and medium enterprises markets.
- It should have financing and organization-restructuring expertise across industries as well as project-based operations and be open to mergers and acquisitions.
- The bank should have a very strong distribution capability across the market.
- The strategy should focus on India; facilities like non-resident Indian (NRI) services, private banking, global corporate banking and investment banking should be in place.
- Technology should be the major driver. Direct banking and global remittances are the order of the day.
- The bank should be able to cater to various customer segments by offering multiple product portfolios.
- It should follow a hybrid channel strategy: branches, partnerships and technology-based delivery

STAKEHOLDERS OF ICICI BANK

- Customers
- Reserve Bank of India (RBI)
- Other banks
- Management
- Employees

CORPORATE STRATEGY TO ADDRESS STAKEHOLDER PERSPECTIVES

Customers: Value should be delivered in terms of saving time (*faster data processing and lesser queueing time*), gaining confidence (higher *transparency* in transactions with regular updates) and stable innovative products (customers are not looking for risks while investing in banks—customer profiling).

RBI: There should be an effective *asset monitoring system* with the implementation of Basel II norms. In the wave of the current crisis, this function assumes greater importance as constant monitoring is required by RBI.

Other banks: There should be greater partnership value by effective scope for large, short-term interbank transactions.

Management: There should be greater ease and effectiveness of operation, at the same time the bank should earn higher margins than its competitors.
Employees: Automation of most of the uninteresting banking tasks (like manual accounting, money counting, etc.) should be carried out with greater control over career path, as a better way to process official transactions.

IT STRATEGY

Manage Risks More Effectively

- In the current environment, ICICI must find better ways to *identify, manage and price* the added credit and operational risks. Identification of the credit worthiness of customers can not only enhance sales but can also provide a more accurate picture of the bank's credit and fraud exposure. This will help in formulating strategies for improving collections and recovery activities.
- The IT strategy should help to measure risk for all of the bank's trading and non-trading products.
- The IT solutions combine calculations for market value and profit-and-loss risk examination in a single function. This can help the bank to meet new regulatory reporting requirements. Also this will provide banks with tools for measuring credit default risk.
- There are also flexible reporting hierarchies for different user groups.

Improve Information Management

- New demands for information necessary for regulatory compliance, risk management, corporate performance management, customer relationship management and making real-time business decisions have increased the need for centralized data management.
- ICICI needs *fully integrated business processes* with IT infrastructures that can *centralize data management across the enterprise* and interface with external data sources, while controlling the expenses for data management.
- This should also help to *automate and standardize business processes* across different business lines and organizational units.
- Thus it needs an *open, component-based* solution that supports third-party applications, can be configured to the organization and is the solution with the lowest cost for these information management needs.

Improve Customer Management

- The key to profitable growth lies in effective cross-selling strategies that accurately identify the most valuable customers and meet their specific needs.
- Such strategies require strong customer trust built on world-class products and services and the means to determine the needs of both new and existing customers.
- To capitalize on individual customer needs and lifetime value, strong background analytics, campaign management, event-triggered marketing and inbound marketing are necessary.
- To provide effective service, the bank must align its customer-oriented processes and support processes with enterprise integration—*from customer-facing applications to back office systems.*
- *So, flexible solutions that can address specific customer needs are to be selected.*

Upgrade Distribution Channels

- Efficient delivery of products and services can further strengthen customer relationships and reduce operational costs. In addition to maximizing both new and existing delivery channels, streamlined delivery means integrating and standardizing business processes and customer interfaces across all distribution channels.
- As banks increasingly use multi-channel integration for routine transactions, ICICI can launch branch-renewal programmes to build customer loyalty.
- ICICI can significantly improve operational efficiency if it replaces its multiple distribution strategies involving disparate channels with one fully integrated strategy that uses a common browser–based architecture.
- ICICI should automate routine transactions and redesign its branches to suit local preferences for products, services and pricing.

Improve Business Process Outsourcing

- In today's competitive environment, many banks are focusing on their core competencies and outsourcing their non-core business processes. In the future, business process outsourcing (BPO) may expand beyond non-core activities to a variety of mission-critical processes.
- Besides freeing resources for other purposes, BPO can give greater cost control while significantly reducing operational risk.
- Outsourcing lets an organization control their business processes while outsourcing specific functions within those processes.
- The solution infrastructure should be able to define and control specific business processes irrespective of their physical location or the applications that run them.

Enhance Business Knowledge

- As reporting requirements expand, consumer privacy laws become more stringent and complex. At the same time, new business strategies require high-quality business information for enhanced decision making. To meet these requirements, the company needs solutions that integrate its business and administrative procedures with its IT system.
- The increased need for reporting transparency and global standardization on the one hand and the need for protection of sensitive customer information on the other require increasingly sophisticated systems for capturing, formatting and distributing information.
- A solution to convert internal and third-party data into actionable information for ensuring effective business outcomes is required.

All the business issues and their solutions are summarized in Table 12.2.

Table 12.2 *Solutions for business issues*

Business Issue	Proposed Practice
Customer and market access	Integrated multi-channel access linked to *credit risk mitigation (CRM) tools for cross-selling; back office* systems; and a single, risk-related view of the customer

(***Continued...***)

Table 12.2 (...*Continued*)

Business Issue	Proposed Practice
Product delivery	Efficiently targeted market segments with an appropriate mix of fast time to market and flexible product development capabilities or focus on high-volume sales combined with low-cost production and economies of scale
Business management	Improved return on equity (ROE) and year-over-year revenue growth through increased business agility via a step change in operational efficiency gained by streamlining business processes and making them more effective
Risk management and regulatory compliance	Leveraged risk management and regulatory compliance efforts for the better understanding of customers, markets, demands and processes, while improving business efficiency and year-over-year revenue growth

ROLE OF CHIEF INFORMATION OFFICER (CIO)

1. Budget:
   - Checking return on investment (ROI)
   - Right size: eliminating clutter, and consolidating or streamlining where and when necessary
   - Finding the balance of savings versus benefits
2. Security and risk:
   - Diagnosing the organization's level of security
   - Preparing to deal with uncertainty, and mitigating risk
   - Enforcing security standards
3. Infrastructure:
   - IT infrastructure blueprint
   - Architecture design
   - Architecture guidelines
4. Integration and interoperability
   - To have a common language
   - To have a common, open architecture
   - Shared information and services
5. Procurement:
   - Evaluating vendors based upon the bid guidelines
   - Vendor management: presales, sales and post-sales support
6. Performance management:
   - By benchmarking
   - By balanced scorecard

IMPLEMENTATION OF MANAGEMENT INFORMATION SYSTEM (MIS)

Table 12.3 shows the MIS design template. The table shows metrics to be measured, their definition, the role as to who would be responsible for publishing the metrics, the tool that will be used for collecting data and the periodicity with which the metrics will be published.

Table 12.3 *Summary of MIS implementation*

Serial Number	Metrics	Numerator/Denominator	Data Collector Tool	Publisher	Periodicity
1	Increase in revenue	Percentage increase in revenue / Average revenue	System	Chief financial officer (CFO)	Quarterly
2	Increased market share	Percentage change in revenue / Total increase in banking industry	System	CFO	Quarterly
3	Customer satisfaction	Percentage reduction in number of complaints / Average number of complaints	Surveys	Customer Relationship Management (CRM)	Semi-annually
4	Number of partnerships and joint ventures	Percentage increase in partnerships / Average number of new partnerships	System	Enterprise resource planning (ERP) department	Annually
5	Brand image	Top-of-mind approach	Surveys	CRM	Annually
6	Data integration	Percentage reduction in number of data entries / Average number of data entries	System	IT department	Monthly
7	Skill upgrades	Percentage increase in number of employees successfully undergoing training programmes / Average number of employees undergoing training programmes	Training system	Human resources department	Annually
8	Increase in information collection	Percentage increase in information volume collection / Volume of information collected	System	IT department	Weekly
9	New schemes introduction	Percentage increase in number of new schemes / Average number of new schemes	System	Vice president, marketing	Yearly
10	New geographic areas covered	Percentage increase in domestic and global coverage	Information system	CIO	Quarterly

(*Continued...*)

Table 12.3 (...*Continued*)

Serial Number	Metrics	Numerator/Denominator	Data Collector Tool	Publisher	Periodicity
11	New customer segments reached	Percentage increase in customers in new segments	Information system	Business head, product line	Half yearly
12	Increased ROIs	$\frac{\text{Incremental revenues}}{\text{Incremental investment in assets}}$	Technology utilization assessment report	Chief technology officer (CTO)	Yearly
13	Better customer needs assessment	BI improvement	BI s/w	CTO	Half yearly
14	Faster demand response	Percentage decrease in new product introduction time	Marketing MIS	Marketing head	Half yearly

An MIS is a system or process that provides the information necessary to manage an organization effectively. MIS and the information it generates are generally considered essential for making prudent and reasonable business decisions.

An institution's MIS is designed to achieve the following goals:

- Enhance communication among employees.
- Deliver complex material throughout the institution.
- Provide an objective system for recording and aggregating information.
- Reduce expenses related to labour-intensive manual activities.
- Support the organization's strategic goals and direction.

ICICI Bank's MIS should focus on the following aspects:

Increase in revenue: It helps the company to know the sources of its revenues (bottom line or top line), whether targets are being met, where the company is lagging and the profitable product lines and customer segments.

Customer satisfaction: It helps the company to know how effectively customer complaints are being handled.

Data integration: It helps in determining the reduction in redundant transaction entries, which is a measure of the success of IT implementation.

New schemes introduction: It helps the top management to keep track of the success of new schemes, the associated costs and the revenues accrued and to make decisions accordingly.

New customer segments reached: This aspect provides information about the profit margins from different customer segments and the degree of penetration of the company into each segment.

Increased market share: It helps to determine the market share in various segments and the difference in market share from its competitors.

Number of partnerships and joint ventures: It gives information regarding the partnerships and joint ventures that ICICI Bank has entered into with other banks and how much the bank has gained as a result of these partnerships.

New geographic areas covered: It gives an idea regarding the number of new areas added to the bank's chain in the current year.

Increased ROIs: It gives an idea regarding the ROI and also gives a comparison of the ROIs over the past few years.

Skills Upgrades: It helps the management to get information regarding the number of employees who have undergone training in various areas and also gives a comparison across the last few years.

PROPOSED BI SYSTEMS FOR ICICI

In these days, companies are facing tough competition in the global market. Decision makers play the most important role in the fray and make crucial decisions to ensure a company's continued success in the market. Companies need good and accurate 'weapons' to gain advantage over their competitors. One of the latest and most innovative weapons available today is BI. According to Herschel and Jones, the effectiveness of BI will be measured in the future based on how well it

1. Promotes and enhances knowledge
2. Improves the mental model(s) and understanding of the decision maker(s)
3. Improves decision making and, hence, a firm's performance

BI software must be a fully integrated and comprehensive suite for

1. *Reporting*: The company must provide fast and simple access to reports and analyses to its decision makers. Individual decision makers must be able to generate reports on their own quickly and easily through a familiar interface.
2. *Query analysis*: All users with different skill levels should be able to access any data source and combine it from multiple platforms in a single query. They must be able to get answers for their questions quickly and easily with no direct involving of IT staff.
3. *OLAP (acronym for online analytical processing)*: Originally introduced by E. F. Codd, OLAP is a decision support counterpart of online transaction processing. OLAP allows users to derive information and BI from data warehouse systems by providing tools for querying and analyzing the information in the warehouse. In particular, OLAP allows multi-dimensional views and analysis of data for decision support processes. Data architects and OLAP cube designers should create consistent data sources for business users so that they can quickly and easily view large volumes of data from multiple angles.
4. *Integrated analytics*: Due to the complexity of businesses, users have to perform more sophisticated analyses without any assistance from statisticians or IT staff. BI software should

provide analytics such as forecasting and optimization with unmatched capabilities for turning data into insightful information, offering accurate insights so that everyone can make better decisions quickly and with confidence.

5. *Visualization*: People are visual creatures, so data should be presented using visual objects such as charts, graphs or maps. These graphics should be implemented in the reports also.
6. *Data mining*: Data mining is the process of applying artificial intelligence techniques to a large data set in order to determine patterns in data. It is the process of scanning large data sets to glean information.
7. *Data warehousing*: Data warehousing enables users to share a common, widely distributed and diverse database and to analytically explore, discover and better comprehend fundamental trends and relationships using all of the available data quickly and correctly.
8. *Anti–money laundering*: All banks should maintain detailed information about their customers. This information should be shared with all regulatory bodies so that credibility of the individuals can be verified. A BI solution should enable the detection of criminal financial activities more accurately, better allocate resources to appropriate cases and provide investigators with the most relevant information.
9. *Credit risk management*: When making credit decisions, banks must juggle a multitude of related and changeable factors (counterparty's credit quality, market conditions, bank goals) that could be elusive, inaccurate or even impossible. A BI solution should assess and report the risk of potential credit losses and calculate the capital reserves needed to cover that risk, calculate current and potential risk exposures, implement appropriate hedging strategies and improve capital allocation.
10. *Credit scoring for banking*: Lenders should rapidly develop, validate, deploy and track credit scorecards. This will make the lending process faster, cheaper and more flexible while controlling credit exposure and minimizing opportunity costs.
11. *Customer retention for banking*: Because the cost of acquiring new customers is much higher than that of retaining old ones, ICICI must determine which of its customers are likely to leave and which of them can be retained. So it needs to analyze huge volumes of data to gain a better understanding of the variables that influence customer attrition and product cancellation.
12. *Fraud detection*: With increasing technology advancements, a new type of electronic fraud has begun. So ICICI needs a new generation of fraud detection measures. The latest anti-fraud measures include chip and PIN technology. The goal is to detect and prevent crimes across the entire spectrum of banking operations and to respond faster to new threats as they arise. It is critical to detect fraud at the point of sale using real-time scoring of accounts by looking at all transactions.
13. *Market risk management*: Due to the market risks faced by banks today, future earnings of a bank, its cash flows and fair market values of assets and liabilities are uncertain. ICICI must find a way to manage these uncertainties through hedging strategies and the use of derivative instruments, and by bringing together inside information or galvanization, combining different instrument types into one portfolio, calculating at-risk measures and performing analyses and tests.
14. *Marketing automation for financial services*: ICICI is trying to maximize customer profitability. In order to achieve this goal, it needs to know more information about its customers so as to execute complex, multi-level and multi-channel marketing campaigns.

15. *Operational risk management*: Sometimes external events disrupt all expectations. Banks should be able to measure operational risk in a scientific way. ICICI should categorize, define and analyze operational risks for preventing or mitigating such risks.
16. *Strategic performance management for financial services*: ICICI should gather data from every source in the enterprise and transform them into the information it needs to make better strategic decisions. Exchanging information across the organization is crucial to ensure that everyone is working towards the same goals.

BI TOOLS USED IN ICICI BANK

Informatica PowerCenter Solution

Dependency on information is particularly critical in the financial sector; in a bid to create a competitive advantage through ensuring fast and accurate access to trusted information, India's second largest bank, ICICI Bank, implemented an Informatica PowerCenter solution earlier from 2007 to 2008. For a unified view of transactions and customer data, all relevant data have to be reliably combined and made available at a central place independent of their originating IT systems, which can be mainframe computers, Web servers or workstations. With demands for up-to-date and accurate information in its data warehouse, the bank opted for Informatica because of the tool's scalability, automation and flexible delivery capabilities.

Along with a team of Informatica's professional services consultants, ICICI Bank's software developers designed, tested and deployed PowerCenter to extract source data from disparate systems, including ATMs, Internet transactions, loans and bonds. The deployment greatly improved ICICI Bank's ability to ensure the integrity of data and to minimize errors as compared to the previously followed manual scripting approach, which suffered from error-handling issues.

PowerCenter gave the bank the capability to make changes swiftly and improve transaction flexibility to respond to new data demands from businesses or IT as they arise. The bank has benefited from greater data immediacy for business users and more reliable information, which results in quicker analysis and timely reporting. Satisfied by the developer productivity and ETL performance gains realized through the deployment of PowerCenter, ICICI Bank officials are now looking to extend the Informatica data integration platform to more thoroughly leverage the power of business information across the enterprise. This is used as a tool for feeding data into the BI system.

SAS9 BI Platform

Enterprise Intelligence

With business transactions growing exponentially, one of the key parameters for the evaluation of a BI solution was its scalability to support the growing volumes of data in ICICI Bank. Key departments involved in evaluating the solution were the technology management group and the retail and corporate technology teams. This scalability has been achieved by using software as service (SaS), which allows the bank to outsource its IT activities while concentrating on its core activities. The SaS Enterprise Intelligence Platform was selected as the ideal tool for this business scenario because it benefits the bank in terms of manageability, interoperability, scalability and usability. Major features of the platform are as follows:

- Usability: The SaS Web-based solution enables ICICI to provide information access to all users across the bank.

- Scalability: The SaS solution can scale upwards and outwards to address a great number of queries from many users.
- Interoperability: The SaS solution can communicate to all of the bank's existing data sources natively.
- Manageability: Security concerns can be addressed using the SaS Management Console, which can be deployed as one point of control in setting up permissions.

BUSINESS INFORMATION STRATEGY (BIS)

ICICI Bank was also interested in a data integration solution for its data warehouses and data marts. This helped to broaden the scope of the SaS solution with the introduction of SaS data integration for the creation of marts. To address issues related to migration and scalability, SaS suggested a proof of concept and involved both the business and the IT users during that important phase. The team of business users and IT managers was impressed by SaS as it took only one-third the time taken by Cognos to build a reporting cube. Cube exploitation clocked in with sub-second response times, and the entire migration of the cube took only 4 hours, including the time taken for understanding the transformations and getting the raw data in place. The successful proof of concept was the key turning point that made ICICI decide to purchase SaS. The vision of consolidating the BI environment and setting up an enterprise-wide BI platform thus became a reality.

RISK MANAGEMENT AND IT SECURITY

The Internet penetrates every sphere of human life today, and this has become a facilitator of growth. But it also creates perils related to IT security. The importance of information security (IS) in the banking industry has grown tremendously over the last five years due to a combination of factors such as regulatory requirements mandating information protection, the growth of electronic banking and the increasing number of individuals (employees, customers and third parties) with access to enterprise data. With the introduction of SOX new laws have been formulated, leading to the business need for greater alignment between IS programmes and business objectives. To make this alignment successful, quarterly risk assessments and reporting are conducted and the information is shared with all stakeholders. However, this requires investment in terms of money, time and manpower.

Currently, the focus is on enhancing controls around employees' access to information. Several banks are implementing employee access rights management solutions that tie an employee's rights specifically to his or her role in the organization, thereby ensuring that employees access only the information and systems that they need in order to perform their jobs. Another area of interest is more secure employee authentication. The focus today is on the implementation of single sign-on platforms that allow employees to use the same user name and password to access all applications. Other major technology projects that are taking shape across banks include investments in detection tools to monitor unauthorized or suspicious movements and access to data and systems.

Impact of IS Breaches

The Indian banking sector has become technology driven. But it needs to move forwards to forestall potential threats of security breaches. India's financial infrastructure has been transformed over the last 10 years. Public and private sector banks have completely networked their operations over the last three years, or they are currently in the process of doing so. Electronic networking was intended to improve the speed of transactions and customer service, and it is true that both of them have improved substantially. But this networking has also made India's banking networks vulnerable to potential breaches.

A devastating attack by cyber criminals on banks' networks could lead to network failures or shutdowns, paralyze transactions, wreak havoc on the banking system and impose unimaginable financial costs on the country's economy. Safety measures in place include firewalls and isolation of banking networks. These networks are not linked to the Internet directly. However, these measures are not fail-safe mechanisms. There could be breaches. The reason is that there are stand-alone personal computers, which have floppy/disc drives, that link to the Internet. In addition, the machines have USB ports that are accessible with pen or flash drives. The discs or pen drives often shuttle between the bank's own network and the Internet for uploading/downloading data or software updates. Parking a dormant bug in these bits of data is child's play for cyber criminals/terrorists.

It is also very important to prevent security breaches because of the following reasons:

- Attacks can happen with catastrophic impact.
  - Today, attacks are getting more financially motivated. Consequently, the financial losses are rising.
  - For breaches with a financial motive, the average loss is US $2.2 million.
- Increasing regulations are mandating information protection (SOX, Basel II, GLBA, data privacy, country regulations).
- In many cases, the board and top management (chief executive officer [CEO]/CFO) is held personally liable for information protection.
- Failure to meet the regulatory requirements give rise to high penalties.

Risk assessment and security systems are critical for any bank. ICICI Bank decided to focus its IT strategy around this core and created a *risk management framework*. Perhaps, the most difficult task for IS professionals is reaching out to a bank's customers to teach them about the risks they incur when they reveal their personal information. Many banks will admit that their greatest security risks come from their customers who fall into the traps designed by fraudsters to capture the customer information that banks work hard to protect. This is why so many of the largest financial institutions are devoting significant marketing and advertising dollars to educate their customers regarding the risks of identity theft.

The problem that many of the banks understand is that as they become more and more technology driven the risks of abuse of technology comes into limelight. Many of the public sector banks as well as the private banks have recently become completely networked and implemented the core banking facility.

IS Governance and Training

During regular assessments of security issues, training assessment is done for different employees. Training on IS has to be given for all the employees of an organization and they should be kept updated on various risk management and risk aversion techniques so that when there is an actual security breach or disaster, its impact can be minimized. A team called the security team is prepared, which consists of security professionals. These individuals are trained in IT security processes. Periodic training programmes are to be conducted for the security team. Classroom training for all IT administrators and system and application owners is also proposed.

Business Value and Technical Benefits of Technology Implementations

The business value and technical benefits expected out of technology implementations are

1. Adaptability
   - 10-day average reduction in time to deploy new servers due to streamlined software licensing
   - More predictable cash flow for infrastructure software purchases leveraging enterprise licensing agreement
2. Availability
   - 99.9 per cent availability sustained for key applications
   - 99.99 per cent availability sustained for server infrastructure
3. Scalability
   - 25 per cent growth in data accommodated with no increase in staff and no extension of backup window
4. Productivity
   - 50 per cent reduction in time to rebuild corrupted servers Option allows, from one hour to 30 minutes
5. Savings in cost
   - 20 per cent anticipated savings on software over the two-year life of ESLA

RISK ASSESMENT AND SECURITY SYSTEMS USED BY ICICI

The following four points give a brief outline of the security measures followed at ICICI:

- Risk assessment processes are reviewed against the bank's security policy framework.
- There is a security operations centre for monitoring the bank's security set-up on a 24×7 basis.
- Critical systems are audited every year by the bank's internal audit department.
- External audits are conducted by one or two of the 'big four' consulting firms and a regulatory body.

TECHNOLOGY AND SYSTEMS THAT ARE SECURED AT ICICI

- ICICI Messenger: This software was developed internally in 2006 to provide secure instant messaging services for internal users.
- FTP server: An open source FTP server application has been customized to meet the requirements of the bank.
- Penetration testing (PT) and vulnerability assessment (VA): PT and VA are done as and when required. The vendors involved are changed every year.
- Unauthorized messaging: Unauthorized messaging is not allowed. Only approved software (ICICI Messenger) is used for messaging services.
- Data security: Encryption software has been loaded on all desktops, servers and laptops associated with the bank.

The architecture in ICICI is secured in various ways. Application security is reviewed periodically, and every application undergoes an assessment before it is implemented in production. Firewalls, intrusion detection systems (IDSs), anti-virus software as well as routers are used to secure the perimeter. With the advent of biotechnology, biometrics devices are now being used as security systems.

Perimeter security is taken care of by using routers, switches, firewalls, IDSs and wireless LAN which should be secured with encryption and authentication. Desktops and laptops are also hardened according to their defined configurations. The operations team monitors IDSs and firewall logs on a 24 × 7 basis, and anti-virus software should also be installed on ATMs.

BUSINESS CONTINUITY PLAN (BCP) AND DISASTER RECOVERY IN ICICI

- The bank has an alternate disaster recovery site.
- The equipment is identical at both the primary site and the secondary site.
- Daily backups are taken on tape.
- Critical data is backed up in real time, whereas the rest of the data is copied at the end of the day.
- BCP has the recovery time objective for each system. The recovery time objective for each application is decided based on the business needs and criticality of the data generated by the application.

RISK MANAGEMENT SOLUTION ARCHITECTURE

The solution consists of three modules:

1. Risks identification module
2. Risk measurement module
3. Risk mitigation module

Risk Identification Module

Data from different sources are extracted and populated into the data repository, which serves as the input engine for the risk measurement module. Table 12.4 represents the details.

Table 12.4 *Risk module*

Name of the Data Source	Data to Be Extracted	Purpose of Extracting the Data
Dedicated Customer Relation Management (CRM) application	Clients' data: clients' payment history, recovery rate, value of loan, maturity, net worth, value of the mortgage (security)	To measure 'credit risk'
Bank's MIS	Bank's financials: rate-sensitive assets, rate-sensitive liability, cash wallet, forex position, exposure in equity, derivative market	To measure 'market risk'
	Internal loss data: history of system failure, process failure, external events and their impact on various business lines (value of operational loss), frequency of occurrences	To measure 'operational risk' (with respect to bank)

(Continued...)

Table 12.4 (*...Continued*)

Name of the Data Source	Data to Be Extracted	Purpose of Extracting the Data
External source	Reports from external rating agencies: list of defaulted clients, credit rating across clients/sectors, credit score for the clients	To measure credit risk
	External operational loss data	To measure operational risk (with respect to the banking industry)

Risk Measurement Module

Data stored in the repository are populated into the risk measurement module, which consists of a 'risk analysis engine' and a 'risk analysis dashboard'.

Risk analysis engine: This engine quantitatively measures each risk and feeds the numbers to the banking dashboard, which is the user interface.

Measurement of Credit Risk

Credit risk is measured based on the 'advanced internal rating approach'. By measuring the 'expected loss', credit risk can be quantitatively measured:

$$\text{Expected loss} = \text{Probability of default (PD)} \times \text{Loss given at default (LGD)} \times \text{Exposure at default (EAD)}$$

Measurement of Market Risk

Market risk consists of

- Interest rate risk
- Foreign exchange risk
- Commodity risk
- Equity risk

The interest risk of the bank is quantitatively measured by measuring the 'duration gap' of the bank's financial assets:

$$\begin{aligned}\text{Duration gap} = {} & \text{Dollar weighted duration of asset portfolio} \\ & - \text{Dollar weighted duration of the bank's liabilities}\end{aligned}$$

There are a number of software available that help in risk assessment. These software use best practices as well as enterprise-wide risk data and suggest different risk mitigation measures. A list of these software is provided in Table 12.5.

Table 12.5 *Comparative analysis of various risk management software*

Name	Vendor	Database	Language	Operating System	Pricing Structure	User interface	Features
Reuters JRisk	Thomson Reuters	NA	NA	NA	NA	NA	■ Functionally rich for trading, trade processing and risk management ■ Future proofed ■ Fast processing speed and real-time updates ■ Cross-asset class capability and consistent view of risk ■ Can be rapidly deployed and easily integrated within the most complex legacy environment ■ Reduced costs for productivity, development and maintenance ■ Service-based architecture
Reuters Kondor Global Risk	Thomson Reuters	NA	NA	NA	NA	NA	■ Counterparty static data maintenance ■ Credit limit calculation ■ Real-time intraday limits monitoring ■ Reporting and revaluation
Basel II Reporting	Hexaware Technologies	NA	NA	NA	NA	NA	This solution offers an integrated solution that encompasses a single technology framework, a common middle layer and a common presentation layer. The Pillar III solution addresses disclosure requirements that meet regulatory expectations based on qualitative and quantitative approaches. Here, it integrates the risk system with well-informed and integrated data management and reporting models.
Adaptiv	SunGuard Corporate	Oracle	C++	Windows XP, Vista	Fixed, volume-based	GUI, Web	Adaptiv assists institutions of varying size and complexity in deploying technology to meet both internal and regulatory requirements for risk management and operational control. It helps financial services institutions from the banking, hedge fund, asset management, insurance and corporate sectors with its deep understanding of risk management and operational processes.

(***Continued...***)

Table 12.5 (*...Continued*)

Name	Vendor	Database	Language	Operating System	Pricing Structure	User interface	Features
Credit Risk Management	Risk Technology International	NA	NA	NA	NA	NA	Credit risk management systems, commercial rating systems, consumer credit scoring, Basel II implementation, data quality and testing, model validation and refinements, internal audit services, stress testing, benchmarking of internal rating systems.
RiskAnalyst	Moody's Analytics	NA	NA	NA	NA	NA	A browser-based internal rating solution RiskAnalyst provides a comprehensive enterprise-wide credit risk management system that deploys a standard set of tools to support internal credit practices for public and private firms. The system is powered by a centralized database that brings together the inputs required by an internal rating system. These inputs can be used to enable model development and model evaluation.
Credit Edge Plus	Moody's Analytics	NA	NA	NA	NA	NA	CreditEdge Plus is a platform that bridges the equity-, bond- and credit-derivative markets, enabling an in-depth understanding of their impact on credit risk that was previously unavailable. This comprehensive solution offers access to the continuously updated Moodys KMV EDF™ (expected default frequency) credit measures and EDF-implied credit spreads. This information, extracted from the equity markets, lets users value the debt and credit derivative instruments that issuers buy, hold, sell, hedge and securitize with a new level of precision. CreditEdge Plus combines industry-standard EDF credit measures with a valuation framework that allows users to overlay their own research and observations to arrive at fair values for bonds, loans and credit default swaps (CDSs).
Moody's KMV RiskCalc	Moody's Analytics	NA	NA	NA	NA	NA	Moody's RiskCalc 3.1 fundamentally changes the middle-market credit process. It enables institutions to accurately characterize the credit risk of thousands of private companies in a matter of minutes for faster

Name	Vendor	Database	Language	Operating System	Pricing Structure	User interface	Features
							loan underwriting decisions and efficient monitoring of portfolio credit trends. Armed with this tool, credit risk professionals can focus their resources on loans with the greatest risk. In addition, accurate default probabilities provide a common metric for communicating with regulators and internal staff.
Misys Basel II	Misys	NA	NA	NA	NA	NA	The Misys 'Basel II in a box' approach is based on an integrated but open and transparent platform, smoothly interfacing with the bank's systems to deliver hassle-free Basel II compliance in the most cost-effective manner. This unique solution combines risk-weighted assets (RWA) and credit risk mitigation calculations with structured processes, audit trails, data modelling, data storage, stress and back testing, regulatory/ management reporting and analysis tools.
Razor	IT and ITES	Oracle	C++	Windows XP	NA	NA	Razor is a new enterprise system created expressly to meet the complex and rigorous risk management demands of today. Plus, its advanced design leverages sophisticated financial engineering principles and makes efficient use of technology, which makes it ready to meet tomorrow's risk management challenges. Whatever the complexity of your risk requirements or the size of your portfolio, Razor can deliver major benefits. Whether your current focus is on improving your limits and use of credit lines, calculating economic capital or meeting the demands of Basel for internal models, Razor can provide the advanced risk functionality you need. Razor provides a fully integrated analysis of market and credit risks within a single application and deals efficiently with the complex interactions of different categories of risk; so it is ideal to develop a firm-wide assessment of risk according to the growing demand.

HARDWARE AND NETWORK AT ICICI

1. High-Power servers running Finacle Core Banking (Infosys), Finn One Retail Loans System (Nucleus Technologies) and CTL (Card Tech Limited) Prime Credit Cards Processing System are used.
2. There are a number of Sun Fire 15K, E6900, E2900 and E6500 enterprise-class servers and various Sun Fire mid-range servers running the Solaris 9 operating system.
3. There are around 800 leased lines, about 600 very small aperture terminals (VSATs), approximately 800 integrated services digital network (ISDN) lines and multiple 34-Mbps lines.
4. Hub and spoke network is used where there is a mix of VSATs, leased lines, ISDN and radio links.
5. *High-end Cisco routers and switches* have been deployed for connectivity.

TRAINING

The term training refers to the acquisition of knowledge, skills and competencies as a result of the teaching of practical skills and knowledge that relate to specific useful competencies. Since the IT strategy revolves around the use of new technology and automation, the end users as well as the security team have to be trained on how to use the implemented technology. Training as a three-pronged process has been proposed, which is outlined as follows:

- Periodic training programmes are conducted for the security team.
- Classroom training should be conducted for all IT administrators and system and application owners.
- All the Web developers should be trained on secure coding practices on a yearly basis.
- End users should be trained to use the new technology effectively.

IT-ENABLED SERVICES

Automated INR Payment Services

This product offers the efficient distribution of inward remittances from exchange houses and banks abroad. The key features of the service include

- Web-based/SWIFT-based messaging facility
- Routing of payment through internal electronic network if the account is with any of ICICI's branches
- If accounts are with other banks, distribution is achieved through bank drafts/cheques sent by courier
- Cover funding through INR account/or through foreign currency accounts
- Online access to INR account if maintained
- MT 950/940 facility
- Dedicated help desk for backup and tracking
- Convenience in funding/providing cover

VOSTRO Accounts

VOSTRO accounts provide INR account services to correspondent banks. All the accounts are held in a special centre located in the Nariman Point branch of ICICI at Mumbai, Maharashtra. The key features include

- Access to the whole ICICI network spread across all major centres
- Internet access to accounts
- Web-based/SWIFT-based messaging facility
- Customized MIS
- Funding convenience
- Competitive tariff

Cross-Border Trade Services

ICICI Bank offers the full range of cross-border trade services to its correspondent banks. This service is available across all major destinations in India with significant foreign trade potential. They have fully integrated communication channels among branches, which directly helps in saving valuable time when facilitating cross-border transactions. Some of the important features include

- Advising and confirming of documentary letters of credit
- Confirmation/reissuance of standby Letter of credit and guarantees
- Documentary collections/open account transactions
- Payment processing and distribution
- Advising and confirming of documentary credits
- Negotiation of documents
- Computerized processing ensuring speedy services

INR Agency Clearing Services

ICICI Bank offers clearing services across all its major centres for facilitating clearing of its customer cheques. The key features include

- Clearing of customer cheques through the bank's code as a sub-member
- Facility to issue demand drafts, which are payable across all the branches, by a particular branch/ branches
- Collection of cheques/instruments through the ICICI network
- Funds transfer service from other centres to a branch/branches through the network
- Facility to issue bankers cheque with a sort code
- Customized MIS and a dedicated help desk

Trust and Retention Account Services

ICICI Bank is one of the leading trust and retention (Escrow) account service providers in India. It has considerable experience in managing various types of trust and retention accounts, including the evolution of a structure that best addresses the concerns of all the institutions involved in the financing of a project/other financing requirements. The key features of this service include

- Waterfall management of cash flows
- Acting as a paying and receiving agent
- Safekeeping and custody for the underlying assets
- Account administration
- Cash escrows and security escrows
- Preconstruction and post-construction management of cash flows
- Regulatory liaison
- Advisory services
- Electronic reporting via the Internet or a specialist online system; customized MIS reporting

CURRENT SYSTEMS IN PLACE

1. ICICI Bank runs its customer-facing services and key enterprise applications such as *Finacle Core Banking (Infosys)*, *FinnOne Retail Loans System (Nucleus Technologies)*, *CTL Prime Credit Cards Processing System*, and *SAP* on highly available servers.
2. *Oracle 9i database* and *Oracle Real Application Clusters (RACs)* provide a robust database component for all its enterprise applications.
3. *Internet banking* and *customer relationship management* use Microsoft SQL Server 2000 Enterprise Edition.

ROI

ROI is explained in the ANNEXURE.

WAY FORWARD

Besides the risk management solutions, some further steps can be taken in the future:

1. Enterprise identity management solution and end point security
2. ICICI Bank's Global Trade Services Unit (GTSU) is currently BS 7799 certified. The certification initiative should be taken forward to other locations.
3. There should be software to analyze real-time online transaction-processing applications.
4. The backup coverage concept should be extended to data on user machines also, that is, to laptop and desktop options.

CONCLUSION

The face of the banking industry is changing rapidly; from a large number of small banks, the industry is moving towards a smaller number of large banks. Banks are providing multiple services to millions of customers across the globe. In such a landscape, technology has become essential for the survival of any bank. Technology is no more the winning criteria, but it has become the qualifying criteria.

All this has to be done without affecting the business drivers and customer convenience and ease; keeping the costs for such measures at the lowest possible level is also important. Hence, banks today have to design their IT strategy keeping in mind all these needs as well as their future needs and the fast-changing nature of technology.

DISCUSSION QUESTIONS

1. What are the characteristics of retail banking?
2. How can you derive a strategy for ICICI Bank using the balanced scorecard approach?
3. How do you calculate ROI for technology investment in ICICI?
4. Perform a SWOT analysis for ICICI Bank.
5. Why is security of prime concern in a bank?

BIBLIOGRAPHY

1. http://www.business-beacon.com/kommon/bin/sr.php?kall=wcos&tab=6010&cocode=96379&ttype=entire_text, 2008.
2. http://www.icicibank.com, 2008.
3. http://www.icicibnk.com, 2008.
4. http://www.moneycontrol.com/annual-report/icicibank/directors-report/ICI02, 2008.
5. http://www.scribd.com/doc/17394690/ICICI-Bank-Annual-Report-FY2009, 2008.
6. ICICI Bank annual reports, 2008.
7. K. Avinash, 2007. Information security policy development and implementation. *Information Systems Security* 16(5):246–56, 11p, 2008.

ANNEXURE

Calculation of ROI is explained as follows: First, the cost involved in the implementation is calculated (see Table A1).

Table A1 *Cost of implementation*

Company Input		
Input prompts	**Response**	
Projected annual revenue	INR 3,36,63,00,00,000	From annual report
Total amount of loans lying as reserve	INR 76,63,00,00,000	From annual report
Material cost of goods sold (COGS) as a percentage of sales	63.00%	From annual report
Cost of idle funds lying with the bank	6.00%	Risk-free interest rate
Annual dollar value of new purchases	INR 84,15,75,00,000	25% of revenue
Margin as a percentage of revenue	13.50%	Growth in the last five years
Average accounts receivable balance	INR 42,78,00,00,000	From annual report

(**Continued...**)

Table A1 (...*Continued*)

Company Input		
Input prompts	**Response**	
Average number of days to recover a loan/advance	60	Last three year's average
Interest earned on cash	3.50%	Interest on savings deposit
Annual direct labour cost	INR 20,78,90,00,000	From annual report
Annual indirect labour cost	INR 4,86,09,00,000	From annual report
Number of office staff directly affected by IT upgrades	2,00,000	Total employees = 4,00,000; 50% are assumed to be affected
Desired cash turns with the new system (how many times an amount can be circulated)	10	Assumed
Estimated cost of server, operating system, database and client licences	INR 10,20,00,00,000	3.03% of annual revenue
Initial cost of software and services	INR 6,80,00,00,000	2.02% of annual revenue

Assumption: The cost of savings due to paperwork and stationery has been ignored; it has been assumed that all IT expenses are incurred at a single point in time to simplify the calculation.

Table A2 *Assumptions in ROI calculation*

ROI Assumptions	
Data Assumptions	
Expected percentage savings in acquisition costs with the new system	2.00%
Improvement in sales due to error reduction and just-in-time receipt of components	5.00%
Improvement in sales due to faster new product improvement and reaching out to new customers	8.00%
Reduction in the number of days to collect invoices	3
Direct labour productivity improvement	4.00%
Estimated reduction in indirect staff	4.00%
Percentage of time spent on tasks that would be automated by ERP	15.00%
Average salary of office worker	INR 2,50,000
Percentage increase in revenue attributed to more accurate costing	0.50%
Percentage increase in revenue attributed to more efficient scheduling	0.33%
Percentage of initial software costs charged for maintenance and support	25.00%
Annual cost of administration	INR 7,00,000

Table A3 *Benefits accrued because of technology investments*

ROI Details
Reduction of idle funds and loss in interest rates
Improvements in reporting and information availability will help in reducing the amount of idle funds, which will reduce the opportunity cost associated with these funds.

Table A3

ROI Details	
Value of current reserve	INR 76,63,00,00,000
Material COGS	INR 2,12,07,69,00,000
Value of reserves after IT enablement	INR 21,20,76,90,000
Total inventory reduction	INR 55,42,23,10,000
Cost of idle funds lying with the bank	6.00%
Total annual savings from improving the timely receipt of materials	*INR 3,32,53,38,600*
Reduction in Acquisition Costs	
The future requirements and needs can be properly identified. This will bring in the economies of scale. IT enablement will also bring in prospective suppliers who can be potential lenders at a lower cost.	
Annual dollar value of new purchases	INR 84,15,75,00,000
Expected percentage savings in acquisition costs with new system	2.00%
Annual savings in acquisition costs	*INR 1,68,31,50,000*
Increased Sales Due to Improved Customer Service	
We can dramatically improve customer service by having immediate access to accurate information regarding past customer requests information, change orders or reschedules. Details of customers can also be kept, which will help us a lot. The date of deposit and loan of a customer can be accurately recorded to give optimum service.	
Current projected sales revenue	INR 3,36,63,00,00,000
Projected profit based on historical profit levels	INR 45,44,50,50,000
Total percentage improvement in sales as a result of improved service levels	13.00%
Resulting projected sales revenue after IT implementation	INR 3,80,39,19,00,000
Profit on new sales revenue based on historical profit levels	INR 51,35,29,06,500
Annual profit improvement from improved customer service levels	*INR 5,90,78,56,500*
Earned Interest on Shorter Collection Cycle	
Reducing the number of days to collect can save the company money on interest cost.	
Average accounts receivable balance	INR 42,78,00,00,000
Percentage reduction in average number of days to collect invoice	5.00%
Resulting monthly return of cash to the business	INR 2,13,90,00,000
Resulting annual return of cash to the business	INR 25,66,80,00,000
Annual interest on additional cash	*INR 89,83,80,000*
Increased Direct Labour Productivity	
Direct labour cost can be reduced by implementing ERP as it will reduce paperwork, which will enable the bank to focus on the core area.	
Current direct labour costs	INR 20,78,90,00,000
Direct labour productivity savings after implementation	4.00%
Annual savings in direct labour productivity	*INR 83,15,60,000*

(**Continued...**)

Table A3 (*...Continued*)

ROI Details	
Decreased Indirect Labour Costs	
Indirect labour cost can be reduced by implementing ERP as it will reduce paperwork, which will enable the bank to focus on the core area.	
Current annual indirect labour costs	INR 42,78,00,00,000
Estimated reduction in indirect staff	4.00%
Annual savings in indirect labour costs	*INR 1,71,12,00,000*
Savings due to Management of Critical Business Processes	
Enterprise business systems administer customer order management, providing services and financials so that the bank stays on track with its business objectives.	
Elimination of work redundancy	INR 7,50,00,00,000
Revenue increase due to more accurate job costing	INR 1,68,31,50,000
Cost savings due to more efficient scheduling	INR 1,11,08,79,000
Annual savings in management of business processes	*INR 10,29,40,29,000*
Solution Cost	
Software and services	INR 6,80,00,00,000
Hardware and infrastructure	INR 10,20,00,00,000
Maintenance and support	INR 85,00,00,000
Administration	INR 5,00,00,000
Total solution cost	*INR 17,90,00,00,000*

Table A4 *ROI calculations*

ROI Summary	
Annual savings summary	
Reduction of idle funds and loss in interest rates	INR 3,32,53,38,600
Reduction in acquisition costs	INR 1,68,31,50,000
Increased sales due to improved customer service	INR 5,90,78,56,500
Earned interest on shorter collection cycle	INR 89,83,80,000
Increased direct labour productivity	INR 83,15,60,000
Decreased indirect labour costs	INR 1,71,12,00,000
Savings due to management of critical business processes	INR 10,29,40,29,000
Total annual savings of an ERP solution	INR 24,65,15,14,100
Total solution cost	INR 17,90,00,00,000
Net benefit	INR 6,75,15,14,100
ROI	38%